The Rhetoric of Intellectual Property

Routledge Studies in Rhetoric and Communication

1. Rhetorics, Literacies, and Narratives of Sustainability
Edited by Peter N. Goggin

2. Queer Temporalities in Gay Male Representation
Tragedy, Normativity, and Futurity
Dustin Bradley Goltz

3. The Rhetoric of Intellectual Property
Copyright Law and the Regulation of Digital Culture
Jessica Reyman

The Rhetoric of Intellectual Property

Copyright Law and the Regulation of Digital Culture

Jessica Reyman

Routledge
Taylor & Francis Group
NEW YORK AND LONDON

First published 2010
by Routledge
605 Third Avenue, New York, NY 10017
4 Park Square, Milton Park, Abingdon, Oxon OX14 4RN

Routledge is an imprint of the Taylor & Francis Group, an informa business

First issued in paperback 2012

Typeset in Sabon by IBT Global.

Library of Congress Cataloging in Publication Data

Reyman, Jessica, 1977–
The rhetoric of intellectual property : copyright law and the regulation of digital culture / Jessica Reyman.
p. cm.—(Routledge studies in rhetoric and communication ; v. 3)
Includes bibliographical references and index.
1. Copyright—United States. I. Title.
KF2994.R49 2009
346.7304'82—dc22
2009033552

ISBN13: 978-0-415-99907-6 (hbk)
ISBN13: 978-0-203-85792-2 (ebk)
ISBN13: 978-0-415-63644-5 (pbk)

Contents

Figures

Acknowledgments

I wish to express thanks to the many colleagues and friends that have contributed to the creation of this book. To begin, I'd like to thank those who gave advice and guidance during the inception and early stages of this project, including Laura Gurak, John Logie, and Mary Lay Schuster of the University of Minnesota, and law professor Dan Burk of the University of California, Irvine.

I'd like to thank my colleagues at Northern Illinois University, especially Michael Day, Jeff Einboden, and Phil Eubanks, who, in different ways, have offered their support during the writing process. In addition, I'd like to give special thanks to the students in my spring 2008 graduate course on Rhetoric, Copyright, and Digital Media, who prompted me to revisit and revise my views on the digital copyright debate in light of their insightful discussions and writings.

I am also grateful for the inspiration that came from other scholars researching and writing on intellectual property issues, including Krista Kennedy, Clancy Ratliff, Danielle DeVoss, Jeff Galin, TyAnna Herrington, Jim Porter, and countless others, whose work has been integral to my own developing thoughts on the issues. Some of these colleagues have offered supportive comments and helpful advice at key moments in this project's development. Others, in their enthusiasm and dedication to the study of copyright and textual ownership, have helped me to understand more clearly the implications of the issues for the field of rhetoric and composition. These individuals' work is what drew me to this line of inquiry in the first place.

Pieces of this research were shared at the Conference on College Composition and Communication, the CCCC Intellectual Property Caucus, and the conference for the Association of Internet Researchers. Thank you to the participants there for their attention, questions, and suggestions.

Special thanks to the four anonymous reviewers of this manuscript for their help in making significant improvements to this text. I'd also like to thank the Routledge Studies in Rhetoric and Communication series editor Erica Wetter and senior editorial assistant Liz Levine for their help with carrying this project through to completion.

Finally, I am grateful for my family, my husband Ryan and my daughter Jordan, for their support and understanding during all stages of the writing process. I especially appreciate their steady encouragement and unwavering confidence in my abilities, and for creating the time and space necessary for carrying this project through to completion.

A version of Chapter 4 appeared as "Property, Theft, Piracy: Rhetoric and Regulation in *MGM Studios v. Grokster,*" *Composition & Copyright: Perspectives on Teaching, Text-making, and Fair Use*, Ed. Steve Westbrook, SUNY Press, 2009, pp. 9–30.

1 Copyright, Authorship, and the Internet

It has now been four decades since Joseph Licklider and Robert Taylor presented one of the earliest visions of what we now know as the Internet. In 1968 they coauthored "The Computer as a Communication Device," in which they predicted a global computer network of "distributed intellectual resources" (28) characterized by its accessibility by multiple users at disparate locations; its ability to help users share, manipulate, and locate data; as well as its facilitation of easy interactive communication among users. Licklider and Taylor's important work eventually contributed to the development of ARPANET, which later became the modern Internet. Their predictions, however, did not focus only on descriptions of human-computer interaction or the technical structure for sharing bits of information across a computer network. They were also interested in human-human interaction, the social dynamics of what they coined a networked "supercommunity." In the introduction to the essay, they made a provocative claim about networked communication:

> [T]o communicate is more than to send and to receive. Do two tape recorders communicate when they play to each other and record from each other? Not really—not in our sense. We believe that communicators have to do something nontrivial with the information they send and receive. And we believe that we are entering a technological age in which we will be able to interact with the richness of living information—not merely in the passive way that we have become accustomed to using books and libraries, but as active participants in an ongoing process, bringing something to it through our interaction with it, and not simply receiving something from it by our connection to it. (21)

In the years since, the suggestion that the Internet is a means for rich, active participation among computer users contributing toward "living information" has become an idealistic model rather than a representation of actual use. Indeed, we would do well to view this utopia with some skepticism, given the understanding that the Internet is not an inherently progressive technology, in and of itself offering the promise of advances in intellectual and creative production.

There is much to be learned by examining the current state of the Internet and its role in cultural production in light of early predictions. Internet technologies carry with them certain social and cultural properties and are not free from the institutional structures that govern users' activities. The physical properties of the Internet have evolved in much the way Licklider and Taylor predicted: bits of information can now be shared across networks that connect with other networks of Internet users. However, the social dynamic is very different. Rather than forming a "supercommunity" of cooperative participants, the Internet in many ways consists of hierarchies of binary roles: producer-consumer, creator-user, writer-reader. The Internet is fraught with limitations imposed by legal structures that govern ownership of information, technical structures that limit how information can be accessed and used, and cultural norms that determine who can participate in creative and intellectual production and in what ways. Licklider and Taylor foresaw some limitations to their vision. At the time of their writing, they recognized a crucial challenge facing the development of the Internet: they asked, "[w]ill 'to be on-line' be a privilege or a right?" (41). While they predicted issues of access restrictions in terms of financial (cost of service) and technological (speed and reach) factors, we have since seen that limitations on activities often take the form of social and cultural norms, practices, and expectations. One such limitation is the increasingly restrictive application of copyright law in cyberspace. In recent years many activities previously taken for granted have become difficult or impossible because of copyright laws. Teachers face infringement notices when attempting to show class-related clips from DVDs to their students as a result of the anti-circumvention provisions in Digital Millennium Copyright Act (DMCA). Critics of strong yet controversial groups such as the Church of Scientology face censorship when copyright infringement claims are filed to prevent citations of key doctrinal content. Technology developers face legal action when developing peer-to-peer software that aids users in sharing files. And everyday Internet users face lawsuits from the Recording Industry Association of America (RIAA) for infringement when accessing and sharing online content. Media scholar Siva Vaidhyanathan calls examples like these copyright "horror stories" ("State of Copyright Activism"), and they have been growing in number in recent history.

OPEN ARCHITECTURE VS. CLOSED LAW

Since the advent of the Internet, we have witnessed a rising tension between the open architecture of the Internet and legal restrictions for online activities. Distributed file-sharing systems have forever changed the expectations of everyday users with regard to digital information. The Internet offers much promise for cultural production in its offering of open access to information and the opportunity for user participation in creation and distribution of intellectual property. And with the introduction of Napster in 1999, peer-to-peer file-sharing technologies offered the types of online activities that took this open architecture a step further to break down the binary between sender and receiver in Internet communication. While in its early forms the Internet allowed interactions among users that were open and free in the sense that anyone with technological access could take part, the model of participation remained hierarchical in another sense, as it was based on a client-server structure. This client-server structure of Internet applications, such as Web browsers, is different from the client-client structure introduced by peer-to-peer technologies in terms of its technical workings. The client-server structure requires that an application, the "client," make a request to another application, the "server." The client waits for a reply from the server, which processes the request and returns the information to the client. Data are centralized, residing on servers that control which users will be granted access to the information. This structure creates an imbalanced relationship between the two participants in the interaction: a client relies on a server that has ultimate control over the exchange. The client-client structure, which is the basis for peer-to-peer file sharing, represents an alternative model of information exchange on the Internet. The client-client model allows each data host to act simultaneously as both a client and a server. Each has equivalent technical responsibilities and equal status in the interaction, and there is no centralized server that controls content. Further, as the number of clients in a client-client network increases, so does capacity on that network.

Internet communication scholars remind us that peer-to-peer file sharing is not a distinct, dramatically different concept but, rather, is one that was built on the existing ideology of the Internet. John Logie notes the continuity between existing Web applications and peer-to-peer file-sharing applications in an effort to show how the peer-to-peer file-sharing debate has implications for the future of the Internet. In fact, he asserts, "*the Internet itself is . . . a peer-to-peer network*" (*Peers, Pirates & Persuasion* 129, italics in original). Logie argues that, long before Napster, the level relationships among users that are created by peer-to-peer file exchanges were present on the Internet in different forms such as participation on Usenet groups, which lack a central server. Internet communication scholar Tarleton Gillespie likewise asks us to reconsider the history of peer-to-peer file sharing as a "dramatic new innovation." Instead, he argues that "[t]he applications that appeared and proliferated alongside Napster were not new; they merely expanded on the architecture of the Internet, building on the same logic as a host of applications that preceded them, and drawing on models of information distribution with a long, if often marginalized, history" (*Wired Shut* 44). Peer-to-peer file sharing, then, was not so much a revolutionary technological development as a conceptual shift in the fundamental structure of existing content distribution models that relied on an imbalanced power differential between producers of content and consumers of content.

At the same time that peer-to-peer file-sharing technologies were being developed and made available, U.S. copyright law demonstrated a decided trend toward more restrictions over what Internet users were able to do with digital materials. The Digital Millennium Copyright Act (DMCA), codified in 1998, asserted new "anti-circumvention" provisions that made illegal any attempt to defeat anti-piracy protections added to copyrighted works and banned circumvention technologies used for that purpose. In 2003, the Supreme Court in *Eldred v. Ashcroft* upheld the constitutionality of the Sonny Bono Copyright Extension Act (1998), which extended copyright ownership an additional 20 years beyond the provisions of the 1976 Copright Act. More recently we have seen the content industries win cases against peer-to-peer file-sharing services (*A&M Records v. Napster*, 2001), file lawsuits against individual users of the networks, and challenge the legality of the technologies themselves (*MGM Studios v. Grokster*, 2005). And the legal battle continues with the ongoing development of new technologies of distribution, such as YouTube (*Viacom v. YouTube*, filed in 2007).

In conflict with recent legal history are many efforts by Internet users to resist increasingly restrictive copyright protections. Copyright activist groups (such as Public Knowledge, Creative Commons, and the Electronic Frontier Foundation), open access publishing initiatives (including the Public Library of Science and PubMed Central), and copyright scholars with public followings (like Lawrence Lessig and Siva Vaidhyanathan) have all sought in their own ways to resist new legal developments. These organized groups and individuals have reached audiences and garnered support through active online presences, public lectures and appearances, exposure through news media, and print publications. In addition, many individual citizens are resisting legal restrictions on the use of intellectual and creative products by simply not acknowledging them. The 2003 Pew Internet & American Life Project report "Music Downloading, File Sharing, and Copyright" indicates that two-thirds of Internet users in the U.S. who download digital music files say they "do not care" if the music is copyrighted. These activities, to various degrees, represent resistance to applications of copyright law that citizens believe curb the benefits of the open architecture of the Internet for the development, distribution, and use of intellectual and creative works.

As a result, a gap has emerged between the reality prescribed by the law and the social reality of Internet users' everyday lives. Recent interpretations and applications of copyright law are in direct conflict with widely accepted social beliefs and practices surrounding cultural production in a digital age. Court cases have become sites of conflict between more than two parties. They are also the battleground for competing value systems in our culture: one of control, which relies heavily on comparisons of intellectual property to physical property and emphasizes ownership, theft, and piracy; and another the value of community participation, seen in the implementation of new concepts such as that of an intellectual "commons," which emphasizes exchange, collaboration, and responsibility to a public good. The question that arises in such courtrooms is, "does the free exchange of copyrighted works on digital networks represent an act of protest to an overly restrictive copyright regime, or is it simple opportunism?" To the content industries, the answer is obvious: "consumers want things for free." I believe the answer is not that simple. While the behavior of file sharers engaging in infringing activities, such as using digital networks to exchange copyrighted text, music, and movie files, may be not be a political act of protest in itself, the development and use of peer-to-peer technologies represents a conceptual challenge to a pre-Internet model of cultural production that relies on increasingly restrictive copyright law and its application in digital environments.

This book focuses on the tensions that are created by this conflict within the ongoing debate surrounding digital copyright law in the U.S. The high-profile public debate has its roots in the enduring legal battle surrounding peer-to-peer file sharing. The legal history of peer-to-peer file sharing can be traced back to 1999, when college student Shawn Fanning developed a technology called Napster, which was one of the first file-sharing applications released on the Internet. The service garnered a large following of music fans that liberally traded copyrighted music files on the network. The recording industry did not approve of such activity, and in 2001 a federal judge forced Napster to shut down (*A&M Records v. Napster*). (Napster has since relaunched under different ownership as a pay-per-use service.) Not long after the Napster decision, a second generation of peer-to-peer file-sharing technologies emerged to take Napster's place. In October 2001, the major music and movie companies sued developers of two of these new peer-to-peer file-sharing applications, Grokster and StreamCast Networks, for contributing to the "theft" of millions of copyrighted music and movie files.

In 2004, the Ninth Circuit Court of Appeals upheld a lower court ruling that file-sharing software could be used for legitimate purposes and was therefore protected under the 1984 *Sony-Betamax* ruling (*Sony v. Universal Studios*). The Supreme Court agreed to hear the case in December of 2004, and on June 27, 2005, the Court held that the developers of peer-to-peer file-sharing technologies are liable for inducing the infringing activities of their users. This ruling was, in effect, in favor of the content industries and soon motivated Grokster to shut down its peer-to-peer file-sharing services[1].

In the wake of the demise of these popular file-sharing services, users have found new ways to share content. At the time of this writing, music lovers continue to download music files through the use of torrents (a file created by a BitTorrent client) or mp3 blogs, and movie and television fans now regularly share videos online through services such as YouTube. And the legal battle continues. Just four months prior to the *Grokster* ruling, the popular online video community YouTube, now with millions of members, was launched. In March of 2007, Viacom filed a $1 billion lawsuit against the video-sharing service YouTube for the more than 150,000 videos that are shared by YouTube users. According to the complaint filed in the U.S. District Court for the Southern District of New York, "YouTube has harnessed technology to willfully infringe copyrights on a huge scale," threatening not just Viacom but "the economic underpinnings of one of the most important sectors of the United States economy" (*Viacom International v. YouTube* Compl. para. 2). This case continues, but certainly will not end, the legal battle over copyright law and digital networks.

Seeking to establish where the line should be drawn between protecting copyright and encouraging innovation, the digital copyright debate reveals the tensions among several interested parties: artists and creators, users of copyrighted works (including students, researchers, and instructors), content industries, and technologists. A look at the history of copyright law in the U.S., as discussed more fully in Chapter 3, shows us that these tensions are not new. Technological development has both presented challenges to and opened new outlets for the creation and distribution of copyrighted works. From the Gutenberg printing press to the player piano to the Xerox machine to the VCR to the CD burner to the mp3 player, new technologies have upset the balance between copyright protection and innovation. What makes the current digital copyright debate significant, however, is that it is situated within a culture marked by increasingly centralized markets for content and a proliferation of legal restrictions for online activity that run counter to the values promised by new Internet technologies: active participation and sharing. As Lawrence Lessig cogently argues in *Free Culture*, "*Never in our history have fewer had a legal right to control more of the development of our culture than now*" (170, italics in original).

INTELLECTUAL PROPERTY IN RHETORIC AND WRITING STUDIES

The implications of this debate are great for rhetoric and writing studies. The field has had a long-standing interest in the relationship between authors (authors, artists, musicians, moviemakers, on the production side) and users (readers, listeners, viewers, on the consumption side), particularly as affected by digital communication technologies. While the Internet is a site for distribution of materials, it is also a site for the range of activities involved in cultural production, or the social processes through which a culture produces, circulates, and consumes creative and intellectual works. The Internet is different from pre-digital technologies used for cultural production (such as the printing press and the videorecorder) in that who can participate and in what ways is more open. The technical structure of the

Internet allows readers/users/consumers to move easily into the role of writers/creators/producers. It is this difference that makes a study of cultural production on the Internet of interest to rhetoric and writing-studies scholars. Discussions of copyright and its application to peer-to-peer file-sharing technologies may seem relatively uninteresting, as the digital copyright debate appears focused on distribution rather than production of information. And rhetoric and composition researchers may very likely not have an interest in the legal fate of a particular peer-to-peer file-sharing service or whether an Internet user can download Brittany Spears' latest album for free. However, copyright debates that address peer-to-peer file-sharing technologies are about more than a particular peer-to-peer file-sharing technology or a particular type of content. The debates have implications for the future of cultural production on the Internet. Analysis of the digital copyright debates reveals not only a clash between users who want to trade copyrighted music files and the RIAA, but also a clash between differing conceptual models for cultural production. Peer-to-peer file-sharing programs are more than a threat to the economic and legal structures for selling music; they are also a challenge to a cultural model for producing and distributing content that is based on exclusivity and centralized control by powerful content industries.

This point is often underemphasized in current scholarship in rhetoric and composition on intellectual property. Too often the academic debate about digital copyright fails on one of two fronts. First, scholars face the danger of conflating the issues of production and consumption, assuming that it is obvious why discussions about technologies that enable peer-to-peer file sharing, which appear primarily to distribute content, have relevance for writing, creativity, and production online. Or, on the other side, researchers fail to address intellectual property issues outside of the classroom, in the context of the important public debate about peer-to-peer file sharing, claiming that the subject falls outside of the realm of what we, as writing scholars, ought to be concerned about. This limited view of the relevance of the digital copyright debate is consistent with how the debate has been framed in public discourse. The content industries have successfully positioned the public debate as one about *distribution* of music and movie files, arguing that peer-to-peer file sharing on the Internet endangers the Internet as a distribution mechanism. The Internet envisioned by the content industry is a digital marketplace, very different from the rich center of participatory cultural production envisioned by writing studies scholars.

As my analysis will reveal, in the rhetoric of the digital copyright debate a binary is reinforced between distribution-production and consumer-creator in discussions about cultural production on the Internet. In fact, the role of the Internet user as creator is often absent or, at best, lacks agency in the debate. Arguments from representatives of the entertainment industry and from legal authorities often present a rather narrow emphasis on the consumption side of the copyright debate, focusing on users as consumers of content products, without recognizing the dual roles that users play: as viewer/readers/consumers as well as writers/creators/producers. However, throughout this book I argue that distribution and production are interrelated concepts in the digital age and that the Internet functions as a site for both. By challenging the distribution-production binary in these rhetorical frameworks, we can see that these issues extend beyond a debate about music file sharing and into a larger debate about the future of cultural production on the Internet. In this way—by explicitly acknowledging that the digital copyright debate is about both distribution *and* production—rhetoric and composition scholars can take a positive step toward helping to clarify the relevance of intellectual property scholarship to our work.

The discourse of digital copyright law offers an ideal site for studying this conflict between models of cultural production, as it addresses these issues in the context of a high-profile public debate. The 2005 Supreme Court decision in *MGM Studios v. Grokster* and the ongoing legal battles that have extended even to college campuses have spurred the debate in recent years, representing the newest developments in a pattern of systematic change toward an imbalance of rights under the current property regime in copyright law. This book tells the story of the digital copyright debate from a rhetorical perspective. A closer look at the language of the debate offers insight into a larger struggle between the open architecture of the Internet and the closed architecture of recent copyright law. Within the debate, several rhetorical frameworks clash, including a discourse of property and control, relying heavily on comparisons of intellectual property to physical property and resting on a history of copyright law that is entrenched in property laws, and another a discourse of freedom and sharing, introducing new legal concepts such as that of an intellectual "commons," and emphasizing exchange, collaboration, and communal responsibility. As my analysis reveals, these frameworks rely on technological determinism, positioning digital technologies as either inherently progressive or destructive. Such frameworks fail to define the Internet in terms of its users, as a space for both production and consumption, as an interactive site of active and nontrivial participation in cultural production.

AUTHORSHIP AND THE RHETORIC OF COPYRIGHT

Rhetoric and composition scholars' interest in copyright, or what is often called "intellectual property studies," can be traced to the study of the concept of a proprietary owner of a work, or "authorship." Authorship has been questioned, challenged, and reconstructed in rhetoric and composition in response to changing understandings of the composing process, particularly as affected by the introduction of new technologies for reading and writing. Drawing on scholarship from the related fields of Internet communication, literary studies, and law, the growing area of research on authorship and intellectual property has evolved over three phases of development: authorship as a construct, digital authorship, and authorship "code." In this section, I review this scholarship in an effort to delineate the current relationship between the study of digital copyright law and the study of rhetoric and writing. While presented as a linear development, this survey is not intended to represent a gradual evolution toward a coherent, contemporary understanding of authorship in a digital age. In fact, as you will see, it is difficult to clearly define and delineate a unified concept of authorship adopted at any given time, including the present. Rather, the phases are general descriptions of shifts in understandings of the concept, and include some overlap.

Internet technologies have often been greeted with optimism by intellectual property scholars, understood as enabling forces for increasingly collaborative interactions (see Bolter; Landow; Barlow, "Economy of Ideas"). These writers highlight the potential of the technological aspects of the Internet to change social and communicative structures. Insofar as the architecture of the Internet allows for freer exchange of intellectual property, they argue, it challenges traditional notions of ownership and encourages revised notions of copyright protections in digital spaces. Internet technologies, however, can just as easily be used to regulate activity on the Internet. Others have responded by arguing that the future of copyright law will be governed by built-in technological protection measures. Digital controls over access to content will determine how we are able to access and use copyrighted works (see Lessig, *Free Culture*). In this way, these scholars emphasize the potential technologies have for restricting online interactions and reinforce a particular legal paradigm for copyright protection. Both views risk reliance on overly simplistic deterministic approaches, explaining changes in authorship practices and copyright law by showing how they are determined by the technical aspects of Internet technology alone.

This point has become particularly relevant in light of criticisms of early work in the field of Internet studies. Many early studies of the effect of the Internet on cultural production have been revisited and revised in recognition of the dangers of such deterministic approaches. For instance, in the last chapter of Howard Rheingold's second edition of *The Virtual Community* (2000; original, 1993), he notes the misleading nature of an argument he made in the original version, namely that technologies are "tools that bring about" certain social activities, and its implication of technological determinism (376). Likewise, composition scholar Jay David Bolter, in the preface to the second edition of *Writing Space* (2001; original, 1991), "made an effort to respond creatively to the criticism of the first edition—in particular on the question of technological determinism." He explains,

> In the first edition I often seemed to portray the computer and earlier technologies of writing as autonomous agents. I seemed to be suggesting that these technologies themselves could change the way we organized

> and expressed our literary and cultural forms and even the way we think. . . . [In this edition] I acknowledge that writing technologies do not alter culture as if from the outside, because they are themselves a part of our cultural dynamic. (xiii)

As these early scholars of digital media and others since them have noted, the relationship between authorship, technology, and intellectual property law is reciprocal; no single concept determines the others, but rather all exist within changing social and cultural contexts. Technologies are not agents by themselves; they are as much a result as a determining factor in social behavior. The concept of authorship, as it relates both to digital technologies and to intellectual property law, both determines and is determined by changes in technology and legal decisions.

While I agree that researchers studying the Internet do well to avoid overly simplified deterministic approaches to the study of communication and technology, at the same time writing and rhetoric scholars should be cautious about rejecting any perception that the structure and architecture of technologies affect use. As far back as what many identify as the "dawn of the Internet," Licklider and Taylor argued that computers facilitate particular types of communicative activity based on their very technical structures. Discussing the differences between the computer as "switch" or as "interactor," Licklider and Taylor argue for the communicative value in a shift from mainframe computers, which store collections of primary data that can be difficult to access and process, to an interactive network that facilitates communication in a mutual environment, which we now call the Internet. More recently, Laura Gurak notes some characteristics of Internet communication that are largely influenced by technical affordances, as shown by the findings of her study of the Lotus Marketplace and Clipper chip cases. She demonstrates that the architecture of the Internet affects the formation of communities, particularly in terms of ethos and delivery.

Likewise, my study of the digital copyright debate rests on the contention that the architecture of peer-to-peer networks affords or encourages certain activities while making others difficult. For instance, peer-to-peer networks allow for user-to-user interactivity and easy exchange of information products without regulation of that exchange or identification of individuals, and without relying on centralized sources for materials. In this way, the technical architecture of peer-to-peer networks does afford certain communication practices, such as the frequent exchange of materials with relative anonymity. It is important for those who study digital copyright debates to note the role of technical design and architecture in influencing use, while at the same time acknowledging the dependence of social behaviors on social, institutional, and cultural structures. It is this relationship, between technical architecture and social practices, that makes a certain Internet technology carry a political charge. Peer-to-peer technologies alone are not political, but the ways in which they are adopted, used, defined, defended, and/or rejected reveal that they do challenge established structures for production and distribution of information.

Authorship as a Construct

The first phase of research in the study of intellectual property hinges on "defining the author," in which the definition and assumptions underlying the concept of authorship are explored. Rhetoric and compositionists began viewing the author as a social construct based on historical accounts of the concept over time. One example is Sean Burke's book-length compilation, *Authorship: From Plato to the Postmodern*, which traces the concept of authorship historically, from ancient Greece to present day. In the introduction, he recounts the ways in which historically the concept of authorship has been understood according to a continuum between two models: the author as imitative and the author as inspired. Such an understanding has developed from accounts of shifts in the concept of authorship over time. In ancient Greece, the author was defined according to Plato and Aristotle's theories of *mimesis*, which posit that art, as a product of mimetic activity, attempts (unsuccessfully) to create copies of ideal forms of reality. In this way, the author was perceived as imitative. Through the Middle Ages, however, the author was perceived as a vehicle for transference of the divine and, thus, as inspired. Interestingly, what distinguishes these premodern conceptions from the modern author is the fact that authorship was not a private activity but rather one of interaction or divine intervention, requiring the influence of other texts to imitate or relying on outside sources for inspiration. (For more on historical accounts of this shift between premodern and modern authorship, see Burke's introductory section, xv–xxx[2].) Martha Woodmansee examines the emergence of the modern Western concept of the author as an individualized, originary, and proprietary creative genius, an author that in some ways still persists today. Martha Woodmansee's landmark essay "The Genius and the Copyright" (1984) asserts that the modern author is a "relatively recent invention," a product of the eighteenth century. She describes this author as "an individual who is solely responsible—and thus exclusively deserving of credit—for the production of a unique, original work" (426). Both Woodmansee's and Burke's historical inquiries into the concept of authorship provided momentum for a critical theory of authorship.

Recognizing that the author is an entity that develops and changes over time allowed authorship scholars to see the concept as a construct rather than a naturally occurring category. Breaking down the notion of authorship as a natural entitlement, the separation of the premodern from the modern author has led to subsequent critique of the Western construct of the author that has previously gone largely unquestioned. Postmodernists Roland Barthes and Michel Foucault were among the first to reject a view of the author as an individual, creative genius and to assert that authorship is, rather, a by-product of a social, historical, and cultural context. Barthes's "The Death of the Author" argues against the "reign of the author," and renames the modern author as the "modern scriptor." Asserting that meaning in a text is constructed by its reader, Barthes writes, "the reader is the space on which all the quotations that make up a writing are inscribed without any of them being lost; a text's unity lies not in its origin but in its destination" (129). It is with this contention that Barthes announces the death of the author as the central figure for discovering meaning in a text. Foucault's "What Is an Author?" is another early theoretical essay identifying the author as a construct and critiquing assumptions underlying authorship. Foucault names the "author-function," arguing that the identification of an author with a creative and solitary individual is a function of discourse, and, in particular, of classification, rather than representative of a singular, natural inspiration for a text. These two landmark texts of the 1960s laid the foundation for critiques of authorship by intellectual-property scholars in future decades by moving attention from an individual figure to the study of a concept developing out of the interchange among texts, readers, and contexts.

To better understand the concept of authorship, scholars began looking not only at how texts are created but also how they are circulated and consumed within a culture. This interchange between texts, readers, and social contexts is facilitated in large part by copyright law. Copyright law, in its original form in the 1709 Statute of Anne in Britain, was the legal mechanism that created and regulated a marketplace for printed works, ensuring the integrity of the text, compensation for writers and publishers, and availability of works at reasonable prices for the public. Viewing the concept of the author as a "function" partly defined by copyright in historical context led scholars over the following decades to seek to demonstrate a relationship between constructions of authorship and the development of copyright law (see Woodmansee; Mark Rose). Providing in-depth historical accounts of the evolution of legal protections for the author over time, these works show how copyright law relies on the identification and sustenance of the individualized author as singular and proprietary owner of a text. Woodmansee's historical study of the late eighteenth-century professionalism of writing in Germany reveals the relationship between understandings of authorship and copyright law. She writes,

> Specifically, it [the modern conception of authorship] is the product of the rise in the eighteenth century of a new group of individuals: writers who sought to earn their livelihood from the sale of their writings to the new and rapidly expanding reading public. . . . [T]his new group of individuals found itself without any of the safeguards for its labors that today are codified in copyright laws. In response to this problem, and in an effort to establish the economic viability of living by the pen, these writers set about redefining the nature of writing. Their

reflections on this subject are what, by and large, gave the concept of authorship its modern form. (416)

Woodmansee links copyright protection with the introduction of the modern author, largely a product of the birth of the professional writer that resulted from a market introduced by the printing press.

Legal scholars also sought to address the relationship between authorship and copyright law during this first phase of study (see Goldstein; Ginsburg, "The Concept of Authorship"; Lange; Litman, "The Public Domain"). They recognize authorship as a construct based on the concepts of originality, natural rights to authors, and proprietorship. They note the implications of these concepts when operating within copyright laws, in particular the upsetting of the balance between individualized reward for intellectual contributions and a public interest in accessing and building on existing works. Consider David Lange's article, "Recognizing the Public Domain," that appeared just a few years (1982) after the codification of the Copyright Act of 1976, which extended the length of the duration of copyright protection and, thus, the reign of the author. In this article, Lange problematizes the notion of authorship by noting its ill-defined boundaries in the actual practice of creation and arguing against extending the concept of "originality" too far. Referencing a case against Universal Studios regarding whether the Dracula character, among others, was copyrightable, Lange argues against an extension of copyright law based on the overly broad concept of original authorship. Jessica Litman questions these same assumptions about authorship and originality in a 1990 article, "The Public Domain." Here, she calls originality a "charming notion," arguing that no work is truly original (965). Litman focuses on the notion of influence of various social and cultural exposures on individual artists, as well as knowledge of a creative or artistic tradition. These two legal scholars reveal the concept of original authorship, or the modern conception of the author, to be unstable and ill defined in copyright law[3].

Accounts such as these, which chronicle the historical evolution of the modern author and its relationship to copyright law, coincided with discussions among rhetoric and composition scholars who study the nature of the composing process. As writing researchers began to recognize dissonances between the modern Western author construct and the activities that occur during actual composing processes, studies of the way that writers actually compose also led researchers to question the currently accepted assumptions about the author. Andrea Lunsford and Lisa Ede's study of collaborative writing in the workplace, *Singular Texts/Plural Authors: Perspectives on Collaborative Writing*, is a notable example. Reiterating some of their well-known views on collaboration, they report, "much or most of the writing produced in professional settings in America is done collaboratively, and that, in fact, much of what we call 'creative' writing is collaborative as well, though it almost always flies under the banner of single authorship" (418). Here, the author construct is revealed as inadequate in its description as individualized and solitary; in fact, as Lunsford and Ede's study supports, writing is *inherently* collaborative.

Karen Burke LeFevre's *Invention as a Social Act* likewise seeks to make more complex the seemingly stable concept of the Western author by exploring the invention stage of the composing process. In this work, LeFevre asserts that invention is a social act and stresses its dialectical nature. Her study places the act of invention within social context and as part of an open, two-way system

> in which an individual who is at the same time a social being interacts in a distinctive way with society and culture to create something. Viewed in this way, rhetorical invention becomes an act that may involve speaking and writing, and that at times involves more than one person; it is furthermore an act initiated by writers and completed by readers, extending over time through a series of transactions of texts. (1)

Invention, previously thought to be a solitary activity in search of original genius, is now revealed as an act of social construction. These works, based on studies of actual composing processes and explorations of writing activities, sought to reveal the activities of the author as collaborative and interactive with other readers, writers, texts, and social contexts, rather than as individualized and isolated. Thus, they built on the existing historical, literary, and legal research of the time by further problematizing the concept of the modern Western author.

Digital Authorship

Intellectual property scholars who study modern authorship often explore the relationship between the author construct and developments in technology. Walter Ong, Eric Havelock, and Elizabeth Eisenstein are a few among many who have chronicled the complex relationships of new technologies to the cultural practices of writing, reading, and exchanging texts throughout different points in history. Whereas it is not within the scope of this chapter to offer a complete historical account of the impact of various technological agents on authorship, these authors offer accounts addressing the relationship of authorship to technology prior to the introduction of digital technologies. Ong's *Orality and Literacy* discusses the impact of the invention of writing itself as a technology. Tracing literacy through three stages, or eras of communication—orality, literacy, and secondary-orality—his work shows how the eras evolved in relation to new "electronic" technologies, such as television and radio, producing a cumulative, rather than exclusive, effect. Havelock's *The Muse Learns to Write* focuses on literacy of Greek periods, arguing that a "crisis in communication" occurred when Greek orality was transformed into literacy through the alphabet and inscribed language, changing both means of communication and consciousness. And Eisenstein's *The Printing Press as an Agent of Change* reveals the impact of one major technological invention, the printing press, on our culture's understanding of authorship. She argues that the printing press allowed for the first time the preservation of knowledge and the accumulation of information that led to a fundamental communications shift in our thoughts about the dissemination of information in our Western culture.

As the Internet emerged as an influential technology, it also introduced new environments for writing and reading. New challenges to authorship arose: how can the author remain an originary, solitary, and proprietary figure when works are being produced, published, and distributed in a network of endless boundaries, links, and collaboratively created structures? With the proliferation of the Internet came the introduction of a new author construct: the "digital author." The digital author, scholars argued, offers a reconceptualization based on changing composing processes within the digital (or, during the 1990s, "electronic") writing spaces of hypertext and other online communication spaces. These online environments for writing locate authorship within relationships among writers, readers, and texts, rather than within the established solitary, modern author.

Early Internet communication researchers and commentators predicted that an online environment characterized by the free and open exchange of information would work to break down established notions of intellectual property. John Perry Barlow, known for his rallying cries about the promise of the Internet, argues in his 1994 essay "The Economy of Ideas" that information on the Internet "wants to be free" (6). He remains idealistic in a 2000 essay on peer-to-peer file-sharing technologies, "The Next Economy of Ideas," in proclaiming, "[t]he war is on, all right, but to my mind it's over. The future will win; there will be no property in cyberspace. Behold DotCommunism" (1). Scholars in rhetoric and composition joined Barlow and other like-minded cyberenthusiasts to articulate the possibilities for new understandings of intellectual property introduced by Internet technologies. These scholars describe the ways in which established models for intellectual property are challenged by the ill-defined boundaries of reader, writer, and text in hypertext environments. Hypertext as a form of writing, they assert, fragments, disperses, and atomizes text, and thus creates a dynamic and unfixed form that is difficult to identify as a piece of "property." Bolter, in the first edition of *Writing Space*, was among the first to address the relationship of writing to digital technology. Credited for coining the term "writing space" in reference to writing in cyberspace, Bolter describes the process:

> An electronic writer is seldom alone with her thoughts. She joins easily and repeatedly with others in the writing of an electronic dialogue—and breaks off just as easily. . . . Because the private and the public, the inner

> self and the outer persona, are so closely connected the writer is never isolated from the material and matrix of her networked culture. (202)

As digital writing spaces call into question the notions of fixity, stability, and isolation of the text, in turn the role of the author also becomes unstable. David Kaufer and Kathleen Carley make the point that writing technologies contribute to the ability of communication to persist across time, space, and sociocultural distance, resulting in the instability of fixed text (34–5). It is in this way that digital communication allows a challenge to the modern paradigm for the author, in which an individual claims exclusive ownership over a discrete, fixed text. George P. Landow, in *Hypertext 2.0: The Convergence of Contemporary Critical Theory and Technology*, agrees that the author is reconfigured in several ways by the Internet: first, the figures of the author and the reader "become more deeply entwined" (90); second, the author becomes a text him- or herself, a "node among other nodes" (91); and, third, the author is revealed as a "decentered self" (95). In new spaces for writing, digital authorship is defined as a relationship between text, reader, and writer, and as such becomes unstable, dynamic, and interactive.

This phase of research is marked by a flood of more focused discussions of intellectual property in rhetoric and composition studies. In 1998, two notable collections of essays on intellectual property appeared in writing studies journals: an issue of the online journal *Kairos* devoted to "Copyright, Plagiarism, and Intellectual Property" and a special issue of *Computers and Composition* on intellectual property, edited by Laura Gurak and Johndan Johnson-Eilola. The articles in these collections range in subject matter from ethical citation of online sources in research to what constitutes student plagiarism, from issues concerning online publication to ownership of online course materials. Along with these collections, book-length discussions of the concept of authorship and textual ownership within the context of writing classes were also published, including Candace Spigelman's book on writing groups and Rebecca Moore Howard's *Standing in the Shadow of Giants* and Lise Buranen and Alice Myers Roy's edited collection, both addressing plagiarism. In each of these works, the concept of authorship is reconsidered in the context of developments in digital communication technologies.

Among these discussions is Andrea Lunsford and Susan West's article in *College Composition and Communication*, "Intellectual Property and Composition Studies." This work is the most cogent and compelling essay to date regarding the importance of intellectual property to the field of rhetoric and composition. In this essay, Lunsford and West present a call for rhetoric and composition scholars to find alternative ways of assigning value to intellectual works, for a revised conception of the author. They write:

> Such re-imagined systems [of textual ownership], we believe, may then locate value not so much in the knowledge products we amass as in the

> processes through which knowledge is produced and used; not in the radical individual or originary author/genius, but in the self-in-relation; not in exclusionary rights and entitlements but in response-abilities that suggest both our accountability for the consequences of what and how we teach and our literal response to students; not in ownership but in owning up to our situatedness within a network of others who shape our language and our notions of how we may be—and whose value, like our own, depends on our very connectedness. (403)

This reimagined author, while not presented as a product of digital technology, holds many of the same characteristics of the digital author—a "situatedness within a network" of other writers, readers, texts.

While these scholars, for the most part, embraced the digital author, encouraging a type of authorship that allowed for collaborative creation, the social construction of meaning, and dynamic and malleable texts, it became clear that writers' activities in online environments supported new constructions that replaced established models of print authorship. Unfortunately, developments in copyright law, digital rights management technologies, and the battle waged by the content industries prevented such reconstructed models from flourishing. In fact, the digital author became an example of one of many unfulfilled promises of the Internet, due to what we might call authorship "code."

Authorship "Code"

While the arguments were inspiring, the anticipated digital author was never realized. Instead, over the years Internet users have seen increasing restrictions on the distribution of information and freedom to use intellectual property circulating online. This conflict, between the open architecture of the Internet and the failed digital author, invited intellectual property scholars to look at online activity from a political perspective, viewing it through the lens of the potential influence of institutional and cultural forces, rather than positioning the Internet as an inherently progressive force. This third phase in intellectual property studies, authorship "code," examines these external forces and activities that have produced resistance to the predicted revolution of the digital author. Authorship "code" describes the ways in which digital technology (or technological "code") has been used to control the terms of authorship by determining who creates, distributes, and consumes content and under what conditions.

In her essay "Rhetoric, Feminism, and the Politics of Textual Ownership," Andrea Lunsford recognizes the ideologies that underlie persistent perceptions of copyright and authorship. She writes,

> [W]hile many have been debating the "death of the author" and theorizing about the possibilities of agency and subjectivity of silenced,

> muted, or disenfranchised groups, the horse is most definitely out of the barn. While most of us watched from the sidelines, the old cloak of the originary author-genius has been . . . spruced up and donned by the corporate entrepreneurial interests. (533)

Lunsford explains that the rise of new forms of authorship has been suppressed by the emergence of a corporate author that content industries diligently seek to preserve. This corporate author figure (or "author-function," as Foucault would call it) serves not the goal of rewarding creators but allowing content owners to maintain ownership of copyrighted works and thus control the digital marketplace. As Lunsford insightfully warns, persistent and dominant paradigms for corporate authorship reward those few who currently have control of economic markets for cultural production at the exclusion of others.

One institutional structure for reinforcing corporate authorship is copyright law. Corporate authorship is sustained on the Internet in part through recent legal decisions such as the DMCA and the 2005 Supreme Court decision in *MGM Studio v. Grokster.* These legal developments are seemingly at odds with the promise of a participatory Internet. TyAnna Herrington examines the divide between the concept of the digital author and legal response to changing contexts for composing. As she points out in *Controlling Voices: Intellectual Property, Humanistic Studies, and the Internet* (2001), "on the whole, the growing trend in academic humanism is to accept that societal belief is constructed from social interaction and dialogue among its participants" (10). On the other hand, she notes, "the legal community's dominant view that knowledge is created in isolation and that the creator should maintain exclusive control over his or her work is consistent with a positivist, authoritarian stance but flies in the face of the beliefs supported by scholars in humanistic studies" (10). While digital authorship relies on the concepts of collaboration and user interaction in the creation of texts, recent developments in case and statutory law work to regulate digital texts and locate value in controlled and proprietary models for ownership.

Herrington rightly points out the tension between rhetoric and composition scholars' views of digital authorship and recent developments in copyright law. Current trends in the application of copyright law to digital texts have shown a steady increase in legal "code" that seeks to control the distribution of copyrighted materials online. But, as researchers have begun to recognize, the way in which restrictions over access to and use of copyrighted works are exercised is often not through the law, but through the technology itself. This type of technological "code" refers to the rules of use that are built into technological systems that affect Internet use. Technologies that include built-in protection measures against copying and certain types of use, called digital rights management tools (DRMs), limit the activities users can perform with copyrighted works in digital form.

DRMs have been used by content owners to restrict what users can do with the content that they have accessed. Technology companies working with content owners can build DRMs into technology devices, software programs, or individual files. For example, music files to be played on mp3 players and personal computers are often marked with DRMs. Restrictions on use might include how many times the file can be played, whether it can be shared on other devices owned by the same user or with other users, whether it can be copied or printed freely, and for how long it can be played. These restrictions are often invisible from the end user, or are presented in the form of wordy license agreements buried within dense legal language. Lawrence Lessig's 2004 *Free Culture* notes the ways in which new technologies have become the agents of the corporate copyright owners. He asserts, "[t]his is the future of copyright law: not so much copyright *law* as copyright *code*. The controls over access to content will not be controls that are ratified by courts; the controls over access to content will be controls that are coded by programmers" (152). Legal scholar James Boyle goes further to show that such technical "solutions" to regulating intellectual property on the Internet operate to "elide the question of power," by presenting this purpose of technology as its natural, inevitable purpose, where "its origins are concealed . . . and its effects are obscured" ("Foucault in Cyberspace"). Through a Foucauldian analysis, Boyle argues that such use of technological regulation measures are coercive, exercising power without full understanding by the end users.

Such "coding" for copyright protection through technological measures thus becomes a coding of a proprietary conception of authorship. The technical structures that do the work of copyright law often reinforce deeply entrenched values of property and control, and they do so largely invisibly. This technological coding that governs use leads to a coding of a particular form of authorship when it becomes aligned with other social, cultural, and legal factors. Tarleton Gillespie calls this a "regime of alignment" (*Wired Shut* 102), an alignment of legal constraints, technological protection measures designed and implemented by allied companies, and public campaign efforts by content industry representatives to gain support from legislators, technology administrators, and users.

TOWARD A NEW RHETORIC OF COPYRIGHT

The body of literature just presented identifies proprietary authorship as a rhetorical construct and argues that authorship constructs are dependent on their historical, technological, social, and cultural contexts. It is clear that as rhetoric and composition scholars seek to better understand composing processes within new digital environments, traditional notions of the Western author become problematic. However, along with new understandings of authorship, established institutions, including the law, have evolved in ways that work against such change. This synthesis of literature might be viewed as a call for more scholarship in the field of rhetoric and composition that addresses this tension between stability and change, between existing legal models for copyright regulation and new forms of authorship and ownership. One line of inquiry taken up by writing and rhetoric scholars interested in intellectual property in particular is further examination of the legal and public discourse that has recently proliferated surrounding the high-profile copyright debate. Through this inquiry, research addressing intellectual property might move to the next phase of study, beyond critique of established models of ownership, and toward consideration of an emerging "new rhetoric" of intellectual property. In 1998, Lunsford called for articulation of such a "new rhetoric of authorship, one that rejects the naïve construction of author as originary genius *or* as entrepreneurial corporate entity, without diminishing the importance of agency" ("Rhetoric, Feminism, and Textual Ownership" 534). For Lunsford, it is important to encourage movement away from current conceptions of "owning" and toward a focus on "owning up," a model that allows for responsibility and answerability, without the sense of entitlement over work as protected "property." A recent rereading of Lunsford's argument marked the beginning of a shift in my own thinking about the rhetoric of authorship and intellectual property. A decade after her call and other assertions of the digital author, I began finding others who have taken interest in identifying, understanding, and facilitating a new rhetoric through critical examination of contemporary public discourse on copyright.

Public discourse about copyright has only recently become the object of examination by intellectual property scholars. As "copyfighters" rally on the Internet, their cries of opposition are often criticized for being extremist or anarchist, their defenses failing due to poor rhetorical choices. John Logie offers one such critique in his 2003 article titled "A Copyright Cold War? The Polarized Rhetoric of the Peer-to-Peer Debates." Here, Logie argues that the rhetorical strategies used in contemporary intellectual property debates are unsuccessful; positive movement toward "fair and appropriate intellectual property policies" is "obscured by the polarizing rhetoric often used by the participants in the debate." Logie builds on this analysis in his book-length rhetorical analysis of the peer-to-peer file-sharing debates, *Peers, Pirates, & Persuasion: Rhetoric in the Peer-to-Peer Debates.* Here, he interrogates key metaphoric frames in the debate and concludes that "the rhetoric of the peer-to-peer debates fails to meet the ethical and logical standards that have long been acknowledged by those who study persuasion" (21). Likewise, cultural studies and media scholar Siva Vaidhyanathan, in a 2004 article "The State of Copyright Activism," notes the potential damage of current rhetoric on the development of a "public consciousness" about intellectual property. This article, based on the afterword to the second edition of his first book, *Copyrights and Copywrongs*, recognizes that the work of activist organizations seeking to resist trends in copyright law is stultified by the fact that "the common rhetoric about copyright obscures much of what is at stake"; he laments that we have only "limited rhetoric frameworks" for talking and thinking about intellectual property in public discourse. Vaidhyanathan closes by arguing for the importance of a new discourse that breaks free from what he calls the "property-talk trap" and moves toward "commons talk."

Law scholar James Boyle, in a 2003 essay "The Second Enclosure Movement and the Construction of the Public Domain," suggests another potential alternative framework. Offering the "vocabulary and analytical tools" that he believes will enable a shift in thinking about copyright, he describes recent movements in copyright law as a "second enclosure movement," analogous to the "first enclosure movement" in sixteenth-century England during which common land was fenced off for private ownership by an elite aristocracy. He then argues for what can best be described as a rhetorical shift, which might be facilitated by looking to the history of the environmental movement:

> The invention of the concept of "the environment" pulls together a string of otherwise disconnected issues, offers analytical insight into the blindness implicit in prior ways of thinking, and leads to perception of common interest where none was seen before. Like the environment, the public domain must be "invented" before it is saved. Like the environment, like "nature," the public domain turns out to be a concept that is considerably more slippery than many of us realize. And, like the environment, the public domain nevertheless turns out to be useful, perhaps even necessary. (52)

The solution that Boyle provides, his "invention," is, essentially, a new rhetorical framework, requiring a shift from conceptualizing intellectual property as owned land to understanding intellectual property as communal, and presently endangered, resources.

These discussions critique the current nature of discourse used in the digital copyright debates, show how it works to undermine resistance to recent copyright law, and offer suggestions for alternative rhetorical frameworks. My study builds on these works and others like them by examining in more depth the public and legal discourse that has appeared in the high-profile online debate surrounding recent copyright legislation and court cases. Evidence of new rhetorical frameworks can be found within the debate over the last decade and in the past several years in particular.

The 2005 Supreme Court case *MGM Studios v. Grokster* has been called by reporters for *Wired* magazine, among others, the most important copyright case in two decades, since the 1984 *Sony-Betamax* case. The case has enjoyed high-profile exposure and participation from representatives of the involved parties, public commentators, journalists, legal experts, and technologists. In addition, the lawsuits brought by the RIAA during the past five years against more than 30,000 individual file sharers has attracted the attention of Internet users, copyright activists, music consumers, and technology administrators. With the help of Internet communication technologies, the debate surrounding these issues has reached the public consciousness in a way that was not possible two decades ago. The Internet has made it possible for the public to easily access legal documents (which were distributed to the public on public websites and peer-to-peer networks), correspondence documents, expert interpretations of the issues at hand, and public forums and discussions about the case. This access enabled the general public to follow and participate in a debate that might otherwise have been limited to those with knowledge of the rather obscure legal process and specialized legal discourse about copyright law. Because of the public nature of online discourse, the current digital copyright debate presents a unique opportunity for studying a culture in conflict over the regulation of intellectual property in the digital age.

Scholars in rhetoric and writing studies have long been interested in the legal, social, and cultural understandings of textual ownership and regulation. This research has much to offer the study of intellectual property across disciplines. Legal scholars with an interest in intellectual property, particularly within digital environments, recognize the central role language plays in the development of legal definitions and applications of copyright law. For instance, several legal scholars have discussed the implications of metaphors on intellectual property as a legal concept: see discussions of cyberspace as place (Hunter; Lemley), intellectual property as physical property (Yen), relevant metaphors of intellectual creation (C. Rose, "Several Futures of Property"), the metaphor of the "public domain" (Boyle, "Second Enclosure Movement"; Cohen), and discussion of the use of the terms "balance" and "bargain" in legal discourse of copyright law (Litman, *Digital Copyright* 77–88). Lessig's *Free Culture* likewise focuses in large part on language, namely the terminology of "property" and "piracy" in intellectual property law. And L. Ray Patterson and Stanley W. Lindberg note the negative implications of copyright statements, such as "[n]o part of this publication may be reproduced, stored in a retrieval system, or transmitted in any form or by any means, electronic, mechanical, photocopying, or otherwise, without the prior written permission of copyright owners," on public perceptions about copyright (*The Nature of Copyright* 10).

Patterson and Lindberg go on to assert that "[i]f fallacies go unchallenged long enough, they are likely to become a substitute for the truth" (11). This assertion reveals recognition that the way we, as a society, talk about intellectual property influences the way we think about it. Repetition of inaccurate statements about legal rights will eventually gain general acceptance as truths about the extent and restrictions of copyright law. Scholarship in rhetoric and writing studies can contribute to legal scholars' study of intellectual property by offering a deeper understanding of how language operates within a given context.

Studying intellectual property from a rhetorical perspective, which I discuss further in Chapter 2, examines language not as inherently truthful or false in its representation of legal concepts, but rather in terms of the underlying assumptions and conditions that determine which statements will emerge as truthful or legitimate statements about how intellectual property should be regulated on the Internet. Looking at the accepted truths about copyright present in contemporary discourse, a study of rhetorical frameworks can show how these statements arise out of particular conditions of a political and cultural context in place of other possible statements. Such a study, then, extends intellectual property research to a larger context, revealing the complexities of the relationships among language, ideology, and practices in contemporary debates about copyright.

What is important about the digital copyright debate is not the underlying technology of digital networks. Rather, I am interested in exploring how the use of that technology introduces a fundamentally different notion of intellectual property than what is presently supported by copyright law. This book examines the public's adoption and adaptation of specialized legal discourse surrounding recent copyright legislation in order to interrogate the tension between technological progress and copyright law. I argue that legal developments are not simply the law's response to the threat of peer-to-peer technology to the recording and movie industries, but, rather, can be seen as a site of negotiation among competing models of cultural production. My analysis illustrates that content owners' discourse of property ownership aligns successfully with the law because both are premised on the notion of exclusive, transmittable information products, rather than the social and relational dimensions of communicative participation.

More specifically, this book addresses three important dimensions of the rhetoric of intellectual property in the digital copyright debate: 1) how the discourse of the content owners supports incentivizing exclusivity in copyright law; 2) how the counterdiscourse of the commons, based on a model of distribution and not exclusivity, fails to prove its value within current legal models for cultural production; and 3) the ways in which these frameworks operate in two particular case studies, *MGM Studios v. Grokster* and the anti-piracy campaigns aimed at college campuses. In the paragraphs that follow, I provide a glimpse of how I will address and interpret the digital copyright debate. The ultimate goal of this exploration is to identify and understand the structures—technological, legal, and rhetorical—operating to sustain a particular model of cultural production in the digital copyright debate. Such an understanding can aid participants in moving toward a new rhetoric of copyright that may help to mobilize the debate and positively shape digital culture.

CHAPTER OVERVIEW

In Chapter 2, I make a case for the usefulness of rhetorical analysis in the study of digital copyright. This chapter defines what I mean by "rhetoric" and provides a framework for appreciating the significance of the discourse operating in the digital copyright debate. This theoretical framework relies on Foucault's understandings of the relationship between discourse, power, and resistance. The framework facilitates the study of discourses on copyright not as dictated by a dominant group of those possessing power, in this case legal authorities, but rather as operating within power instantiated through mundane and everyday social practices and relations. This approach reveals that it is through discourse that we can understand the conditions for (and against) change in the legal landscape. I show how a rhetorical analysis of the debate, including both the dominant discourses of legal authorities and content owners and the counterdiscourses of copyright activist groups, is useful for understanding how particular beliefs and values in the regulation of intellectual property on digital networks are legitimized.

Chapter 3 establishes the tension between digital technology development and copyright law as it has developed historically. In this chapter, I offer a historical look at selected cases and legislation in U.S. copyright law over time, with particular attention given to the foundations for copyright protections. Such a history demonstrates the contentious relationship between technological developments and expansions to legal authors' rights throughout the history of U.S. copyright law.

In Chapter 4, I identify a primary narrative employed by content owners—representatives of the music and motion picture industries, recording companies, songwriters, and music publishers—that tells their version of the copyright story. I argue that the metaphor of "property" at the heart of the narrative posed by content owners is premised on a value of individual reward for creative activity and exclusive, transmittable information products. As such, it positions technology as destructive to creative and intellectual activity and supports the regulation of digital communication technologies.

My analysis in Chapter 5 focuses on a narrative employed by technologists and copyright activists. I examine a central metaphor in this narrative as a counterdiscourse that has emerged in response to the dominant discourse of property ownership, that of "the commons." This rhetoric of resistance can be seen in the discourse of technology companies and their advocates, including the Electronic Frontier Foundation, Public Knowledge, and P2P United. This discourse, based on the metaphor of "the commons," highlights the democratizing nature of digital networks and the values of cooperation and community. My analysis reveals that this discourse fails, however, to make a clear distinction between a free pass to consume entertainment products and the freedom to access, build on, and contribute to an information commons.

Chapter 6 examines the legal discourse in the debate in the context of the most recent copyright case to reach the Supreme Court, *MGM Studios v. Grokster* (2005). Through examination of key legal documents in the case—including petitioner, respondent, and amicus briefs and the judicial opinion—I note the assertion of a tension between the "competing values" of creativity and technological innovation. My analysis reveals that what is determined to be "progress in the arts and sciences" requires that cultural production be regulated to fit the economic models existing for print- and analog creativity. By introducing a new "inducement rule," the decision in *Grokster* supports the transformation of creative activity into monetary forms and the reduction of the complex social systems that produce intellectual works into business transactions between corporate authors and consumer citizens.

Chapter 7 offers a second case study of the rhetorical work of narratives in the digital copyright debate. In this chapter, I analyze the anti-piracy messages aiming to educate college students about digital copyright. These messages, presented by content industries and their supporters over the past several years, have gained support from university administrators and Congress. Namely, their efforts follow the Higher Education Opportunity Act of 2008, which asks universities to offer "alternatives" and "technology-based deterrents" to peer-to-peer file sharing. An analysis of the narratives and characters presented in these campaigns reveals how the anti-piracy messages fail to recognize the complex roles of computer users as producers of content as well as consumers.

Copyright law has the potential to regulate digital culture by fitting it to increasingly commercial patterns that threaten to undermine the democratic potential of a networked society. An underlying assumption in this book is that researchers studying rhetorical practices in online debates surrounding legal issues can help shape public debate and, ultimately, public policy. In Chapter 8, I describe the larger implications of the digital copyright debate for the future of cultural production. I conclude by arguing for an ethical and responsible enactment of a new rhetoric of copyright.

2 Rhetoric, Law, and Power in the Copyright Debate

The discourse surrounding copyright law in recent years has been plagued by a series of polarized oppositions between villain pirates and victimized businesses, corporate greed and technological revolution, law and lawlessness, right and wrong. As discussed in Chapter 1, such binaries arise out of an increasing tension between the development of "open" digital technologies for production and distribution of intellectual property and the increasingly "closed" legal structure for regulating those activities. Recent court cases and legislative activities have become sites of conflict between competing value systems surrounding cultural production. These value systems have been largely purported through stories that describe the origin, function, and role of copyright law and, ultimately, the role of the Internet in creative and intellectual activity. These "narratives" (a term I define later in this chapter) serve to support the polarized oppositions in discourse about copyright law by suggesting that one value is the only value in intellectual property, or that one model for regulating intellectual property on the Internet is the correct model and another inherently destructive to cultural production. The question arises, "whose story counts?" The upcoming chapters consider how these disparate narratives normalize and legitimize particular structures for managing copyright. As I will show, the tensions among them reveal a culture in conflict over what ownership, authorship, and copyright mean in the digital age. In this chapter, I describe my approach to analyzing the discourse of the digital copyright debate and explain the usefulness of rhetorical inquiry for understanding copyright law.

My approach relies on rhetorical analysis of the discourse of the digital copyright debate. In looking at the rhetorical features of the discourse about what is and is not legal on digital networks, I identify competing frameworks operating in the debate and the implied assumptions underlying them. My analysis assumes that the language in the debate does not reflect intrinsic values or represent a fixed, objective truth about copyright law but rather constitutes the meaning and values arising from the specific conditions of a particular time in the history of cultural production. As such, this book seeks to address the following lines of inquiry:

- What are the rhetorical features and frameworks operating in the digital copyright debate, and how are these features articulated publicly by content owners, Internet users, legal experts, and technologists?
- How do these features and frameworks function to legitimize/normalize beliefs and behaviors associated with cultural production on digital networks while excluding others?

Through analysis of the discourse of the law, governmental officials, popular media, content owners, and technology developers, we can better understand how intellectual property is defined and its regulation defended within a contemporary context. In this study, I identify key discursive constructions that resonate in contemporary discourse, understanding the digital copyright debate as representative of a society in conflict over changing models of cultural production.

A rhetorical study of the digital copyright debate is fruitful for several reasons. First, as noted in Chapter 1, a public debate is taking place in the context of rapidly developing and at times inconsistent[4] legal directives regarding copyright and digital networks. Second, as the legal experts debate the issues, the exchange of copyrighted materials on digital networks remains rampant in our culture. For instance, according to one study from media measurement company BigChampagne, the number of people logging on to peer-to-peer networks has increased steadily, doubling between 2003 and 2005 alone (Aughton) and continuing to rise since. It appears that individual lawsuits filed by the RIAA and recent court opinions have not thwarted the use of digital networks by the general public. In fact, as of December 2008 the RIAA's strategy of pursuing legal action against individual music file sharers was dropped completely (though, according to the *Wall Street Journal,* RIAA chairman Mitch Bainwol reports that the lawsuits were abandoned only to pursue another strategy of working through ISPs that he feels could be more successful [McBride and Smith]). Because conflicts over digital copyright law are not so easily resolved within the realm of the law or among communities of Internet users, they have been widely discussed among disparate groups across cyberspace, generating a high-profile public debate about a complex legal issue.

The following chapters examine the legal and public discourse of the digital copyright debate. I look at the language used by lawyers and judges, content owners, technology developers, and their supporters to illuminate what is at stake in this debate. One implicit argument in this study is that Internet communication technologies offer the potential for more public debate about specialized issues and a blurring of public and legal discourse about copyright law. The digital copyright debate has been covered by the major news programs at the local, national, and public broadcasting levels; in advertisements; on streamed video; and on Web sites and blogs. The result has been an interesting blurring of the specialized (legal) and nonspecialized (public) discourse at work in the debate. I argue, further, that such a blending between discourses has created the opportunity for the subsequent emergence of a "new rhetoric" of copyright, which, as I will show, is still in a critical period of formation.

As this debate helps to demonstrate, the categories of "public" and "legal" discourse in the digital copyright debate are not stable, distinct communities of discourse, especially in today's public sphere of online communication. Rather, there is much crossover between specialized and nonspecialized discourse, in addition to a blurring of what is presented as information and as advocacy. For instance, what is traditionally considered the specialized discourse of the law—such as legal briefs and text from legislative action—has been circulated among the public on various Web sites and even via file-sharing networks themselves. This legal discourse is then quickly quoted and analyzed on blogs, news sites, and online forums by technologists and file sharers across the Internet. In addition, legal experts such as Lawrence Lessig and Fred von Lohmann have become well known and widely read among the general public, contributing to the production and distribution of materials on technology advocacy Web sites. The lines between what is categorized as "legal" and "public" discourse have become blurred in the online digital copyright debate, and a new rhetoric is emerging that has the potential to transform critique into praxis.

RHETORIC AND RESISTANCE IN THE DIGITAL COPYRIGHT DEBATE

In the broadest sense, this book approaches the digital copyright debate from a rhetorical perspective. It takes the stance that language not only works to persuade and convince audiences to act in a particular manner but that it also constitutes knowledge and perceptions, including complex legal concepts such as copyright, within a particular cultural context. My analysis focuses on the relationship between power and rhetoric, relying on Michel Foucault's view of power and his understanding of discourse as constitutive of power structures within social and political contexts. Foucault's work sheds light on how power structures operate by facilitating the examination of the position of the speaker within a cultural context and the role of institutional sites in authorizing particular discourses. He encourages those who study discourse to ask not only what statements are being made but also "[h]ow is it that one particular statement appeared rather than another?" (*Archaeology of Knowledge* 27). Following Foucault, I explicate various statements that have appeared about copyright in the debate and explore how these statements shape understandings about cultural production on the Internet. This approach is useful for understanding the copyright debate because it highlights the ways in which the stories being told are more than simple morality tales about right and wrong in the context of music file sharing. Rather, by examining the relationship among competing discourses about copyright law, my analysis reveals underlying assumptions about who should get to participate in cultural production and in what ways. This analysis demonstrates the role of discourse in shaping the future of digital copyright law and, ultimately, the future of cultural production on the Internet.

The term "rhetoric" is often misunderstood by the general public as a stylistic device that at best serves as decoration and at worst serves to misrepresent or hide the truth. However, rhetoric scholars understand rhetoric as central to the creation of new knowledge: the ways in which individuals talk about social and cultural activities and processes can serve to shape those activities and processes. In this way, they highlight the interactive aspect of rhetoric and its epistemological consequences. In *The Rhetorical Tradition*, Patricia Bizzell and Bruce Herzberg offer a definition that reflects this understanding of rhetoric:

> *Rhetoric* is synonymous with meaning, for meaning is in use and context, not words themselves. Knowledge and belief are products of persuasion, which seeks to make the arguable seem to be natural, to turn positions into premises—and it is rhetoric's responsibility to reveal these ideological operations. (15)

Following this definition, the study of rhetoric aims to illuminate the sources and statuses of knowledge, regarding language not only as stylistic but as powerful and contributory to the creation of meaning. The result of this conception of rhetoric, according to Stanley Fish, "is to move rhetoric from the disreputable periphery to the necessary center . . . [T]he skill which produces belief and therefore establishes what, in a particular time and particular space, is true, is the skill essential to the building and maintaining of a civilized society" ("Rhetoric" 1614). It is this notion of rhetoric that connects language use to social and cultural activity. If human beings participate in the making of meaning as participants in discourse, then the study of rhetoric contributes to understandings that lead us closer toward more idealized uses of language and, ultimately, more idealized existences. It is with this goal in mind that this book undertakes a study of the rhetoric of the digital copyright debate. It is my hope that by illuminating the rhetorical processes through which participants in the debate create new knowledge about copyright law, I can help to guide participants toward a new rhetoric that more ethically and responsibly contributes to new understandings of cultural production in a digital age.

While Foucault does not directly address the concept of rhetoric specifically, his work has been adopted by those who study rhetoric for his treatment of "discourse," not as a "majestically unfolding manifestation of a thinking, knowing speaking subject, but, on the contrary, a totality, in which the dispersion of the subject and his discontinuity with himself may be determined" (*Archaeology of Knowledge* 55). For Foucault, discourse does not simply describe or represent external objects in a manner determined by an individual human subject. Rather, he recognizes discourse as a system of dispersed subjectivities, and the production of discourse as "deployment" of this system. Therefore, much like Bizzell and Herzberg's assertion that "knowledge and belief are products of persuasion," Foucault recognizes discourse as generative of knowledge that produces power within a given time and context. Foucault builds on this concept by positioning discourse within a complex web of power relations. My interest in revealing the underlying assumptions evident in the rhetoric of the digital copyright debate is based on a concern with how uses of language might contribute to changes in what counts as meaningful or what discourses have status in the legal and cultural landscape for copyright law. Foucault's theories of power and resistance help explain how change or resistance to current copyright law might occur in the context of the ongoing debate surrounding digital technologies, leading to a more idealized state of cultural production in a digital age. If rhetoric has the power to shape new meanings and alter power structures, then the rhetorical frameworks used in this debate can quite possibly shape cultural understandings of copyright law in ways that differ from the model of control and exclusivity currently legitimized through the legal system.

Barbara Biesecker claims, "there is in Foucault's work quite an elaborate theory of resistance, but one that can be grasped only by coming to terms with his decidedly non-monumentalized conception of power" (354). For Foucault, power is not located in a sovereign body or a dominating structure such as "the law." Rather, he notes its "omnipresence," asserting, "power is everywhere; not because it embraces everything, but because it comes from everywhere" (*History of Sexuality* 93). Foucault describes the operation of power: "[p]ower is not an institution, and not a structure; neither is it a certain strength we are endowed with; it is the name that one attributes to a complex strategical situation in a particular society" (93). By resisting assigning power solely to dominating groups, Foucault avoids what Nancy Fraser identifies as a problematic distinction between legitimate and illegitimate power and concentrates instead on "the actual ways in which power operates" (18). She notes further that Foucault encourages the examination of power "instantiated in mundane social practices and relations" (26). In the analysis of the digital copyright debate, Foucault's work can be applied to illuminate the ways specific practices and relations operate through discourse to legitimize a particular form of intellectual property regulation in the digital age. This framework helps to show that the legal actions that establish rules for developing and using digital networks do not emerge solely from legal discourse and case precedent, but also originate from the more localized discourses of participants in the public debate, which are largely based on fear of technological development (e.g., "viruses"), violation of moral code (e.g., "stealing"), and a breakdown of capitalist values (e.g., the value of "property").

Particularly helpful to uncovering the possibility of resistance to the legal landscape of contemporary copyright law is Foucault's assertion that change arises from "mobile and transitory points of resistance" (*History of Sexuality* 96) in cultures of conflict. Observers will not necessarily find a single point or locus for resistance to copyright laws; that is, resistance cannot reside within or be effected by an individual (such as a particular copyright activist) or by one particular institution (such as the law), but rather successful acts of resistance exist in pluralities:

> [T]hey too are distributed in irregular fashion: the points, knots, or focuses of resistance are spread over time and space at various densities, at times mobilizing groups or individuals in a definitive way, inflaming certain points of the body, certain moments in life, certain types of behavior. . . . Just as the network of power relations ends by forming a dense web that passes through apparatuses and institutions, without being exactly localized in them, so too the swarm of points of resistance traverse social stratifications and individual unities. And it is doubtless the strategic codification of these points of resistance that makes a revolution possible. (*History of Sexuality* 96)

Foucault asserts that change, such as copyright reform, can be set into action only by a dense web of forces of resistance. While individual agency in the traditional sense does not seem to find a place in Foucault's work, his notion of resistance does allow for situational changes in beliefs and practices that make resistance possible.

Foucault's theory of resistance has been highly scrutinized, particularly by feminist scholars like Nancy Fraser, Nancy Hartsock, and Jana Sawicki, who perceive it as deficient, gendered, contradictory, or even impossible (Hekman). The question of the subject and the possibility of resistance in Foucault's work is highly contested because, as Sawicki notes, Foucault seems to establish a subject who is "the product of dominating mechanisms of disciplinary power" and, at the same time, to offer the possibility of resistance to such disciplinary power (Hekman 161). Sawicki observes that if power is so deeply insinuated within an individual—in an individual's very identity, norms, and practices—"it is difficult to imagine how change might be possible" (161). Nancy Hartsock argues further that Foucault's failure to develop an adequate notion of resistance is a result of positioning the individual as a product of power relations. She asserts that Foucault's understanding of power reduces individuals to determined creatures, victims of disciplinary technologies or the effects of power, rather than agents with the capacity to resist (171–72). Such criticisms of Foucault's theory of resistance might be answered by arguing that Foucault does not posit resistance as external to power relations, but rather shows that resistance relies upon and grows out of the very situation against which it struggles. While this view of resistance does not allow for individual emancipation from power, it does allow for specific, local struggles against particular forms of power that may, when forming a "dense web" across a society, create space for the possibility of change.

Foucault's theory of resistance may prove incomplete, but his work is useful to the study of the digital copyright debate in that it reveals the role of constantly shifting power relations in the emergence of new forms of cultural production. The future of the copyright debate appears, on first encounter, to be determined by the dominant legal system that governs copyright law. Whether a particular file-sharing service is deemed lawful appears to rest on the process of the courts objectively applying established legal code to the new technology. Foucault's theories on power encourage us to see the future of the digital copyright debate not as dictated by one dominant system (i.e., the law) but rather as formed through discourses operating out of the mundane and everyday social practices surrounding Internet use. While a particular legal ruling in a peer-to-peer file-sharing case, in and of itself, does not lead to the destruction of digital networks, the moral story propagated by the content industries does shape the future of cultural production when adopted and rearticulated by millions of users across the Internet. And while the introduction of the concept of an information commons in the digital copyright debate is not individually liberating, user perceptions about the value of online production as communicated at various sites online have the potential to come together to shape the debate. The public debate about digital copyright, therefore, becomes as important as the legislative action governing copyright law to ensure a future for cultural production on the Internet.

Jana Sawicki helps to explain how Foucault can be useful to the study of resistance to dominant legal structures. She observes that for Foucault, liberty or freedom is not granted by an institutional structure but through practice:

> [Liberty] is never assured by the institutions and laws that are intended to guarantee them. This is why almost all of these laws and institutions are quite capable of being turned around. Not because they are ambiguous, but simply because "liberty" is what must be exercised. (Foucault, "Space, Knowledge, Power" 245)

In other words, laws will only hold power insofar as they are not viewed by citizens as an arbitrary exercise of authority. In her study of five court cases involving midwives, Mary Lay refers to Sawicki when considering why certain discourses proved ineffective within the court system: "[s]he proposes that Foucauldian theory urges us to ask not only whether laws are capable of being turned around but also whether the practices of freedom are in place" ("Midwifery on Trial" 74). Lay explains that Sawicki defines such "practices of freedom" as "new attitudes and patterns of behavior, new cultural forms that give legal reforms their force" (74). In the digital copyright debate, some participants do view recent legal developments as arbitrary, or at least ill-fitting, for digital cultural production. And "practices of freedom" include users' persistence in downloading and distributing copyrighted content via digital networks, public support for technology developers, and unconventional modes of collaborating, creating new works, and circulating texts online. While these practices and beliefs exist, they are still limited in scope and frequency. Only when they enjoy the consistent, widespread adoption as "calculated actions" will the necessary conditions for new forms of cultural production lead to legal change.

Foucault's relevance to the study of groups in conflict amidst legal change or uncertainty has been demonstrated by Mary Lay and Elizabeth Britt, in their respective studies, who apply Foucault's theories to the study of the relationship between reproductive technologies and the law. In *The Rhetoric of Midwifery*, Lay uses Foucault's concept of normalization, "which not only 'imposes homogeneity' but also makes it possible to classify and rank, 'to measure gaps, to determine levels, to fix specialties' " (Lay 108), to interpret the normalizing effects of a 1999 Minnesota law establishing licensing regulations for direct-entry midwives. While such licensing rules normalized midwives' practices through professionalization and granted them access to certain technologies, they at the same time limited the midwives' autonomy in making decisions in their work (108–10). As Lay points out, the process of normalization has the potential to create both order and tension for midwives. While licensing allows certain midwifery practices to gain status within the medical community, it often obscures the fact that what is normal versus what is abnormal is contingent upon that social and cultural context. The rhetorical process of normalization has the potential to present what appears to be a natural order according to which other systems must be compared, often at the expense of traditionally silenced and excluded systems of thought and practice. Elizabeth Britt, in her rhetorical analysis of a 1987 Massachusetts law affecting infertility treatment, also uses Foucault to facilitate an understanding of order as a culturally contingent concept. As Foucault notes in *The Order of Things*, the "fundamental codes of a culture—those governing its language, its schemas of perception, its exchanges, its techniques, its values, the hierarchy of its practices—establish for every man, from the very first, the empirical orders [with] which he will be dealing and within which he will be at home" (xx, qtd. in Britt 96). Britt argues that by establishing infertility as a medical condition, it at the same time establishes infertility as deviant and abnormal. Legal attempts at creating order in the digital copyright debate, namely the legal regulation of peer-to-peer file-sharing technology, likewise has the adverse effect of normalizing a print- and analog-based model of cultural production while establishing digital cultural production as deviant. For instance, as I discuss in Chapter 6, when the Supreme Court in *MGM Studios v.*

Grokster attempts to create order by establishing the "inducement rule" for developing and using peer-to-peer networks, it at the same time normalizes a particular structure of property ownership over copyrighted works and a limited role of technology in cultural production, making abnormal possible new models for copyright management. Likewise, by casting college students in the role of music fans and consumers in anti-piracy campaigns, as I show in Chapter 7, the Internet is defined as a place of digital commerce rather than one of participatory production.

Foucault's theories of power and resistance help to show that it is within networks or systems of localized behaviors, practices, and discourses that legal change is possible. Several central tenets of his work contribute to the understanding of copyright law as inseparable from the technological and social developments surrounding the issue. To examine the tension between the current legal model for intellectual property regulation and that which is introduced by digital information technologies, my analysis examines how legal structures for copyright law are reified and resisted through acts of discourse, and how meaning is negotiated among dispersed points of power in the digital copyright debate.

LAW AND RHETORIC

Many discussions among the public media present the digital copyright debate as a legal dispute between the content industries and peer-to-peer file sharers over how best to adapt existing copyright law, which is based on pre-digital production models, to a digital world. Leaders in the music and movie industries often characterize their strife as one that seeks to find "new methods for copyright enforcement" and to explore "how to protect [the content industry's] works in a digital age" (Harmon). Viewed from this perspective, the debate centers on how copyright law—a necessary and just legal structure—can be reinforced in response to the threats posed by digital technologies, including:

- Ease of reproduction. When a work is created in digital form, it is as simple as clicking a button to make perfect or near-perfect copies of that work. Rather than relying on specialized equipment, publishing houses, or production studios, which were required in a pre-digital age, copies can be made on a mass scale by end users. In addition, each time a user accesses, reads, downloads, and shares a digital work, a copy is made. Copies can no longer be limited or controlled.
- Ease of distribution. Internet access is widely, even globally, available among everyday citizens. Access to digital networks allows the free exchange of materials from one-to-one and, even more importantly, from one-to-many. These exchanges create more copies among more users in very little time.

By viewing these technological advances as threats, content industry representatives in the copyright debate suggest that the law should be extended to ensure that copyright holders' rights are protected. Ensuring such protection requires legal developments that expand control over copyrighted works, as demonstrated by the myriad of extensions to copyright law in the last 50 years.

This understanding of the copyright debate positions the law as a closed, static set of rules, a system relying on fact-finding and subsequent decision making to maintain its integrity over time. In this view, legal statutes and court decisions appear to result from a stable system of logic that performs the function of complete and just control over property, behavior, and relations among citizens. Such a view supports extensions of copyright law in order to continue an established model of cultural production, once the very origin of copyright protection but ill fitting in a digital age. The law as an institution, however, does not always operate as a stable and self-contained system. Rather, it is shaped by social, political, and economic practices.

Extensions to copyright law have been defended by content industry representatives and legal authorities alike as necessary for applying legal precedent to current digital media. But these legal developments have not emerged without response from others participating in the public debate. Internet users who find such laws unjust continue to develop their own models and methods for cultural production in a digital age, even when those do not abide by the rules of the law. Individuals are finding alternatives such as using Creative Commons licenses on their videos, photos, and digital creations, which give preemptive permission to others to reuse or republish works. These licenses allow them to bypass the default protections of strict copyright law, functioning as a contractual agreement among individual Internet users. And still others are using the tools of digital media creation to participate in cultural production in ways that may be considered unlawful under copyright law, such as reusing and remixing copyrighted content without permission. In these ways, digital network users are sorting out the rules for cultural production in the digital age through their own means, without necessarily applying legal principles of copyright. These Internet users understand themselves not as merely consumers of another's copyrighted content nor as copyright criminals but as participants in cultural production on the Internet. They want to access, rip, and remix their culture, to engage in activities prohibited under copyright law. Thus, while legal developments may appear, on the surface, as neutral applications of legal precedent to contemporary situations, they are only one instantiation of a larger cultural battle about the appropriateness of applying the rules and norms of an analog era in a digital world. Viewing the debate within its larger social context sheds light on how copyright law shapes, reflects, and is in tension with societal understandings of cultural production in a digital age.

In the introduction to the collection of essays *The Rhetoric of Law*, editors Sarat and Kearns point out that research addressing the "rhetorical nature of law," by which they mean the persuasive nature of legal discourse, may arouse anxiety in its potential to reveal the "unscrupulous, unattractive ways legal processes can be manipulated" (3). While legal scholars may recognize the law as "the very profession of rhetoric" (Wetlaufer 1555), legal discourse often relies on the denial of the law's rhetorical nature. Legal discourse makes claims of its own authority through appeals to reason and logic, asserting objectivity and self-evidence, and denying a rhetorical or persuasive quality. Sarat and Kearns note that legal discourse is persuasive, and not only informative or prescriptive, when addressing citizens. Law and literature scholar James Boyd White also recognizes that legal discourse does more than say, "[h]ere is how the case is decided": It also functions to say, "[h]ere—in this language—is the way this case and similar cases should be talked about. The language I am speaking is the proper language of justice in our culture" (*Heracles' Bow* 34). In this sense, White identifies the rhetorical function of legal discourse in shaping cultural understandings of justice. The discourse that presents a ruling in a given copyright case, for instance, defines what is lawful in terms of creating, distributing, and exchanging copyrighted works, but it also functions to present a certain framework through which to understand the relationship of digital technologies and cultural production.

In addition to shaping citizens' perceptions, legal discourse itself is shaped by social definitions of what behavior is fair and just. Because citizens do not always view a ruling as "correct," they may pose resistance in the form of noncompliance. One common example is drivers who consistently drive above the speed limit, and another is file sharers who continue to illegally share files on peer-to-peer networks. Studying copyright law from a rhetorical perspective, then, considers not only how understandings of copyright have been shaped by legal discourse but how cultural understandings of cultural production shape that discourse as well. To do so requires consideration of both formal legal discourse and the public debate among interested parties, including the content industry representatives, technologists, creators, copyright activists, and file sharers themselves.

Narrative

One rhetorical device used by participants in the digital copyright debate is *narrative*. Participants use narratives as a primary means through which to describe and justify a given legal model for copyright regulation. Examples are numerous, aimed at addressing audiences that vary widely in terms of education, background, and experience with copyright issues, from lawyers and judges to university officials to college student file sharers to information technologists. For instance, interested parties create and circulate stories in the form of comic books with engaging characters and interesting battles between copyright villains and heroes. One such comic, the "Donny the Downloader Experience," was presented in 2007 by ASCAP (American Society of Composers, Authors and Publishers) and i-SAFE, a nonprofit organization that specializes in Internet safety education. The comic, presented as part of a multimedia program aimed at middle-school students to educate them on why music piracy is harmful, features interspersed and compelling stories from Donny, a 14-year-old music file sharer, and Sonya Bender, a 17-year-old aspiring songwriter. Another example of the use of a narrative in the copyright debate can be found in "Tales from the Public Domain: Bound by Law?" presented in 2006 by Duke Law School's Center for the Study of the Public Domain. The comic features a hero, Akiko, who battles—literally, with a laser gun—a cyclopean "Rights Monster." These elaborate stories, only two among many, seek to present complex legal concepts in ways that the general public of Internet users can understand.

The use of narratives in the digital copyright debate is not surprising given that storytelling is an easy-to-understand and memorable language structure and, as such, mitigates the difficulties of understanding complex legal concepts. Copyright law is a complex subject, relying on slippery definitions and shifting over time in response to market demands and new technologies. Also, legal processes lend themselves to narrative structures: the fact-finding and decision making in the legal process are largely dependent on (re)interpretation of statutes and precedential judicial opinions, oral arguments, witness accounts, and various other representations of what happened in a conflict. These versions of experience, accounts, or narratives as I'll call them, play a central role in legal processes. Legal action always begins with a narrative, the story the client tells his lawyer about what happened. Legal action is carried out through narrative forms. Parties tell what happened and why it should be justified or punished. And legal action ends with a narrative, the narrative the court relates in its ruling and judicial opinion—what the court says happened and what it means. In addition, in public discourse about complex legal subjects, nonexpert rhetors also use narrative structures to describe what they perceive to be the correct version of the copyright story and what they understand as a just and fair form of law. The primary work of discourse about the law, within the courtroom and in the public sphere, is to negotiate versions of experience that appear in cooperation or competition with others.

Narratives about copyright have played a key role in the cultural acceptance of particular conceptions of authorship and modes of regulating technology in copyright law. Debora Halbert, in her 1999 *Intellectual Property in the Information Age*, applies a narrative methodological approach to the study of intellectual property discourse to "document the types of stories being told about intellectual property and who is telling those stories" (xiii). Noting the pervasiveness of narratives of private property ownership in contemporary discourse, she asserts,

> This narrative process serves to establish property lines in new technology and socializes the average citizen to an understanding of what is and is not acceptable. If the copyright message can be uncritically passed on through narratives to the general population, then the property rights of current owners will be reinforced. (xiii)

As Halbert predicted, the concept of the proprietary author has, in fact, been passed on throughout the recent history of copyright through narratives. In U.S. copyright law, the concept of intellectual property as property and author as exclusive owner has been reinforced with the development of increasingly restrictive provisions extending the terms of copyright. Such extensions of owners' rights over copyrighted works largely stem from the perceived need to protect what is understood to be the absolute and intrinsic property rights of creators. However, at the same time, new narratives are being proposed to counter this story of property ownership. By examining more closely the use of these narratives in contemporary discourse, we can begin to see the ways in which understandings of cultural production develop and arise within contemporary contexts rife with tension between technology and copyright law.

Narratives, and in particular legal narratives, contain certain characteristics. In *Minding the Law*, Anthony G. Amsterdam and Jerome Bruner present an "austere definition" of the elements of a narrative:

> (1) an initial *steady state* grounded in the legitimate ordinariness of things
> (2) that gets disrupted by a *Trouble* consisting of circumstances attributable to human agency or susceptible to change by human intervention,
> (3) in turn evoking *efforts* at redress or transformation, which succeed or fail,
> (4) so that the old steady state is *restored* or a new (*transformed*) steady state is created,
> (5) and the story concludes by drawing the then-and-there of the tale that has been told into the here-and-now of the telling through some coda—say, for example, Aesop's characteristic moral of the story. (113–14)

Examining narratives according to this structure helps to reveal the ways in which they come to constitute truths about copyright and, ultimately, cultural production online. As Amsterdam and Bruner point out, it is important to understand that narratives are deeply concerned with legitimacy: they are about threats ("Trouble") to a normatively valued state of affairs ("steady state") and what it takes to overcome those threats (efforts at "restoration" or "transformation"). In distinguishing between the normative state and the troubled state, narratives separate the conventional, legitimate, or ordinary from the unexpected, aberrant, and illegal challenge to it[5]. It is in this way that the stories about copyright law do more than recount history and dictate action; they also function to construct a particular reality of social order in cultural production. Narratives operating within the context of legal debates establish a particular state of being as "normal," identify a disruption of that normalized state of justice, and prescribe an action to restore, maintain, or transform the social order. As Amsterdam and Bruner assert, "narrative is a mode of discourse that takes directly into account the normative element upon which the law is based—the existence of a legitimate, canonical state of things that has been complicated by some human action in some particular context or setting" (141). Narratives in discourse about digital copyright, then, support a particular legal order in what has proven to be a complicated new digital context.

Further, narratives, particularly as they appear in discourse about the law, participate in legitimizing and normalizing certain states through their selection of content. Narratives do not relate objective facts and complete pictures of the way the world operates, but rather offer different versions of the truth from various perspectives about the way the world should be. While narratives appear as coherent wholes, no story can include all there is to tell; a narrative is, by nature, a rendering. It is constrained by time, with a set cast of characters, a selection of events, and a resolution point. James Boyd White argues,

> In looking at competing stories, and trying to decide between them, or upon a third, we thus naturally think in terms of inclusion and exclusion: what—or who—is present that can be dropped? Where should it begin, how should it end? The lawyer who reads and remakes a story . . . is constantly at work seeking to integrate tension and consistency into a coherent whole, to comprehend contraries: different languages, different inclusions and exclusions, different senses of ending and beginning. (*Heracles' Bow* 175)

White points out that narratives are constructed based on selections of characters, events, and timing. These selections contribute to the rhetorical work of narratives, creating versions of experience that define the terms of a conflict and its appropriate resolution while presenting a given version as the natural or complete story. The rhetorical study of narratives in the digital copyright debate, then, becomes a study of what is included (and excluded) and to what end.

Metaphor

Metaphor is another powerful rhetorical device used frequently in the discourse of the digital copyright debate. Metaphors of intellectual property as physical *property*, information resources as an intellectual or creative *commons*, the use of intellectual works as *theft*, and the development of digital technologies as the spreading of a *virus* or *disease* are among the many metaphors in the debate that help particular narratives to take shape. From a rhetorical perspective, metaphors are more than language devices that describe a concept through comparison with another seemingly unrelated subject. In addition, metaphors are constitutive of our understandings of new concepts, theories, and knowledge. George Lakoff and Mark Johnson's *Metaphors We Live By* is an important work for discussing the ways in which the use of metaphor shapes understandings of the world. The authors make a strong case that metaphors pervade our conceptualization—the way we think and act—and largely define our everyday experiences. People tend not to recognize common and accepted metaphors as such, however, and metaphors therefore often function on a level of which many people may not be consciously aware. Because metaphors are transparent and circulate imperceptibly in the discourse of a group or culture, it is difficult to see from within the implications of particular metaphors.

Viewing metaphors from a rhetorical standpoint, and in terms of their power to shape cultural understandings of copyright law, requires that we view them within the particular rhetorical situation in which they are uttered. Within given rhetorical situations, many metaphors, variations on a particular metaphor, and related concepts emerge. Rhetors create, select, and shape certain metaphors, while rejecting others, when using metaphoric language in persuasive discourse. Philip Eubanks, in his discussion of what he calls the "rhetorical constitution of metaphor," notes the importance of examining closely "the recruiting and rendering of conceptual metaphors" as "an integral function of rhetoric" rather than understanding metaphors as only a relationship between two terms (29). To examine the persuasive use of metaphors in the digital copyright debate, then, it is important to view them in the contexts in which they are adopted, adapted, and altered.

One aspect of metaphors that makes them more visible, or rhetorically powerful, is their dynamism within a given rhetorical context. Metaphors become more visible when they appear as new metaphors or when existing metaphors are adopted and adapted within new situations. When this occurs, metaphors are particularly potent and "alive." As Ken Baake asserts in his study of metaphors in science writing, metaphors "are vital only when they remain in constant motion" (62). Metaphors do more than transfer meaning from one term to another. They also constitute new meanings and new conceptualizations that differ depending on situation. This view of metaphors as agents that create and "carry" meaning is useful in that it allows us to view the ways in which such figures of speech change. As such, metaphors employed in the digital copyright debate constitute understandings of cultural production based on their movement against the background of a particular ideology and structure of cultural production at any given point in history. Even while the terms of metaphors employed may remain the same over time, what changes are the rhetorical values assigned to those terms. For example, although property-based metaphors continue to describe creative and communicative activities (i.e., intellectual property is physical property), they at the same time contribute to constantly changing conceptualizations of intellectual property when applied to new and emerging environments. The use of property metaphors, which may have operated in a print culture to provide publishers with incentives to invest in authors, a positive connation, more recently has led to misunderstandings of the use of digital technologies as destructive devices that encourage "theft," a decidedly negative association.

Many legal scholars over the past two decades have begun the work of critiquing particular metaphors in discussions about intellectual property in digital form and argue that courts must resist the pull of uncritical adoption of what they perceive as harmful analogies when telling the story of copyright. These works discuss the implications of the metaphor of "cyberspace" as place on the advancement of the property metaphor (see Hunter; Lemley); consider the development and application of metaphors of the public domain (see Boyle, "Second Enclosure Movement"; Cohen); and introduce alternative models to more aptly describe the actual structure of ownership of online intellectual property (Yen's feudal society metaphor for the social organization of the Internet) and the exchange of intellectual goods (Carol Rose's call for a new form of "limited common property"). The discussions recognize that legal discourse and, consequently, legal decisions[6] often rely on comparisons to physical space and property in deliberations regarding intellectual property rights on the Internet.

Such comparisons do more than *describe* how copyright is viewed by members of a culture; they also work rhetorically to *prescribe* a particular structure for regulating cultural production. In "Place and Cyberspace," Stanford law professor Mark Lemley argues,

> The cyberspace as place metaphor can be valuable. Thinking about the Internet by reference to the physical world is fine, if for no other reason than that courts must apply a host of physical-world laws to the Internet. But blind application of the metaphor to reach a particular result obscures more than it illumines. The metaphor will serve its purpose only if we understand its limitations—the ways in which the Internet is not like the physical world. (543)

Lemley recognizes the persistence of the space- and place-based metaphors and their limitations for the purposes of legal analysis. He does not, however, explore the implications of that language use on social practices and cultural understandings of intellectual property:

> "Property" is a doctrinal tool that we use to create a just society. To reify it—to make it a talisman whose very invocation renders us

> incapable of thinking through the optimal social result—is to exalt form over substance. Choosing form over substance is rarely a good idea; and certainly not on the Internet, where the form itself is nothing but a metaphor. (543)

Whereas arguing for a separation of "form" from "substance" and asserting that form is "nothing but a metaphor" denies the rhetorical power of metaphors in legal decisions, Lemley aptly identifies a problem: language used to describe intellectual property obscures the nature of cultural production in the digital world. It is useful to understand that the use of the language of property serves as a powerful rhetorical device that contributes to an understanding of cultural production as reliant on scarcity and exclusivity. The metaphor does more than describe the regulation of intellectual and creative works; it argues for a property-based model of regulation as the natural system of cultural production in our culture.

*****

This chapter has presented a description of the usefulness of rhetorical analysis, and in particular analysis of narratives and metaphors as rhetorical devices, for better understanding the digital copyright debate. With the recent proliferation of digital information technologies comes new ways for reproducing, using, and distributing intellectual and creative products in digital forms across networks. In response, creators, users, and owners of these cultural works seek to establish the rules for using the new technology and socializing others to an understanding of what is and is not acceptable. Yet, what is acceptable is not easily discernable within the new and unfamiliar context of the Internet. In order to make sense of what the rules and expectations should be, disparate groups construct narratives and adopt metaphors to assert what they view as the proper application of copyright law. While the entertainment industries look to the history of property rights and economic market effects to justify regulating copyrighted materials, technologists and user advocates rely on narratives about saving endangered intellectual resources and the benefits of an intellectual commons. Each story has a collection of metaphors, cast of characters, setting, sequence of events, and moral of the story that may be included in or excluded from another story. As my analysis reveals in the pages that follow, these competing narratives reveal a deep conflict between a value in individualized ownership and a value in a participatory Internet. It is within this deeper conflict that a problematic model for copyright regulation is established, the privileging of a state of cultural production based on individualism, exclusivity, and private reward over one based on community, participation, and collective responsibility.

Foucault asks those who study discourse to reject reliance on certain "unities of discourse" that draw attention to groupings, links, likenesses, and categorizations but may not offer a "pure description of discursive events" (*Archaeology of Knowledge* 27). Instead, we should ask, "[h]ow is it that one particular statement appeared rather than another?" (27). Following Foucault, I explore how certain narratives or metaphors appear where others do not. This study of inclusivity and exclusivity in the digital copyright debate is helpful in sorting out the complex role of rhetoric in the conflict between technological development and copyright law. This approach reveals that the regulation of cultural production involves more than the authority of legislation and case law; it also manifests itself through power exercised locally at multiple social sites removed from the formal legal system. Foucault treats the law as "a multiple and mobile field of force relations, wherein far-reaching, but never completely stable, effects of domination are produced" ("Two Lectures" 102). Part of this "field of force relations" in the digital copyright debate is the rhetorical work of the involved parties, which prescribes a solution to the digital copyright "problem." And in defining an appropriate model of copyright regulation, the rhetoric of the debate also defines an appropriate model of cultural production in a digital age.

3 Striking a Balance
Copyright Law and Technological Change

The rise of peer-to-peer file sharing has recently put copyright on the radar of important issues concerning the public for many Internet users, writers, musicians, artists, students, parents, and educators. However, the tension between copyright law and technology development is not new, beginning well before the advent of peer-to-peer file-sharing programs. Throughout history, when faced with new developments in technology that allow intellectual and creative works to circulate through different means, those who make their living from the business of creating and distributing works have often offered resistance. Some creators and content owners have responded to the introduction of new technologies with skepticism or fear. And the content industries often defend their rights passionately, appealing to the legal system for satisfactory response to these new threats by way of strict enforcement of copyright law to control unrestrained copying and distribution. In a contemporary context, it is easy to forget amidst the media hype about peer-to-peer file sharing that this conflict is not specific to pop music nor even to digital technologies. Such tension between copyright law and technology innovation has arisen in light of many new inventions that have challenged the status quo in print, entertainment, and music industries throughout our nation's history.

As an example, in Lawrence Lessig's most recent book, *Remix: Making Art and Commerce Thrive in the Hybrid Economy*, he recalls American composer John Philip Sousa's response to the introduction of new music technologies at the turn of the century, including the player piano and the phonograph. These inventions, which gave rise to "mechanical music," changed the way that listeners accessed music, in addition to changing people's relationship to the activities of cultural production. Sousa feared the economic effect of the capability of copying, where copies of musical productions could be shared easily at a fairly low cost. But he also feared the changes facing cultural production, namely the death of "amateur" culture, or a culture in which everyday citizens are practiced in producing and playing their own music. To the *Washington Post* in 1906 he wrote,

> When I was a boy . . . in front of every house in the summer evenings you would find young people together singing the songs of the day or

> the old songs. Today you hear these infernal machines going night and day. We will not have a vocal cord left. The vocal cords will be eliminated by a process of evolution, as was the tail of the man when he came from the ape. (qtd. in Lessig, *Remix* 24–5)

Sousa saw that the reproduction of music by new technologies posed a danger to the familiar activities of cultural production: if the "infernal machines" were allowed to flourish, humans would "evolve" into a species of consumers rather than producers of culture. Everyday citizens would no longer participate in music making, but rather would become passive listeners of the music produced by an elite few. Sousa's fear was not only about an economic market but also about redefining the roles in cultural production, effectively limiting who produces. He argued that U.S. copyright law should respond in a way that supports participatory culture, which flourished prior to the introduction of the phonograph and player piano by allowing as many citizens as possible to engage in acts of music making. The premise was simple: the existing model for cultural production, in its reliance on amateur participation, led to more cultural production and a more robust artistic and intellectual landscape. What is most notable about Sousa's comments, however, is his focus on the technology itself as the destructive force of this production model. He understood the machines as a threat to the future of cultural production in that they would eliminate the practice of amateur participation. Therefore, he argued, copyright law must be applied to regulate the machines themselves.

This argument, at first glance, seems very different from that of content owners and publishing bodies today. In fact, Lessig notes that Sousa's claims could be applied to support what Lessig calls the "read/write culture" of the Internet age, which some content industries are working so diligently to prevent. Today, the movie and music industries seek to sustain a model of cultural production that relies on intermediaries to produce and distribute intellectual and creative works from a select few, a very different model from the amateur culture Sousa valued. Before music products are released to the public, for instance, artists must work within an established business model for recording and releasing music, usually for one of the four major labels that dominate the music industry (Sony, EMI, Universal, and Warner). This business model employs music publishers, producers, and record labels who produce and circulate the recorded music; online music stores and performance rights organizations, who help to distribute their music online; and booking agents, road crews, and promotional staff to handle live music performances; among others. This model of music production, and similar models in movie production and book publishing, has little use for amateur participation, with the goal of producing a finalized, professional product to the consuming public. However, perhaps surprisingly given all that has changed in terms of technological development, the debate about copyright law and its relationship to technology remains similar in many ways to the one that engaged Sousa a century earlier. The debate today continues to be characterized by a fear that new technological developments will alter the cultural landscape in such a way that the production of intellectual and creative works will fundamentally change in a negative way, perhaps even ceasing to exist altogether.

As an example of the fear circulating within the contemporary digital copyright debate that technology will destroy cultural production, "Donny the Downloader," an educational video released in 2007 that is geared toward middle-school-age children, features a 17-year-old singer/songwriter identified as Sonya, interviewing Michelle Lewis, a recording artist/songwriter representing ASCAP. In this conversation, the teenager wants to enter into the activities of cultural production in the only way imaginable: as a songwriter working within the established music business. She is interviewing a representative from ASCAP about how peer-to-peer file sharing might affect her future in music. Their conversation reveals this fear of the implications of new technologies for the future of music:

> *Sonya*: What do you think is going to happen to the music industry if everyone keeps illegally downloading?
> *Michelle Lewis*: I'm worried that songs will go away. I'm worried that making music will become a hobby for most people and people won't take it as seriously. People value what they pay for and if it's free, it's like wallpaper, it's like air, it's like water. It becomes disposable. It's not good for music ultimately to treat it like it's free . . . like it's worthless.

Lewis is concerned about music losing value because production will no longer be professionalized ("making music will become a hobby"). Sousa argued the opposite when he expressed concern for the loss of amateur culture. However, the premise of this contemporary argument about the value of copyright in sustaining a rich musical culture is consistent with Sousa's: technology will endanger the future of copyright and, in turn, the future of cultural production ("songs will go away"). Thus, the argument goes, copyright law needs to be updated, or at least more rigorously applied, to regulate technology and protect the future of cultural production from extinction.

The relationship between copyright law and technological innovation is complex, interdependent, and often contentious. Developments in copyright law reveal much about how we, as a culture, perceive new technologies. Often applications or interpretations of copyright law rely on the assumption that technology, if unregulated, is potentially destructive to society by inhibiting cultural production. Given this history of tension between copyright law and technological change, we can see that more is at stake in contemporary digital copyright debates than how popular music will be distributed on the Internet. Rather, what is at issue are the production models themselves. The legal rights and social practices associated with who produces and who consumes are being redefined. A brief, selective history of U.S. copyright law can tell us more about the relationship between copyright and technology. This chapter begins with a brief overview of the basics of copyright law, moves to discuss the theoretical foundations for copyright protections, and then outlines certain expansions to the scope, duration, and nature of copyright protections that highlight the contentious relationship between copyright law and technology development. While this discussion primarily addresses readers who are unfamiliar with copyright law and the recent digital copyright debate, even those well versed in the issues will find some new approaches for considering the debate.

OVERVIEW OF U.S. COPYRIGHT LAW

A discussion of U.S. copyright law and its foundations necessarily begins with a look at the Constitution's Intellectual Property Clause, Article I, §8, Clause 8, which states,

> Congress shall have power . . . to promote the progress of science and useful arts, by securing for limited times to authors and inventors the exclusive right to their respective writings and discoveries.

As copyright scholars often point out, this clause is important because it offers insight into the original aims of copyright law in the United States. According to this constitutional justification for copyright, as described in the short phrase "to promote the progress of science and useful arts," the law grants individual creators ownership rights with the goal of providing a larger societal good of promoting progress through intellectual and creative production. Protection of creators' rights is not an end in itself but rather serves the purpose of providing incentive for the creation of more works, as a means for incentivizing future creation. It is this intended balance between individual ownership rights and public good that often gets overlooked or misconstrued in the digital copyright debate. Too often participants in the debate rely on the assumption that the end goal of copyright is to reward creators for their contributions, as commonly argued by the movie and music industry representatives in the digital copyright debate over peer-to-peer file sharing. However, the purpose for granting ownership rights, as suggested in the Constitution, is to stimulate future creation that will lead to societal progress.

Having undergone major revisions throughout our nation's history, U.S. copyright law today applies to any "original work of authorship fixed in a tangible medium of expression." These works include literary, dramatic, musical, visual, multimedia, and other intellectual and creative works (Title 17, Chapter I, §102). Copyright law grants what is referred to as "exclusive rights" to copyright owners in §106 of the statute. These exclusive rights include the rights to copy, distribute, and create derivative works from the original, in addition to others. Copyright law in its current form is far reaching in duration, as works created today are protected for the life of the author plus 70 years (for corporate authorship, the duration is 95 years from the point of creation). Copyright protections are also automatically applied to any eligible work, which means that many works are copyrighted without any conscious decision or effort from the copyright owner to seek such protections. For example, even the informal notes you make in a file on your laptop or with a pen in your notebook as you read this text are protected by copyright law for the duration of your life plus 70 years.

When copyright law offers rights to an "author," this author is a legal appointee rather than necessarily the person who created a copyrighted work. While sometimes copyrights belong to creators themselves, many times rights are assigned to a different owner, an individual, or a corporation that becomes the legal author through a contractual agreement or under the "work-for-hire" clause (§201(b)). The work-for-hire clause states that a work created within the scope of employment becomes the property of the employer. This means that work created under contract, as with a book publisher or recording company, is often not owned not by the artist or creator but by the publishing body or company. Many creators, including writers, filmmakers, and musicians, are surprised to discover that they do not retain the copyright to a work they have created.

Further, as information and entertainment products become more widespread in our economy, many "authors" that own the copyright for, produce, and distribute these goods have grown into large industries. Representatives from these same content industries—including the music and movie industries, music publishing, print publishing, the computer software industry, and radio, television, and cable broadcasting—often initiate and contribute to legislative processes. Jessica Litman chronicles the legislative story behind the 1998 Digital Millennium Copyright Act (DMCA), demonstrating how the content owners' "seats at the bargaining table" influence the legal process. As Litman reports, the DMCA was largely shaped by a working group on intellectual property that was chaired by Bruce Lehman, the newly appointed patent commissioner and a former copyright lawyer for the computer industry. Lehman's senior staff included former lobbyists for the copyright industries, and the group of major information-industry partners together contributed to a report on the state of copyright law that made recommendations for copyright reform. In addition, once the language of the DMCA was drafted, representatives of the motion picture and recording industries responded with support of copyright reform (in particular, the adoption negotiation of anti-circumvention provisions) by sharing cautionary tales of the problems of widespread international piracy. This example shows, Litman argues, "[c]opyright legislation written by multiparty negotiation is long, detailed, counterintuitive, kind to the status quo, and hostile to potential new competitors" (*Digital Copyright* 144). Amidst negotiations among the motion picture industry, the music recording industry, book publishers, the software publishing industry, the Internet service provider industry, and technology manufacturers, it was the public interest that got lost in copyright reform activities surrounding the DMCA.

While the rights granted to legal authors are identified as exclusive rights, limitations to rights of copyright owners are built in to establish the appropriate balance between authors' rights and public welfare. These exceptions help to create limits on the interests of those who develop intellectual and creative works and allow access to and use of works in support of the original intention of copyright referred to in the Constitution's Intellectual Property Clause. One such limitation to copyright owners' exclusive rights is "fair use," which allows users of copyrighted works to access, copy, and use copyrighted works under certain circumstances without seeking permission or paying royalties to the content owner. The fair use doctrine (§107) is probably the most important limitation to copyright protections for academic settings, allowing many uses of copyrighted works for the purposes of teaching, research, and criticism. The statutory language of fair use stipulates that determinations of fair use are handled on a case-by-case analysis based on four factors: 1) the purpose and character of the use, 2) the nature of the copyrighted work, 3) the amount and substantiality of the portion to be used, and 4) the effect of the use on the potential market for or value of the work. In addition, the fair use statute notes several specific instances that are fair use, including copying "for purposes such as criticism, comment, news reporting, teaching (including multiple copies for classroom use), scholarship, or research."

Many copyright experts and activists argue that the courts' interpretation of fair use is moving toward the point of rendering it unusable. Some lawyers perceive the standards for fair use becoming more difficult to satisfy, even involving the addition of a fifth "good faith principle" to a fair use analysis (San Martin). In the digital age, there are many obstacles to fair use as a legal defense for certain uses of copyrighted works that, in a pre-digital world, were permissible. As noted in "Will Fair Use Survive?", a report published by the Brennan Center for Justice at the NYU School of Law, "[t]aking advantage of fair use has always been difficult because of its unpredictability, the high cost of defending it in court, and the crushing liability that may result if one guesses wrong" (Heines and Beckles 4). The report goes further to assert that in the digital copyright age, there are additional obstacles to applying fair use. Some of the obstacles for using fair use include

- The widespread distribution of "cease-and-desist letters" by copyright owners to those who are engaging in uses of works that they view as fair use. At times these letters can be legally inaccurate or overstate threats about legal consequences for activities.

- Adoption of fair use guidelines, such as the 1976 "Classroom Guidelines," as legally binding rules about fair use. These guidelines suggest bright-line rules about using copyright works—such as meeting tests of "brevity" (e.g., 1,000 words or 10% of the work) and "spontaneity" (copying is at the instructor's "instance and inspiration" and needs to be so close in time to classroom use "that it would be unreasonable to expect a timely reply to a request for permissions")—that do not find support in copyright law itself ("Agreement on Guidelines for Classroom Copying"). As such, they have the potential effect of limiting uses that could be considered fair uses.
- The potential for the DMCA to limit fair use with its "anti-circumvention" provision, which makes bypassing digital rights management systems unlawful for most purposes.
- The proliferation of licensing intermediaries, such as the Copyright Clearance Center, that offer pay-per-use licenses for the use of copyrighted works. These intermediaries offer ease of use but potentially obscure the fair use rights of users.

While many of these barriers to fair use are not legislative acts, each relies on the threat of legal punishment for using copyrighted works without paying royalties or securing permission, even when that use may be defensible under fair use. Together, they result in a cultural perception that fair use, arguably the most important limitation on exclusive copyright protections, is very limited in scope and applies only to very few circumstances in the digital age.

THEORETICAL FOUNDATIONS FOR COPYRIGHT LAW

The basic tenets of copyright law previously described—defining what is copyrighted, who holds a copyright to a work, and what the exceptions are to these exclusive rights—set the stage for better understanding the complex relationship between copyright and technology today. These tenets arose from the ongoing balancing act between authors' rights and users' rights, a balancing act that has more recently become destabilized with the introduction of digital communication technologies. Legal experts and analysts have explored the origin and implications of this balancing act, noting the role of foundational principles of copyright regulation that give rise to conflicts. On the one hand, copyright law is intended to support a democratic society by creating a marketplace that makes creative and intellectual works available to the public, who can enjoy them, learn from them, critique them, and build on them, with the end result of societal progress. On the other hand, the creators of such works deserve compensation for their hard work and creativity. It is these two foundational principles—the value of a marketplace of ideas to a democratic society and the notion of authors' rights—that underlie the uneasy balancing act inherent to copyright law.

Democratic Production, Democratic Society

One fundamental goal for copyright focuses on the necessity of copyright protections for supporting a democratic society. This rationale for copyright focuses on the ways in which creativity and cultural production work to support a particular social structure. Following the framers of the U.S. Constitution, who noted the role of copyright law in providing incentives to spur more creative and intellectual work to support "progress," this viewpoint assumes the value of an uncensored marketplace of ideas in the sustenance and progress of democratic society at large. In this sense, copyright law serves what copyright scholar Neil Netanel calls a "structural function" in addition to its "production function" that together create a marketplace characterized by diversity of expression. Copyright law serves a production function by providing incentives to authors who create new works. In addition, it encourages a democratic structure in public processes by encouraging the dissemination of works and ensuring that participants in democratic society have the information they need to participate. Netanel explains,

> Democratic governance requires not simply the diffusion of knowledge per se, but also an autonomous sphere of print-mediated [and, to bring this up to date, digital] citizen deliberation and public education. . . . By underwriting a flourishing national market in authors' writings, copyright would help to secure authors' and printers' freedom from the corruptive influence of state, church, and aristocratic patronage. (357–58)

According to this view, copyright law is intended (though not always applied) to make participation in cultural production more democratic, that is, independent of special status or hierarchy within a particular corporation or the government. This justification for copyright law aims for participation by many rather than control over content creation and information distribution by a few. As Netanel points out, however, "[t]oday's media conglomerates have attained an agenda-setting power that rivals that of state officials and, in the view of some commentators, undermines the democratic character of public discourse by skewing it towards those with the financial wherewithal to obtain access or buy advertised products" (358). While many are hopeful about the potential of digital production capabilities (the ability to compose professional works at relatively low cost and distribute them with a click of a button on digital networks) to bypass media conglomerates and make cultural production more democratic, recent history tells us that the tensions between copyright law and new digital communication technologies are rife. No single technological structure—including the ability to produce, download, and distribute material on the Internet—will revolutionize established markets for making money from entertainment products. Instead of supporting democratic cultural production and social processes, copyright law has been applied to regulate the Internet in such a way that it becomes a mechanism that bolsters the financial gain of a privileged few.

The democratic function of copyright law has also been challenged recently due to copyright's uneasy relationship to the First Amendment of the U.S. Constitution. Copyright scholars point out that the while the First Amendment grants freedom of speech, copyright protections can actually place limitations on who can speak about what subject and in what way by protecting a content owner's exclusive rights. In fact, copyright law has been cited, most likely incorrectly, as a rationale for censoring unwanted speech. As an example, in 1999 Zack Exley created a parody Web site, viewable by the public, about George W. Bush that received a lot of attention during the 2000 U.S. presidential campaign. The Web site mimicked the layout and design of the Bush campaign Web site and included parodic stories about the presidential candidate. The creators of the site argued that they could present the design and content of the site, which relied heavily on the design and content of original campaign Web site, under the fair use provision. The Bush campaign subsequently made an infringement claim against Exley, stating that the use of the material was not fair use. As Alfred Yen points out about this case, the Bush campaign "had no interest in protecting revenue associated with the sale of its copyrighted material. Instead, it wanted to use copyright law to silence one of the candidate's political critics" (102). The foundational principle of copyright law that links it to an uncensored marketplace of ideas supporting democratic society has recently faced challenges from both powerful content owners who seek financial gain and from political forces seeking to censor speech.

Authors' Rights

On the other side of the copyright balance is the concept of authors' rights. In the contemporary digital copyright debate, the movie and music industries attempt to show in their arguments against peer-to-peer file sharing that the *reason* copyright exists is to protect those who create works from pilfering. This rationale—the idea that copyright law's primary purpose is to reward individual authors for their contributions—is based in part on the notion of "moral rights" or "natural rights" for individuals. The notion of "moral rights" can be traced to some European countries, where copyright laws depict an intimate bond between authors and their works. Law professor Jane Ginsburg notes in her essay "A Tale of Two Copyrights: Literary Property in Revolutionary France and America," "post-revolutionary French laws and theorists portray the existence of an intimate and almost sacred bond between authors and their works as the source of a strong literary and artistic property right" (991–92). In support of this observation, she presents a claim about French copyright law by France's leading modern copyright theorist, the late Henri Desbois, who asserted,

> The author is protected as an author, in his status as a creator, because a bond unites him to the object of his creation. In the French tradition, Parliament has repudiated the utilitarian concept of protecting works of authorship in order to stimulate literary and artistic activity. (qtd. in Ginsburg 991–92)

This concept of moral rights extends to the U.S. as specified in the Berne Convention for the Protection of Literary and Artistic Works, the international copyright agreement signed by the U.S. in 1989. The agreement establishes that each country that has signed must provide protection for copyrighted works first created and/or published in other countries of the Berne Convention. Further, the rights granted to an author must be the same rights granted under the citizen's own national copyright law. The Berne Convention affords moral rights to authors, including the right to attribution (also called a paternity right) and the right to the integrity of the work (or the right to protect a work from mutilation or distortion that could damage an author's reputation), although the U.S. does not formally recognize the full extent of moral rights of authors as upheld in some foreign countries.

In U.S. copyright law, we can see traces of the moral author in the concept of "originality" as defined through key legal cases. In *Bleistein v. Donaldson Lithographing Co.* (1903), the Supreme Court asserted an intimate and sacred bond between creator and a work of lithography. Although lithography, relying on new technology at the time, produces a close replica of an image, in the opinion Justice Holmes notes a personal imprint in its creation:

> The copy is the personal reaction of an individual upon nature. Personality always contains something unique. It expresses its singularity even in handwriting, and a very modest grade of art has in it something irreducible, which is one man's alone.

In this case, the act of creating a lithograph produces something original because it is the "personal reaction of an individual." This close connection, between a work and its author, is similar to the sacred bond between artists and their works as presented in French copyright law. In 1991, the U.S. Supreme Court revisited the notion of "originality" by setting a slightly higher standard: "[o]riginal, as the term is used in copyright, means only that the work is independently created . . . and that it possesses at least some minimal degree of creativity" (*Feist Publications v. Rural Telephone Service* [1991]). In order for a work to be protected by copyright, it needs to not only be the product of an individual's hard work (such as collecting names and contact information in a phone book), but also must exhibit a level of originality, though only an "extremely low" level. *Feist* determined that for a work to be copyrightable, it needs to do more than collate information; it also needs to offer something new and original.

This standard of originality in U.S. copyright law also has roots in a Lockean natural right theory, as exposited in Locke's *Two Treatises on Government*, which is often viewed as seminal to property rights in the U.S. In this work, Locke connects labor to property ownership, in this case, the ownership of land:

> The *Labour* of his Body, and the *Work* of his Hands, we may say, are properly his. Whatsoever he then removes out of the State that Nature hath provided, and left it in, he hath mixed his *Labour* with, and joined to it something that is his own, and thereby makes it his *Property*. . . . [I]t hath by this *labour* something annexed to it, that excludes the common right of other Men. (Book II, Chapter V)

According to Locke, the fruit of one's labor belongs to the individual when he or she takes objects from the common and attaches his or her labor to them to produce something new. The labor a person invests leads naturally to a claim of exclusive ownership over what is created. The justification for property ownership relies on two interdependent standards: that an individual has put forth effort in its creation ("sweat of the brow") and that he or she has made a personal or individual contribution to what already exists (i.e., created something original). In this model, as in *Bleistein*, meeting one standard leads to meeting the other, as individual labor invested leaves a personal imprint on the object and thus creates a piece of property owned by the individual.

However, throughout the years it has proven difficult for copyright theorists and litigators to apply the moral and natural rights theory that provides a rationale for property ownership to the intangible property that is the subject of copyright law, particularly in a digital age. Applying the principles behind property rights to intellectual property is complex and ill fitting. Tarleton Gillespie addresses this problem of property rights when applied to intellectual works, noting that to equate intellectual property with tangible property is "awkward and potentially problematic" because, unlike physical property, cultural expression is "nonrivalrous" and "nonexcludable" (*Wired Shut* 25). As Gillespie points out, intellectual property is nonrivalrous in that using and sharing an intellectual or creative work does not deplete the original resource. Two people can read the same text, and while the delivery mechanism itself (the book, the pages, or the CD or computer on which the work is stored) may wear out, the ideas within it, as passed along through copies or through memorization, cannot be "used up." Intellectual property is also nonexcludable, particularly in digital form, in that it is difficult to take back once it has been shared. When reading online in particular, where each viewing of a page creates another copy of that page on a computer, it is virtually impossible to control each individual copy made of a work. The characteristics of nonrivalry and nonexclusivity are distinctly different from the characteristics of objects of physical property, such as a chair or a car or the land Locke refers to, or anything else that can only be owned and used by one person at a time. (I discuss the problem of the metaphor of "property" in the digital copyright debate more fully in Chapter 4.)

A RECENT HISTORY OF EXPANSIONS TO U.S. COPYRIGHT LAW

A brief look at foundational principles for U.S. copyright law and the challenges they've faced shows how technological developments, like the phonograph, the lithograph, the Internet, and digital social networks, to name a few, create an imbalance in copyright protections. Technological advances allow users to create and distribute works in ways that redefine the roles of creators, publishing bodies, and copyright law itself in the production process. What was once intended to establish a balance between authors' rights and users' rights and facilitate "progress" has more recently become an imbalanced system serving more and more the interests of the content owners at the expense of social progress. In the early forms of copyright laws, the Copyright Act of 1909 established many formalities for copyright protections: original works were protected only when they were published and included a notice of copyright. In addition, the 1909 Act required that a content owner take formal steps to renew the copyright of a work, usually for a total term of 28 years. The 1909 Act's formalities and its renewal structure required content owners who were genuinely interested in pursuing rewards for their copyrighted works to take affirmative steps indicating their intent, and if they failed to act, their work was free for others to use. The 1976 Copyright Act, however, changed much of these formal requirements, and since then the U.S. Copyright Act has been amended more than 20 times, offering increased protection for copyright owners (and not necessarily for creators) (Cohen et al. 36–37). These expansions have affected the subject matter of copyright, duration, penalties for infringement, and the use of technology to support copyright protections.

One area of expansion in copyright law is the designation of the subject matter of copyrightable material, or what copyright protects. According to the 1976 U.S. Copyright Act, copyright protections applied to literary works, musical works, dramatic works, pantomimes and choreographic works, pictorial, graphic, and structural works, motion pictures and audiovisual recordings, and sound recordings, and in 1990, it was amended to include an eighth category, architectural works (Architectural Works

Copyright Protection Act). In 1980, §117 of the Act was revised to apply to computer software. The revision specified that while it is lawful to make a backup (or "archival") copy of software, it is unlawful to make or sell copies of software to third parties. In addition, through the 1990s ensued a dispute about whether characters in stories should be copyrightable. While copyright law traditionally has protected expression of ideas rather than the ideas themselves (what is "fixed in a tangible medium of expression"), in several cases in recent history this boundary between expression and ideas has been challenged when considering the copyrightability of characters. Copyright law now protects highly delineated characters that are central to the story or characters that constitute the "story being told" (see *MGM v. American Honda Motor Company* [1995], in which a Honda commercial that used a James Bond–like character to advertise a car was ruled unlawful according to the "story being told" test, which stipulates that a character that constitutes the story being told is protected by copyright). Similar tests have also been applied to fan fiction shared on the Internet. The courts in at least one ruling have indicated that fan fiction in the form of unauthorized sequels infringes the derivative work rights of authors and is not fair use (*Warner Bros. v. RDR Books* [2008]).

Copyright law has also recently been expanded in terms of the duration of copyright protections. The Copyright Act of 1790 stipulated a duration of 14 years, renewable for another 14-year term. The Copyright Act of 1909 changed the terms to 28 years plus a possible renewal of 28 more years. The Copyright Act of 1976 granted protections for the life of the author plus 50 years. And with the Copyright Term Extension Act of 1998, U.S. copyright law extended copyright protections to the life of the author plus 70 years. This last extension was challenged on grounds of unconstitutionality at the Supreme Court level. The copyright term extension was protested because the Constitution stipulates that Congress grant copyright protection "for a limited time." The Supreme Court, however, did not agree that regular increases of the copyright term effectively make copyright protection last indefinitely (*Eldred v. Ashcroft* [2002]).

Other expansions to copyright law have imposed regulations on the use of technologies to distribute or exchange copyrighted works in the Internet age. In 1997, with the No Electronic Theft Act (NET Act), willful copyright infringement became a criminal activity, punishable by up to three years of jail time and $250,000 in fines. As it was introduced in Congress, The NET Act was intended to "criminalize computer theft of copyrighted works, whether or not the defendant derives a direct financial benefit from the act(s) of misappropriation, thereby preventing such willful conduct from destroying businesses, especially small businesses, that depend on licensing agreements and royalties for survival" ("No Electronic Theft [Net] Act"). The NET Act also had the effect of making infringing activity on peer-to-peer file-sharing networks a federal felony. A year later, in 1998, the Digital Millennium Copyright Act (DMCA) established anti-circumvention laws, which prohibits acts of circumventing a technological protection measure used by content owners to prevent access to works (e.g., encrypting DVDs). And, soon after, courts began applying secondary liability doctrines to digital-file-sharing sites and networks for music and videos, pursuing technology companies themselves (and not only users) as contributors to copyright infringement on their networks (*UMG Recordings v. MP3.com* [2000], *A&M v. Napster* [2001], *MGM Studios v. Grokster* [2005], *Viacom v. YouTube* [ongoing]). And, finally, the proposed Inducing Infringement of Copyrights Act of 2004, or "INDUCE Act," sought to establish liability for anyone who "induces infringement" of copyright, such as those who develop software and digital networks.

Together, these expansions to copyright law have tipped the balance away from the interest of the public and social progress and toward the rights of content owners, usually media conglomerates rather than individuals. These expansions have been well documented and analyzed fully by copyright experts (see, for a sampling, Lessig, *Free Culture*; Pamela Samuelson; Patterson and Lindberg, *The Nature of Copyright*), but a cursory glace at the recent history of copyright law allows even the casual observer to notice the tensions introduced with the introduction of digital communication technologies.

RETHINKING THE COPYRIGHT "BALANCE"

Copyright law and technological development are inseparable. In fact, it was technological advancement that served as the impetus for the development of copyright law in the first place. It was not until the introduction of a new technology that made mass reproduction a reality—the printing press—that copyright was spurred into existence in England with the 1710 Statute of Anne. This statute, considered the birth of modern copyright law and serving as the basis for U.S. copyright system, might be viewed as an endorsement of the new technology that allowed a more democratic mode of publishing, free from state censorship and publisher monopolies (Lessig, *Free Culture* 85–94). While the legal regulation of digital communication technologies is often justified by the notion of authors' rights, copyright law originated to embrace the democratic potential of new technology (the printing press, in particular) to free cultural production from state censorship and monopolizing publishing bodies.

In recent years, however, the relationship between copyright and technology development has changed considerably, now to protect authors' rights often at the expense of cultural production. As new technologies have been introduced, the law has been adapted to regulate new forms of creation and distribution of content, including photography, music recordings, and computer software. New copyright legislation has sought to control the creation and distribution of digital copies that everyday users regularly engage in. Further, even particular technologies have been branded, in legal terms, as dangerous and destructive to creative and intellectual production, which has forced their extinction (such as mp3.com and Grokster). The problem of digital copyright is commonly described by content owners as one of saving cultural production from the destructive force of digital technologies as unregulated copying and distribution mechanisms. But this description ignores the goal of copyright to maintain an essential balance between creators' and users' rights. If copyright law is to serve the purpose outlined in the Constitution—to promote progress—then the public, many of whom are Internet users, need access to information, tools, and channels of expression. And it becomes even more important to maintain the balance between authors' and users' rights in a digital age in which the dichotomy between content creators and content consumers has become blurred. With the help of social networking tools and digital networks in general, Internet users easily assume the dual roles of both content creators and content users. And it is the Internet itself that has removed some of the barriers between the two, making it easier than ever to create content by building on others' ideas, free from censorship, and to make contributions freely available to the public.

Copyright law has recently been expanded to lock down digital copies and computer programs, regulate closely the right to make derivative works, and even incorporate some moral rights' protections for legal authors. The formalities that used to pertain to U.S. copyright law, affecting both the assignment of protections and duration, have been all but abandoned. And legal principles now regulate not only copies of works themselves, but the technologies of cultural production that are central to creative and intellectual processes. The revisions just presented seek to regulate activities of users of the Internet, and to regulate technology development itself. Collectively, they bolster the concepts of authors' moral and natural rights and seek to maintain nonscarce Internet resources as rivalrous and exclusive. These revisions to and applications of copyright law are ill fitting to new forms of creativity, and often result in an imbalance in favor of authors' rights without the mechanisms that spur future creativity.

4 Property Stewardship and the Regulation of Technology

In the rhetoric of the digital copyright debate, a common story told by the entertainment industries is the property stewardship narrative. In this chapter, I examine the property stewardship narrative as it appears in the rhetoric of the entertainment industries and their supporters in the debate. Through analysis of the discourse of these powerful groups, including that which is present in amicus briefs filed in recent cases, and the groups' public Web sites, press releases, and consumer awareness campaigns, I argue that the property stewardship narrative normalizes ownership-based structures for copyright and identifies regulation of technology as destructive to cultural production. Through its selection of characters and establishment of a particular "steady state" and "moral of the story," the narrative gains strength by suggesting coherence with legal history and privileging property, exclusivity, and originality as foundational principles in copyright law.

The property stewardship narrative identifies the conflict in the digital copyright debate as one of victimized businesses versus predatory technology developers and their opportunistic consumers. According to this story, the U.S. system of copyright law protects the interests of content owners from those who would otherwise exploit their works through unauthorized reproduction and distribution. Such protections are necessary because they protect the role of content owners—including the movie and music industry producers and publishers—as stewards of intellectual property, who secure for creators economic rewards for their efforts. According to this narrative, organizations such as the Recording Industry Association of America (RIAA) and the Motion Picture Association of America (MPAA) play the vital role of stewards who manage and sustain the market value of intellectual property for creators. A conflict arises with the introduction of digital technologies like peer-to-peer file sharing technologies, which threaten this established management system by enabling consumers to bypass the property stewards and exchange, reproduce, and distribute content directly with one another on a large scale. In order to restore the proper, fair state of copyright, property stewards are essential for protecting artists from exploitation and ensuring that creators get paid for their contributions. And according to the property stewardship narrative, the best way to maintain this steady state is to regulate digital technology itself, which threatens to disrupt the current business model for cultural production.

It may be surprising to note that the language of "stewardship" has been used in the copyright debate by both supporters of increasingly regulatory copyright protections and proponents of less restrictive copyright laws. The content owners in the digital copyright debate have used the language of property stewardship to show the necessity of their role as guardians of property and protectors of intellectual goods. But the language of stewardship has also appeared, in more limited instances, in academic scholarship that argues for less restrictive regulations of cultural production through copyright law. This latter group of scholars argues for a form of stewardship of intellectual property based on a land trust model, which restricts the state's ability to privatize public resources and turn them over to private parties (see Boyle, "Second Enclosure Movement"; van Houweling). As I will show in the next chapter, the notion of a "cultural conservancy" in managing intellectual property has connections to forms of stewardship: like a land trust or nature preserve, an intellectual property conservancy serves to protect works of special public value from exclusionary private ownership, and thus from obsolescence, due to overly restrictive copyright protections. The role of the "steward" might be understood as protector of something valuable to the public from privatized interest, as employed in the cultural conservancy narrative I discuss in Chapter 5. But the language of stewardship has been adopted most widely by entertainment industry representatives and their supporters, who attempt to demonstrate their role as guardians of property, which requires increased privatized control of goods and punishment of those who do not respect the property rights of owners.

I described in Chapter 2 the concept of the "steady state" and its normalizing function in the context of narrative structures. The "steady state" in a given narrative establishes the normatively valued state of affairs, presenting an initial setting that is "grounded in the legitimate ordinariness of things" (Amsterdam and Bruner 113). It functions to distinguish between the normative state and the threat to it, or the reason for the conflict. Within the property stewardship narrative, the steady state is one based on a metaphor between intellectual property and property, where value is assigned according to market forces and economic worth of owned creative and intellectual goods. Treating intellectual property as property serves to give the intangible, nonrivalrous works of intellectual property, for which the cost of creating works is often high and the cost of reproducing them is low, monetary value as consumable goods. While enlisting stewards to protect authors from those who may pilfer their works may be the *effect* of copyright law, it is not the primary *reason* that copyright law exists. As discussed more fully in Chapter 3, the U.S. Constitution's Intellectual Property Clause identifies the fundamental purpose of copyright as to "promote the progress of science and useful arts" through a balancing of rights between creators and the public. This constitutional language raises more questions than it answers, however, about what form copyright should take in a digital age: what is "progress"? How is it best promoted? The property stewardship narrative within the rhetoric of the digital copyright debate assumes a particular type of "progress" in cultural production. This progress relies on individualized creation of original works of authorship, works created by professional artists and creators, produced with the help of the entertainment and publishing industries, and distributed to consumers via channels of mass entertainment.

This "steady state" of cultural production as promoted through the property stewardship narrative suggests that copyright law can best accomplish its goals by providing economic incentives for authors and offering protection of this monetary value through the use of entertainment and publishing industry stewards. Applications of copyright law, to maintain this steady state, must create or sustain exclusivity (limits on copying and distribution), which enables an economic value in intangible intellectual and creative works. A threat, then, is introduced when modern technology endangers this exclusivity by making copies widely and freely available without passing through the hands of stewards. It is in this way that digital networks have the potential to disrupt a "normalized" steady state and create a conflict. In order to return to the healthy and proper state of affairs, according to the property stewardship narrative, digital technology needs to be highly regulated through copyright law.

During the past five years or more, during which a high-profile debate about digital copyright has emerged in response to legal battles over peer-to-peer file sharing, many supporters of the movie and music industries have relied on versions of the property stewardship narrative in their arguments about the perceived threat posed by digital technologies. The most adamant proponents of the narrative of property stewardship are organizations such as the RIAA and the MPAA, who among others tell their stories publicly through several channels. Most notably, these organizations have launched consumer awareness campaigns and public statements to fight peer-to-peer "piracy" in support of the lawsuits against individual users of file-sharing networks and of the motion picture studios who brought the high profile *MGM Studios v. Grokster* case. Through these public statements, these organizations have taken a proactive approach to defending the rights of property stewards to regulate the intellectual goods that have been entrusted to their care. While the entertainment industry has long engaged in a battle against "piracy," this type of piracy is different: rather than using the term to refer to large-scale commercial infringement operations, such as the international for-profit piracy of movie and sound recordings occurring in China and Russia, it is used in the digital copyright debate to describe individual copying, private conduct that is not for profit (for more on this distinction between types of piracy, see the U.S. Copyright Office's "Piracy of Intellectual Property"). Such shifting of the rhetoric toward hyperbole serves to obscure the differences between organized criminal activity on a massive scale and private offenses.

In the war on piracy, the entertainment industry representatives have repeated the property stewardship narrative in legal briefs, press releases, Web site content, and "educational" campaigns that tell their story about how intellectual property should be managed in a digital age. One example appeared in the months leading up to the 2005 *MGM Studios v. Grokster* decision, when the Motion Picture Studio and Recording Company petitioners (one of two groups of petitioners) filed a legal brief with the Supreme Court on January 25, 2005. In this brief, they offered a narrative of what happened leading up to the lawsuit, in a section titled "Statement of the Case":

> Respondents Grokster and StreamCast operate Internet-based services that contribute to copyright infringement on a "mind-boggling" scale. Their services make it possible for millions of users to reproduce and distribute copyrighted sound recordings and motion pictures without permission—and without paying for them. Virtually all those who use Grokster and StreamCast are committing unlawful copyright infringement, and they commit millions of acts of infringement each day. Grokster and StreamCast exploit this massive infringement for profit, and petitioners are suffering extreme harms as a consequence.
>
> The question is whether Grokster and StreamCast will be held responsible for their conduct under well-established principles of copyright liability, or whether they have a perpetual free pass to inflict these harms because a tiny fraction of the material available on their services may not be infringing. . . . *Sony-Betamax* calls for a balance between "effective—and not merely symbolic—protection" of copyright, and "the rights of others freely to engage in substantially unrelated areas of commerce." Ignoring the need for balance, the Ninth Circuit denied petitioners any possibility of "effective protection" of their copyrighted works in the digital era, while shielding enterprises that profit directly from brazen expropriation of the value of those works. (Motion Picture Studio and Recording Company Br. 1–2)

The first point of interest in this version of the story is the cast of characters. The conflict presented is one between entertainment companies and technology developers. Creators and users of copyrighted works are only indirectly implicated: they do not demonstrate a great deal of agency within this context, beyond their opportunistic actions "made possible" by the availability of the technology. Later in the brief, the creators appear as circumstantial victims ("creators of the copyrighted material must stand by helplessly as the value of their copyrighted works vanishes" [50]) and users of peer-to-peer networks are unaware of how they are being manipulated by the technology companies ("[u]sers whose computers are commandeered for this purpose are almost never aware of the role they have been conscripted to play" [10]). This cast of characters positions property stewards—the corporate copyright owners—as the wronged parties harmed by technology developers.

In the age of print, the role of the corporate copyright owner in cultural production was more clearly defined, necessary to make possible the availability of materials from writer/artist/creator to reader/consumer/public. Copyright law provided publishers and distributors with incentives for investing in finding creators, and printing, publishing, marketing, and distributing their works. In more recent times, however, the role of the publisher in cultural production has become uncertain. In the digital age, the cost of copying and distributing intellectual property can be minimal. The ease of distribution directly to users on a digital network makes the very presence of a publisher or content owner unnecessary. The cast of characters in the preceding passage focuses on a conflict between entertainment companies opposing technology developers, without emphasizing the role of authors or consumers as agents who have the power to shape the future of cultural production on the Internet. Instead, without the leadership of property stewards, creators are "helpless" and consumers are unaware of their "conscripted role." In this way, the narrative defines the digital copyright conflict as one to be resolved between legal owners, or stewards, and distributors of consumable goods, and fails to acknowledge the challenges of modern technology to the customary role and very existence of the property stewards themselves.

Outside of the context of this legal brief, users of copyrighted works in other instances of the property stewardship narrative do not always appear as so passively implicated. In the high-profile online debate, users of digital networks are not "unaware of the role they have been conscripted to play," but actually become conscious, active contributors to a crime. A new character is introduced in this context: the pirate, criminal, or thief. The RIAA's public Web site, MusicUnited.org, includes one of the more pejorative statements about users of digital networks:

> No black flags with skull and crossbones, no cutlasses, cannons, or daggers identify today's pirates. You can't see them coming; there's no warning shot across your bow. Yet rest assured the pirates are out there because today there is plenty of gold (and platinum and diamonds) to be had. . . . The pirate's credo is still the same—why pay for it when it's so easy to steal? The credo is as wrong as it ever was. Stealing is still illegal, unethical, and all too frequent in today's digital age. ("Antipiracy")

The introduction of the character of the pirate into the copyright story attempts to raise the stakes in the debate by assigning an intention of harm to the user of digital networks, and thus frames the activity of using technology as a moral violation. The user of a digital network is no longer an innocent pawn in disrupting cultural production, but a thief with criminal intent. Without the protection of an outside party acting as steward (e.g., the movie and recording industries), copyrighted works are exposed to uncharted waters (digital networks), and are subject to hijacking (copying) by pirates (network users).

The MPAA, known for the late Jack Valenti's use of hyperbolic rhetoric and the fight against piracy[7], joined the RIAA in announcing its own round of lawsuits filed against individual file sharers on November 16, 2004. At this time, president and CEO Dan Glickman stated in a press release, "[t]hese initiatives are part of our efforts to ensure the Digital Age does not get commandeered by thieves who see it as an open grab bag" ("Studios File First Wave of Suits"). With this statement, Glickman presents the character of the thief, a robber who "commandeers," or takes arbitrarily by force, property that does not belong to him or her. These examples of the rhetoric of the entertainment industry assign blame to the users of digital technologies for disrupting the steady state of cultural production, thus implicating their own consumers in the high-profile public debate. Although this strategy has had questionable market effects on music and movie sales, it adds force to the message of content owners as they attempt to ward off use of digital networks to share copyrighted works by creating two villains, technology developers and technology users themselves. Despite the differences in who carries the blame for creating the threat, public messengers supporting the entertainment industries agree that the existence of new digital technologies endangers the established, and appropriate, system for cultural production. This casting of blame creates a conflict between the "good" businesses and the "bad" technologies designed for destructive purposes, presenting a dichotomy between proper copyright regulation and wayward digital technology in the promotion of progress through cultural production.

While copyright law in its original form intended to balance creators' rights and the rights of the public to support future creation, the property stewardship narrative presents economic incentives for authors as the purpose of copyright. Because the development and use of digital technology becomes an obstacle to ensuring economic incentives, returning to the "natural order" for cultural production requires increased regulation of technology through copyright law. In the preceding "Statement of the Case" example, the reasoning for legal recourse is based on what is referred to as the "well-established principles of copyright liability" and the "foundational principles of copyright law." The brief argues, "reversing the Ninth Circuit [the lower court decision that did not hold technology companies liable for contributing to the infringing activities of users] is necessary to preserv[e] the 'economic incentive to create and disseminate ideas,' and ensur[e] that copyright remains the 'engine of free expression' the Framers intended" (20–21). Further, the brief argues, "permitting businesses to profit from products or services used primarily for infringement undermines the fundamental purpose of copyright protection" (31). This brief refers to "foundational principles" and the "fundamental purpose" of copyright law, a reference to the steady state in the property stewardship narrative. According to this narrative, it becomes necessary to secure the economic value of intellectual property to "preserve" the natural state of cultural production and to apply copyright law toward its intended purpose. The identified fundamental purpose of copyright law, or its normalized state, is decidedly economic in nature. And as such, this normalized state assumes a permanent, intrinsic right of intellectual property as "property" of owners of copyrighted goods.

As stewards of intellectual and creative works as property, the entertainment industries must serve first and foremost the creators of those works. While within the cultural conservancy narrative discussed in Chapter 5 the primary responsibility is to the public who benefits from access to intellectual resources, in the property stewardship narrative the primary responsibility of stewardship rests on protecting artists' and creators' economic rights to their property. The rhetoric of the entertainment industry representatives assumes a natural property right to creators, as evidenced most strongly on the 2005 versions of the RIAA's MusicUnited.org and the MPAA's RespectCopyrights.org public Web sites. (The examples in this chapter are from 2005; both Web sites have since been updated.) The MusicUnited Web site makes the point that downloading music is "wrong" because it deprives creators of their natural right to the fruits of their labor. To humanize the effects of consumers' lack of respect for this natural right, the Web site highlights details about the labor-intensive process of creating music. It states, "[m]usic doesn't just happen. It's made, note by note, beat by beat, by people who work hard to get it right" ("Why You Shouldn't Do it"). The RIAA-sponsored Web site goes further to point out that the people who contribute to the intellectual or creative work deserve economic reward ("It's about putting food on the table and covering the rent") for their intrinsic qualities of "imagination, soul, and courage." Probably the most convincing claims on the site come from artists themselves. On a page dedicated to accounts from artists about peer-to-peer file sharing appears this quote from James Grundler, singer/songwriter and member of band Paloalto:

> I live with my drummer and guitarist and we have no money. Our survival is based solely on the purchase of our music. Music is not free. Even the street performer gets a dime in his box. ("What the Artists and Songwriters Have to Say")

This language follows from the notion of absolute and intrinsic rights to property, in particular John Locke's idea that an individual person is his own property, and, as such, has a natural right to what results from his labor. In this case that right is the right to an economic reward for an intellectual work. In the now famous passage of his chapter on property, Locke gives a defense of the right of unilateral appropriation, the right to "exclude the common right of other Men" his property, or that to which he has "annexed" through labor something to it. The MPAA's RespectCopyrights Web site shows the relevance of this argument today:

> Copyrights allow the people who create movies, music, art, dance, software and books—and other creative and expressive works—to be paid and to earn a living from their jobs, just like a clerk at a store and a businesswoman behind a desk. Without the protection of copyrights, creators would not be able to survive by doing what they do best, and they would be forced out of their creative fields to find other jobs. Eventually, there would be fewer and fewer new works for all of us to enjoy.

In a contemporary context, Locke's description of "the Labour of his Body and the Work of his Hands" becomes the work of the clerk, the businesswoman, and the "people who create movies, music, art, dance, software, and books."

The notion of property rights for authors that appears in the property stewardship narrative has strong historical basis in the metaphor of authorial property in copyright law. The metaphor of property is a central tenet to the origin of the legal rights of the author: according to a Western view of authorship on which copyright was designed, texts are objects of appropriation and authors are the solitary, *natural* owners of the textual objects they create. Providing historical accounts of the evolution of legal protections for works of authorship over time, copyright scholars emphasize that copyright law relies on the identification and sustenance of the individualized author as singular and proprietary owner of a commodified text (see Patterson and Lindberg, *Copyright in Historical Perspective*; Mark Rose; Woodmansee; Woodmansee and Jaszi). They show that proprietary authorship, while seemingly a natural right, emerged by the late seventeenth and early eighteenth centuries when the London bookselling trade flourished and gained a monopoly over printing privileges.

Mark Rose, in his study of literary authorship in the eighteenth century, notes that the discourse of intellectual works as property arose at a time when the liberal discourse of property and the literary discourse of original genius came together in the context of a legal battle over perpetual copyright (see *Tonson v. Collins* [1761], *Millar v. Taylor* [1769], and *Donaldson v. Becket* [1774]). Rose argues that it was at this time that intellectual property rights came to be seen as *natural* rights, fueled by the discourse of property rights promulgated by John Locke's *Second Treatise on Government*. Rose writes, "The key to John Locke's thought was the axiom that an individual 'person' was his own property. From this it could be demonstrated that through labor an individual might convert raw materials of nature into private property" (5). An individual's right to what results from his or her labor, such as the land he or she has cultivated, was a natural right, and this right had to be protected by legal order. When applied to intellectual property, this right became an author's rights to the fruits of his or her labor, a copyrighted work, that had to be protected. Such protections came in the form of commercialized ownership of copyrighted works: they were largely assigned to booksellers, not authors, who were in the practice of selling their works outright to the booksellers for printing and distribution.

In addition to this discourse of property rights, the concept of proprietary authorship also has historically relied on the notion of "original genius." Law professor Peter Jaszi collaborated with Martha Woodmansee in the introduction to their edited collection *The Construction of Authorship* to offer a historical look at authorship in the Romantic period. They write,

> The modern regime of authorship, far from being timeless and universal, is a relatively recent formation—the result of a quite radical reconceptualization of the creative process that culminated less than 200 years ago in the heroic self-presentation of the Romantic poets. (2-3)

This "relatively recent formation," they note, draws heavily on the notion of authorship as "originary": an intellectual work "results not in a variation, an imitation, or an adaptation . . . but in an utterly new, unique—in a word, 'original'—work which, accordingly, may be said to be the property of its creator" (3). According to Rose, it was the combination of this discourse of property rights coupled with the Romantic notion of the individual genius that shaped the construction of the foundational principle of property ownership in copyright law.

The RIAA and MPAA rely on this idea of a natural, absolute property right of a copyright owner to support the concept of "theft" that pervades their discourse. The moral of their story seems simple: "don't steal." The RIAA's MusicUnited Web site compares downloading the recorded songs of popular artists to the petty theft of items from a friend:

> Most of us would never even consider stealing something—say, a picture or a piece of clothing—from a friend's house. Our sense of right and wrong keeps most of us from doing something so selfish and antisocial. ("Who Really Cares?")

In this way, the RIAA presents a familiar morality lesson that music listeners will remember from childhood: taking what's not yours is wrong. Like their music industry counterpart, the MPAA presents analogies between theft and movie piracy. As part of their educational campaign is a 47-second film titled "Piracy—It's a Crime" that has been shown widely on the big screen during previews of Hollywood films. This short film presents a series of excerpts in which criminals are stealing others' property: a car, a handbag, a cellular phone. The analogy is clear: movie piracy, like these other criminal acts, is the same as theft of physical goods. The text of the film reads as follows, coupled with the images of crimes, like stealing a car, as pictured in Figure 4.1:

> You wouldn't steal a car.
> You wouldn't steal a handbag.
> You wouldn't steal a mobile phone.
> You wouldn't steal a DVD.
> Buying pirated films is stealing.
> Piracy. It's a crime. (*Piracy—It's a Crime*)

Whether referring to buying pirated copies of films or downloading and distributing copies on peer-to-peer networks, the messages from the entertainment industry representatives apply the same in both contexts: the copies are private property and taking them is the same as stealing someone's clothing, car, handbag, phone, or other personal possessions. This language of theft relies on three questionable assumptions. First, it assumes that intellectual property is the same as physical property. This assumption neglects the distinctions of rivalrous and nonrivalrous resources, and suggests that intellectual property has value only as commodified goods. The rivalrous versus nonrivalrous distinction in intellectual property scholarship can be traced back to economic terminology. Paul Samuelson's 1954 article that develops a theory of public goods, "The Pure Theory of Public Expenditure," argues

Figure 4.1 Image from MPAA's *Piracy—It's a Crime.* Copyright 2005, Motion Picture Association of America. Source: RespectCopyrights.org.

that a public good, which intellectual property arguably is, is a nonrivalrous resource, meaning that an unlimited number of people may "consume" the work without depleting it. Second, the metaphor of intellectual property as property assumes that a creator has an individualized, absolute, natural right to his or her creations, which fails to recognize the solitary, originary, and proprietary author as a cultural and historical construct. Third, the language of theft in the digital copyright debate does not clearly identify a victim of the crime. While the language of theft suggests that the losers of the copyright battle are the creators of copyrighted works, through other accounts the victims in the property stewardship narrative are actually the content owners whose role as stewards is challenged in light of the unique conditions of digital music and movie distribution.

Despite these questionable assumptions, entertainment industry representatives present a simple and startling message with the property metaphor. They argue that free and open digital networks, in contributing to the infringement of the natural rights of copyright owners to economic rewards, are the accomplices to theft. As such, they disrupt not only established markets for copyrighted works but also the very democratic ideals of our society. On one level, the danger appears to be the threat of a breakdown of copyright law into a lawless free-for-all on digital networks. The petitioners' legal brief in *MGM Studios v. Grokster* identifies this danger: "[t]heir [Grokster and StreamCast] services breed a culture of contempt for intellectual property, and for the right of others generally, in cyberspace" (Motion Picture Studio and Music Publisher Br. 13). In addition to "erod[ing] respect for the very foundations of copyright law in the digital age" (14), digital technologies present the even larger threat of a breakdown of the fundamental democratic right to property. Creating a sense of fear of the effects of such lawlessness, the entertainment companies suggest connections between criminals of much more dangerous crimes and participation on peer-to-peer file-sharing networks. In two print advertisements circulated by the RIAA, we can see attempts to create a comparison between use of peer-to-peer networks and violence. Figure 4.2 presents an ominous glow, dark shadows, and a positioning of the computer mouse to look much like a dangerous weapon. And another advertisement (Figure 4.3) creates a connection between Internet predators and peer-to-peer file-sharing activity. It plays on the fear parents may have of the dangers of pornography, child predators, and other threats children and teenagers face on the Internet. These images suggest that file sharing does more than rob content owners of their paychecks; it poses a risk to the order of society by subjecting innocent people, even children, to immanent dangers. The images suggest that technology itself is dangerous (a weapon) and that peer-to-peer file-sharing networks must be regulated for the very safety and well-being of society.

When the opinion for *MGM Studios v. Grokster* was announced on June 27, 2005, the decision was viewed by the entertainment industries as

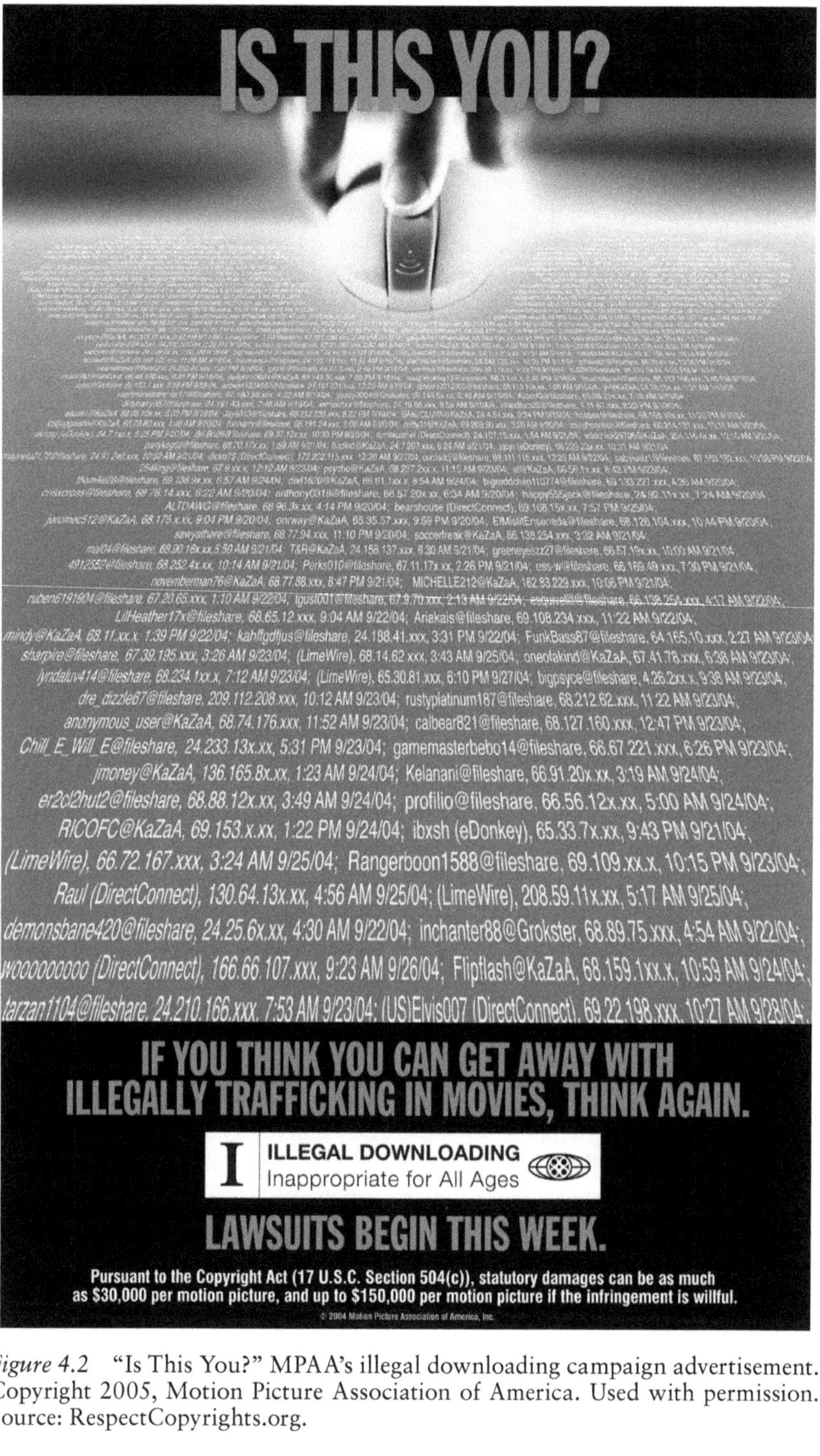

Figure 4.2 "Is This You?" MPAA's illegal downloading campaign advertisement. Copyright 2005, Motion Picture Association of America. Used with permission. Source: RespectCopyrights.org.

Figure 4.3 "Parental Guidance Suggested." MPAA's illegal downloading campaign advertisement. Copyright 2005, Motion Picture Association of America. Used with permission. Source: RespectCopyrights.org.

a clear victory for the content industries. In a flurry of media coverage of the case on June 27 and 28, 2005, the content industries released public statements and participated in interviews offering responses to the ruling. Dan Glickman, the president and CEO of the MPAA, in a statement about the ruling said, "[t]his case speaks to the values we hold dear as a nation. It is wrong to promote stealing. Grokster promotes stealing, and it ought to be held responsible for its actions" (Press Release). Invoking another contemporary court ruling involving display of the Ten Commandments, Mitch Bainwol, head of the Recording Industry Association of America, said the court affirmed the notion that "thou shalt not steal" (Krim A1). And in the official "RIAA Statement on *MGM v. Grokster* Supreme Court Ruling," he added,

> With this unanimous decision, the Supreme Court has addressed a significant threat to the U.S. economy and moved to protect the livelihoods of the more than 11 million Americans employed by the copyright industries. The Supreme Court has helped to power the digital future for legitimate online businesses—including legal file sharing networks—by holding accountable those who promote and profit from theft. (A1)

From the entertainment companies' perspective, digital technologies present dangers larger than the disruption of legitimate business models; they threaten the moral fabric of our society. From their perspective, it is "wrong"—in both the legal and moral sense—to use technology in this way. According to the entertainment industry and their supporters, the natural state of copyright regulation is based on property rights and can be properly maintained with the help of property stewards. By supporting the regulation of the use of new technologies, copyright law can serve to restore our society's respect for the fundamental value of private property.

In showing the ways in which use of digital networks both threatens the foundations of copyright law (endangers "economic incentives") and is morally wrong ("file sharing is stealing"), petitioners establish both the natural order of the property stewardship model of copyright and the conflict posed to that natural order by digital technologies. As I discuss in Chapter 2, what is defined as "legal" is not a self-evident ruling based on case precedent about the way intellectual property should be regulated, but instead reflects what has been established as the natural or normal system of justice by a particular society's set of beliefs and mores about appropriate conduct. Foucault reminds us that such privileging of a particular order of things is constructed through discourse:

> Order is, at one and the same time, that which is given in things as the inner law, the hidden network that determines the way they confront one another, and also that which has no existence except in the grid created by a glance, an examination, a language. (*Order of Things* xx)

Foucault helps us to understand how in making a claim for regulating peer-to-peer networks to support established property stewardship models of cultural production, litigants, entertainment industry representatives, and supporters highlight one set of uses of technology and applications of copyright law as their natural, inevitable purposes. Here, that set of uses involves peer-to-peer file-sharing technologies as distribution mechanisms, used to support the producer-consumer relationship that necessitates property stewards in cultural production. Such uses also require regulation of technology through copyright law—both in terms of punishing file sharers' activities and regulating technology development—that supports current methods for buying and selling individualized copies. Because digital networks permit the cultivation of an alternative value of wide distribution and amateur cultural production, they do not even appear on the "grid" of the property stewardship narrative and, thus, can only be viewed as deviant.

It is not within the scope of this chapter to explore whether the content industries' messages have effectively shaped their target audience's perception of file sharing[8]. However, we can look at the ways in which the narrative of property stewardship gains legitimacy in the legal debate, that is, how it operates to constitute a particular understanding of the role of technology during a contentious time in the legal history of copyright. Examining the discourse of property stewardship in the digital copyright debate reveals that the use of property-based narratives to discuss copyright establishes a normalized state of copyright enforcement in which technology must be regulated to sustain current business models for cultural production. In doing so, the value of intellectual property is defined in terms of exclusivity and competition in markets for packaged, transmittable intellectual and creative goods. This view of cultural production gains force based on its asserted alignment with the foundational principles of property and naturalized authors' rights in copyright law. It allows a sense of coherence with legal history within new contexts, rather than giving in to a state of lawlessness and social chaos on the Internet. In addition, it also demonstrates consistency with the foundation principle of private property in our democratic society by equating file sharing with theft.

Relying on a property-rights approach to copyright emphasizes the individual benefit of economic reward and advancement and the natural right of the author, perhaps at the expense of the community. While a property stewardship narrative of copyright calls on Internet users to respect and reward the contributions of individuals, it fails to highlight the relatedness of intellectual and creative activity—the inherently collaborative nature of composition, a sense of communal responsibility, and the common good of sharing and access to information. The "steady state" of copyright law in the property stewardship narrative appears as the natural and inevitable structure for regulating digital technologies, but it is only one of many possible structures. The property stewardship narrative in the digital copyright debate presents a natural order of exclusivity and private property in copyright law that is neither necessary nor inevitable. Digital technologies, including peer-to-peer file-sharing technologies, have many applications in many contexts, and while our culture has until now relied on a property stewardship system for the exchange of intellectual works, there are other forms of content creation and exchange that may serve just as well—or better—for these activities in a digital age. The Internet offers a place where artists and producers can respond to and adapt their activities and services to the unique and changing digital landscape. The challenge for copyright law does not necessarily lie in reinforcing established rules of order within the seemingly chaotic, lawless Internet. Rather, the challenge could be finding ways to create and maintain a system on the Internet where contributors and artists could be properly compensated, and both creators and users could take advantage of the distinctive features of digital distribution technologies. In the next chapter I examine the discourse that presents such an alternative framework for intellectual and creative activity introduced by digital technology advocates, a cultural conservancy.

5 Inventing the Commons

The Cultural Conservancy of Intellectual Property

In the previous chapter, I argued that the property stewardship narrative told by the entertainment industry normalizes the regulation of technology through copyright law and identifies the use of digital networks to distribute cultural goods to consumers as its natural, inevitable purpose. The narrative, while failing to take into account the distinctive topology of cultural production in a digital age, gains strength by suggesting coherence with legal history and the "natural right" of proprietary authorship in copyright law. In tension with this property stewardship narrative is another narrative told by the technology companies and their supporters: the *cultural conservancy narrative*. This version of the digital copyright story identifies the conflict as one between stultified creators and a powerful entertainment industry that seeks increased legal protections over already overregulated cultural production. According to the narrative of cultural conservancy, recent expansions of U.S. copyright law are unnecessary and unprincipled, damaging information flow and inhibiting the future creation of works by perpetually affording more rights to self-interested corporate copyright owners. Supporters of the cultural conservancy model of intellectual property regulation argue that technological developments have made visible the fact that the current regime of copyright law does not work well to balance creativity and technology innovation. Legal protections for intellectual and creative works, based on notions of property, do not offer creators the freedoms necessary to access and build on existing works and to create new ones. Very different from the property stewardship narrative, the cultural conservancy narrative emphasizes the importance of protecting access to existing works, which have become "endangered resources," for ongoing intellectual and creative expression in our culture. In order to ensure the continuation of the production of intellectual property in the twenty-first century, or a "healthy" environment of cultural production, the use of digital technologies for sharing, creating, collaborating, and distributing intellectual and creative works should be encouraged through less restrictive copyright law.

In this chapter I show how the fairly new cultural conservancy narrative, and in particular the underlying metaphor of the "commons," has developed over the past decade in the digital copyright debate in the discourse of representatives of technology companies, copyright activists, and their supporters. I examine instances of the narrative as they appear in legal briefs, press releases, and public Web sites from both peer-to-peer file-sharing technology companies and three nonprofit copyright activist organizations that actively support the development of digital technology, P2P United, the Electronic Frontier Foundation (EFF), and Public Knowledge. This analysis highlights again the concept of the "steady state" in narratives about intellectual property regulation, particularly in contrast to the steady state presented by the property stewardship narrative. The steady state established in the cultural conservancy narrative, like that of the property stewardship narrative, is grounded in references to the "foundational principles" of copyright law. However, what are asserted as foundational principles of copyright law is very different from that of the property stewardship model. Instead of focusing on protecting authorial rights to intellectual property, the cultural conservancy narrative focuses on ensuring the public right to access creative and intellectual resources. The cultural conservancy narrative highlights the values of collaboration and interactivity in the creative process, which is aided by an intellectual commons.

As shown in Chapter 4, the property stewardship narrative from the entertainment companies appears consistently and repeatedly on Web sites, print advertisements, and even during movie theater previews. By contrast, the narrative of cultural conservancy appears at only dispersed points in fragmented form. Copyright activists and technology supporters rely on central concepts that work together to form a coherent narrative of cultural conservancy, but none of these groups alone offers much in the way of a complete version of the story. The cultural conservancy narrative is still in formation, emerging from technology companies, copyright activists, and their advocates as a rhetoric of resistance in the digital copyright debate.

The notion of cultural conservancy, and the central metaphor on which it is based, the "commons," first appeared in academic and legal expert circles before being adopted in the public discourse of the digital copyright debate. The concept of the commons as a model for cultural production emerged largely from academic discussions about the impact of copyright law on Internet communication practices and from lawyers' perspectives in news sources and in law review articles. It can be traced back to James Boyle's *Shamans, Software, and Spleens*, published in 1996. Boyle is often credited with first introducing the idea of "cultural environmentalism," a metaphor intended to facilitate thinking about intellectual property policy as environmental policy and intellectual resources as part of a commons. Boyle draws an analogy between copyright and environmentalism, arguing that we need to establish a more unified rhetorical framework that reflects a collective responsibility for valuable intellectual resources. By doing so, he says, we may be able to "invent" new ways of conceiving of intellectual property:

> Just as the duck hunter finds common cause with the bird-watcher and the salmon geneticist by coming to think about "the environment," so an emergent concept of the public domain could tie together the interests of groups currently engaged in individual struggles with no sense of the larger context. This notion, in turn, allows people to solve collective action problems in a number of different ways, including the creation of specialized organizations whose technical expertise and lobbying proficiency allows the diffuse interests of a wider public to be better articulated. Here, too, we can learn. The public domain should have its Greenpeace, its Environmental Defense Fund, its Nature Conservancy, its Environmentally Concerned Scientists. In fact, organizations paralleling each of these functions are currently being created. ("Second Enclosure Movement" 73)

Boyle recognizes the power of discourse as he argues for a rhetoric of cultural conservation in efforts to save the public domain, which is endangered by extensions to copyright law. But "like the environment," he writes, "the public domain must be invented before it can be saved."

The language of cultural conservancy in the contemporary digital copyright debate sounds much like Boyle's envisioned cultural environmentalism. While not focused specifically on the public domain, it relies on the idea that intellectual and creative resources need to be saved from privatization that will eventually lead to their extinction, a tragedy facing a wider public of "diffuse interests." And just as cultural environmentalism relies on the invention of the public domain, in order to save cultural production in a digital age the cultural conservancy narrative must successfully invent the concept of the commons.

The usefulness of the concept of the commons, the basis of the cultural conservancy narrative, has been widely discussed in intellectual property expert circles, developing over the past decade into its current form in the public digital copyright debate. For the purposes of this discussion, I define a "commons" as a collection of materials and resources that are not subject to individual or privatized control but rather are under the care and responsibility of a larger, collective group. As such, a private party cannot exclude access to and use of what is in the commons. I want to stress that within the cultural conservancy narrative the commons does not mean "free," in terms of being free of charge or completely free to use as desired; rather, it means free from individualized ownership. Lawrence Lessig makes this point in his definition of a commons in "The Architecture of Innovation":

> By a commons I mean a resource that is free. Not necessarily zero cost, but if there is a cost, it is a neutrally imposed, or equally imposed cost. . . . [Central Park, public streets, open source software] are commons because they are within the reach of members of the relevant community without the permission of anyone else. They are resources that are

> protected by a liability rule rather than a property rule. . . . The point is not that no control is present; but rather that the kind of control is different from the control we grant to property. (62–63)

A commons is not a free-for-all, unmanaged space, but rather is governed by a community that both protects and shares its collective resources.

The notion of a commons in cultural production, what might be called an "information commons," rests on the idea that intellectual property holds value not in its exclusivity but in its wide availability to others. Ideas contained in intellectual and creative works—even expressions of those ideas, which are the subject of copyright law—are not physical objects whose ownership excludes others from exposure to them. In other words, a person having "consumed" a particular intellectual work does not exclude another's consumption of that work; intellectual products cannot be "used up." If you read an article and I read the same article, you still have the knowledge you've gained from that article; my consumption of it doesn't take anything away from you[9]. Intellectual property, by nature, is not exclusionary. While legal restrictions and technological measures may be applied to limit access to and use of a work, they cannot take back the value of the work once it has been encountered and shared. It might even be conversely argued that intellectual works don't hold more value when made exclusive, but rather gain value through sharing and public access. The value in intellectual and creative works, when understood as resources within a commons, stems not only from the economic worth established by content owners; in fact, this value is relatively small in comparison with the value in the interaction of, attention to, and social activity surrounding creative and intellectual works in digital spaces. The value in an intellectual commons amounts to more than the sum of its parts; rather, it is the sum of access to the works plus the unpredictable interactions and productions that arise out of it.

Arguments touting the virtues of the general concept of the commons (both in the realm of the copyright debate and in other contexts) face criticism based on what is known as the "tragedy of the commons," usually traced back to an essay by Garrett Hardin published in *Science* magazine in 1968:

> The tragedy of the commons develops in this way. Picture a pasture open to all. It is to be expected that each herdsman will try to keep as many cattle as possible on the commons. . . . As a rational being, each herdsman seeks to maximize his gain . . . the rational herdsman concludes that the only sensible course for him to pursue is to add another animal to his herd. And another; and another. . . . [T]his is the conclusion reached by each and every rational herdsman sharing a commons. Therein is the tragedy. Each man is locked into a system that compels him to increase his herd without limit—in a world that is limited. Ruin

> is the destination toward which all men rush, each pursuing his own best interest in a society that believes in the freedom of the commons. Freedom in a commons brings ruin to all.

While this tragedy of the commons, in which "freedom in a commons brings ruin to all," appears to be that to which all "rational men" would naturally strive, Carol M. Rose raises an interesting point about the naturalness of such narratives. While Hardin, John Locke, and others assert that such self-interest in the treatment of property is human nature, others, including those whom Rose would call the "Mom" or "Good Citizen," might assert that the common good of cooperation or public interest over individual property rights—even if facing risk of cheating or stealing—may be another human tendency (*Property and Persuasion*). Citing Carol Gilligan, she argues that the caring, cooperative person "is just as much 'there' as the indifferent noncooperator John Doe" (*Property and Persuasion* 39). Gilligan, in *In a Different Voice*, makes this point in a larger context by looking at the concept of morality by noting a difference in the ways in which men and women decide what is right and wrong and concludes, "in the different voice of women lies the truth of an ethic of care, the tie between relationships and responsibility, and the origins of aggression in the failure of connection" (173). This ethic of care is in contrast to the ethic of equality, that "everyone should be treated the same," and instead relies on the notion that "no one should be hurt." Applying this difference in ethics to the difference in systems for regulating copyrighted materials, we might see that an understanding of property and the subsequent rational tragedy of the commons is not the only construct for the management of intellectual resources in cultural production[10]. Intellectual and creative works might be governed according to an ethic of care, or an intellectual commons, that relies on cooperation and shared responsibility, focusing on the relational aspects of composing and creating in digital environments rather than a value in individualized reward and self-interest purported by the property stewardship model.

While the metaphor of property in the property stewardship narrative measures value according to numbers of consumed goods and monetary worth, the concept of the commons assigns value to intellectual property according to its situatedness within a network of relationships and responsibility for cultural production. It would protect not—primarily—the rights of authors to seek rewards for contributions, but would instead focus on the rights of the public to access, use, and build upon those materials, the relationships among participants. Internet scholars often assert a value of the Internet as a network that facilitates interactivity and relationally constructed meanings in its hypertextual form. Lawrence Lessig in his second book, *The Future of Ideas: The Fate of the Commons in a Connected World*, argues that the Internet is "the most important innovation commons that we have ever known" (26). He describes the Internet as forming a commons in its very architectural structure: the "code" of the Internet, the technical architecture on which it is built, allows information to be exchanged without the permission of anyone. This information is shared among members of community itself, without a mediator, between users who have the potential to become creators themselves. There is no central governing system, and it thus remains open to whatever innovative contributions or content are sent across the wires. Because digital networks are "free," growing larger and stronger with increased participation and defying means for regulation, they offer opportunities for the development of an information commons.

Lessig is largely responsible for one of the earliest introductions to the concept of the commons and the value of cultural conservancy to the general public as cofounder of the successful Creative Commons organization. According to its Web site, the Creative Commons organization describes its mission as "expanding the range of creative work available for others to build upon and share" (http://creativecommons.org/). The organization offers models of contractual agreements (Creative Commons licenses) to complement traditional copyright models for creators who desire less restrictive protections over their work. Creative Commons is a widely supported grassroots effort that provides services and educational materials for the general public. With this audience and purpose in mind, the organization often communicates its mission on the Internet through accessible and easy-to-understand multimedia movies (for examples, see http://mirrors.creativecommons.org/). These movies explain the mission of the organization by telling the story of cultural conservancy. Among these movies are three two-minute multimedia films that were entered into a 2003 contest that invited users of Creative Commons to communicate the Creative Commons mission[11]. These films, early contributors to the development of public discourse about the commons, are rich with metaphor and present artistic, compelling examples of the cultural conservancy narrative through their use of visual images, music, and text.

The film that was awarded first place, titled *Building on the Past*, explains the mission of Creative Commons through the idea that all works build on past works, essentially, a challenge to the premise of originality in the property stewardship narrative. The film opens and closes with the statement "[c]reativity always builds on the past," which is reinforced through both spoken word and text on the screen (Cone). The film challenges the notion of originality in the creation of intellectual works in favor of the idea that all works are influenced by and build upon previous works. In this filmmaker's view, if all works build on others, then the interpretation of copyright law as protecting original creativity against others' use of them impedes future creative activity. The film shows how Creative Commons licenses allow for building on the past, and thus encourage creative and intellectual activity.

Arguments against the property metaphor and for an intellectual commons in intellectual property law are explicit in the short film. In one scene, we see a stark, colorless image of two men engaging in a physical battle over a chair (see Figure 5.1). This scene is accompanied by text describing how application of copyright law "restricts other people's access." It is clear that this image, which relies on the metaphor of intellectual property as holding the physical properties of a chair, is a negative one, representing violence and battle for appropriation, rather than the result of a collaborative and fruitful creative process.

In another scene, the filmmaker again challenges the understanding of intellectual property as property in copyright law. In this scene, we see the creation of a stock car as a replacement metaphor for intellectual property. This act of constructing the car appears against a sunny, colorful backdrop, and is a result of a collaboration of three men working together. Figure 5.2 shows the result of such efforts. It is this act of collaborative creation, as opposed to the tug-of-war contest to gain control of the chair, that represents the concept of a commons. While this metaphor is still one with physical characteristics (a car), the object is not privately owned and access is not exclusive, but rather it only comes into being when it is contributed to by many elements from many individual efforts. This alternative metaphor

Figure 5.1 Chair image from Creative Commons' *Building on the Past.* Copyright 2003, Justin Cone, Attribution-Noncommercial 1.0 Generic Creative Commons License. Source: mirrors.creativecommons.org/movingimages/Building_on_the_Past.mpg.

Figure 5.2 Stock car image from Creative Commons' *Building on the Past.* Copyright 2003, Justin Cone, Attribution-Noncommercial 1.0 Generic Creative Commons License. Source: mirrors.creativecommons.org/movingimages/Building_on_the_Past.mpg.

Figure 5.3 Building blocks image from Creative Commons' *Building on the Past.* Copyright 2003, Justin Cone, Attribution-Noncommercial 1.0 Generic Creative Commons License. Source: mirrors.creativecommons.org/movingimages/Building_on_the_Past.mpg.

Figure 5.4 Denim skirt image from Creative Commons' *Mix Tape*. Copyright 2003, Sheryl Seibert. Attribution-Noncommercial-Share Alike 1.0 Creative Commons Generic License. Source: mirrors.creativecommons.org/movingimages/Mix_Tape.mov.

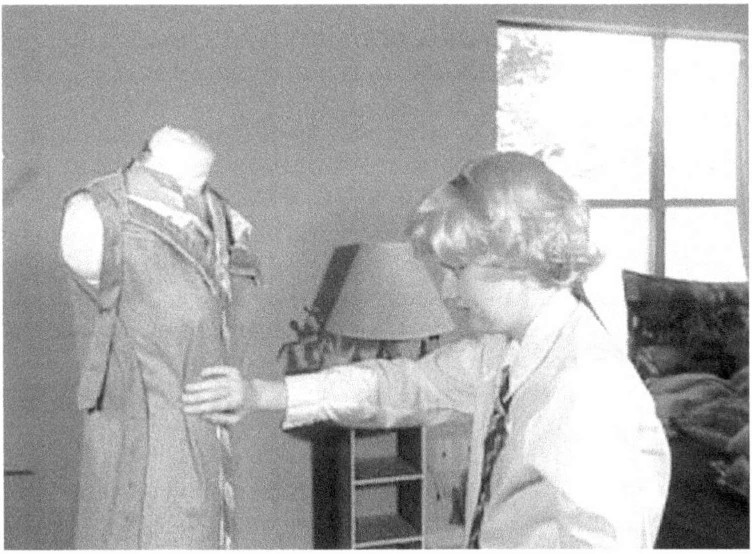

Figure 5.5 Denim skirt image from Creative Commons' *Mix Tape*. Copyright 2003, Sheryl Seibert. Attribution-Noncommercial-Share Alike 1.0 Creative Commons Generic License. Source: mirrors.creativecommons.org/movingimages/Mix_Tape.mov.

Figure 5.6 Scraps image from Creative Commons' *Mix Tape*. Copyright 2003, Sheryl Seibert, Attribution-Noncommercial-Share Alike 1.0 Generic Creative Commons License. Source: mirrors.creativecommons.org/movingimages/Mix_Tape.mov.

of a commons presents the value of a collaborative, fruitful, and positive interaction that builds on existing parts, rather than that of engaging in a battle of ownership of a physical object.

The concept of the commons can be further explained by looking at the filmmaker's reliance on the central metaphor of intellectual property as building blocks (see Figure 5.3). Building blocks are of little use when taken alone, but together can create something of larger value. Just as with intellectual property, it is not the ownership of one creator over an object but the work's contribution toward derivative or transformative works that gives it value. Not only does this image communicate the idea that access to and use of creative works contribute to the development of future works, but that Creative Commons licensing for such use is an easy, elementary task.

The second-place entry in the Creative Commons contest is entitled *Mix Tape* (Seibert). Like the first-place entry, this film relies upon the central idea that new works are generated from previous works. The visual, textual, and audio channels in this film collectively promote recycling, reusing, and remixing creative works. Visually, the story focuses on a denim skirt, purchased new in one of the first scenes. The skirt, bought by one individual, is subsequently sold at a yard sale, transformed into a dress, tossed into a dumpster, and finally recovered from the dumpster to be made into a handcrafted work at the film's close (see Figures 5.4, 5.5, and 5.6). The visual narrative is accompanied by a song about "mix tapes," as well as by captions that reinforce the overall message: creativity is not an individual enterprise, and the works of the past are what those of the future are built upon.

Again, as with the first-place entry, the breakdown of the property metaphor is explicit. The film rejects comparisons between intellectual property and privatized property to be exclusively owned, and instead draws a parallel between intellectual property and recyclable resources. The images of the transformation of the denim skirt extol the virtues of reusing and repurposing existing materials. The lyrics in the film describe the remixing that used to be done with analog cassette tapes:

> This song could be between two of your favorites in the middle of the "b" side of your mix tape. Downloaded it from the web, burned it onto a disc, bounced it on a cassette 'cause it's an old car.

As the lyrics reinforce the transfer of a song from one medium to another, in this case from digital to analog format, the visual narrative shows the transformation of the denim skirt into a dress and, finally, into scraps for another craft project, paralleling the shifts that the lyrics describe. The narratives here, which follow the reuse and repurposing of a denim skirt and the remixing of a song, do not portray independent objects whose use is determined by a single creator; rather, the property becomes valued as it is recycled, exchanged, transformed, and reused.

The captions used throughout the film reinforce the idea of remixing shared resources. An excerpt from the written text reads,

> Today, creative works are treated like disposable products. Things you buy and sell. And discard when you are done. But what if creative works were building blocks? Ingredients that could be used by others, like artists, and musicians? Then art becomes something organic and growing until it exceeds the imagination of any single creator.

As in the first film, the metaphor of building blocks is used to describe creative works. Older works serve as blocks from which new works can be built. In contrast to the metaphor of creative works as disposable property, to be purchased and consumed, the filmmaker suggests that works may also be repurposed and reused by others, by consumers turned artists.

The filmmakers in both films see Creative Commons as a way to facilitate repurposing and to help creators collaborate, mainly by allowing them to identify these creative building blocks available for use. In addition, the emphasis on reuse and recycling of materials in these films (whether parts for a car or a piece of clothing) evokes an environmentalist moral of the story consistent with other iterations of the cultural conservancy narrative.

Recycling and environmentalism are based upon the threat of privatized ownership and depletion of resources. While intellectual property has been considered physical property among many participants in the digital copyright debate, an emerging narrative of cultural conservancy communicates the dangers associated with the reduction in available intellectual resources as a result of overreaching copyright laws. In the Creative Commons films there is evidence of the use of alternative metaphors to the property metaphor: intellectual property as building blocks or as recyclable and reusable resources. Each of these metaphors relies on the notion of intellectual property as existing within a commons, suggesting an alternative to property ownership in copyright law.

This same narrative of cultural conservancy appears in the discourse from technology companies themselves. The makers of peer-to-peer file-sharing technologies, such as Grokster and StreamCast Networks, employ the language of the commons in their public rhetoric. These technology companies argue that their products and/or services help to facilitate an information commons, maintaining a healthy environment for creativity in an age of endangered intellectual resources. Key to the metaphor of a commons for Grokster and StreamCast Networks is the rhetoric of "sharing." The rhetoric of sharing is particularly potent in the discourse of the digital copyright debate; in fact, the activity of using the peer-to-peer network itself is called "file sharing." This term suggests an inherent value of contribution to and use of communal resources, rather than exclusivity and proprietary ownership. The peer-to-peer technology companies embrace this notion on their public Web sites. In 2005, prior to the shutdown of their file-sharing services, the Grokster Web site asserted, "[r]esponsible, active sharing is the key to useful peer-to-peer experiences" ("Quick Guide"), and StreamCast Networks posited that their peer-to-peer file-sharing product Morpheus "allows people to connect directly and share information. The peer-to-peer user network becomes richer and more fulfilling the more people use Morpheus" ("Products"). These sentiments reveal that it is the activity of sharing that brings value to the technology as facilitator of a commons. If users actively contribute resources and do not merely passively download them, then the commons will flourish and grow. In addition, if users fulfill their "responsibility" to share, then digital networks can create a commons.

The Electronic Frontier Foundation (EFF), an Internet technology advocacy group, has likewise made attempts to communicate the value of the commons to the public by introducing their own version of the cultural conservancy narrative of copyright. Relying on a metaphor similar to Boyle's environmentalism analogy, their "Endangered Gizmos" campaign likens technological innovations to endangered species and copyright law to a dinosaur, suggesting that copyright law is an outdated system unable to adapt to changing circumstances introduced by digital distribution technologies and thus facing dire consequences. The Endangered Gizmos campaign relies on the notion of a commons of shared resources that can "flourish" and "grow" when given the freedom from overly restrictive legal regulations. The campaign focuses on technological innovation, and presents various technology inventions that are extinct, endangered, or that have been saved, presumably by those fighting against an overly restrictive copyright regime. These inventions include the Sony-Betamax videorecorder (saved), the CD burner (endangered), and Napster (extinct), to name a few. The implicit argument is that within a system of cultural conservancy based on an information commons, technological innovations would be allowed to flourish and "enhance our lives" rather than becoming extinct. This point is brought to life in a short film that shows a monster's foot crushing an unsuspecting iPod. The animated short shows the destructive role that copyright, a lumbering monster, plays in disrupting the harmonious balance of a cultural commons, portrayed as a sunny pasture containing colorful flowers and animated technologies frolicking in the field (see Figures 5.7 and 5.8). When these innovations are not allowed to flourish, they become extinct. In this narrative, copyright law is the monster, creating a hostile climate for the innocent, weaker gizmos. In the Endangered Gizmos video, the monster's foot might also conjure images of a dinosaur, representing an old regime of copyright, a system in need of adaptation to a rapidly changing climate. The campaign relies on the notion that current applications of copyright law are harmful, and suggests that the existence of copyright in its current form destroys innovation. The message suggests its own natural order of cultural production: the evolution of technology development has revealed copyright law as a monster or dinosaur, deviant or ill suited for the contemporary climate of cultural production. Further, the campaign implies a contest between two species facing extinction, dinosaur/copyright versus gizmos/technological innovation.

It is helpful to note further that the images from the Endangered Gizmos video are likely drawn from the 1969 animated short *Bambi Meets Godzilla*, the monster/dinosaur referencing the character of Godzilla in the film. *Bambi Meets Godzilla*, a two-minute film created independently by Marv Newland, is now considered an animated classic as an early example of an independent effort on a low budget, produced outside of the traditional Hollywood model for film production. In addition, *Bambi Meets Godzilla* parodied the *Godzilla* films to offer a critique of Disney's animated film *Bambi*. The likeness of the foot to a dinosaur's foot seems fitting given the Endangered Gizmos campaign's reliance on "extinct" and "endangered" species, and the reference to the Bambi-Godzilla conflict shows the ways in which the battle between copyright law (Godzilla) and new digital technologies (Bambi) has a predictable outcome: Godzilla gets Bambi. In addition, as a parody of an existing work, the creative production of the Endangered Gizmos film as a remixing of *Bambi Meets Godzilla* serves to reinforce the value of a commons, in which intellectual resources are available for reuse.

Technology companies and their supporters argue that the appropriate approach to managing intellectual property is to establish a commons that

Figure 5.7 Technologies flourish image from EFF's Endangered Gizmos Campaign. Copyright 2005, Electronic Frontier Foundation. Used with permission. Source: www.eff.org/endangered.

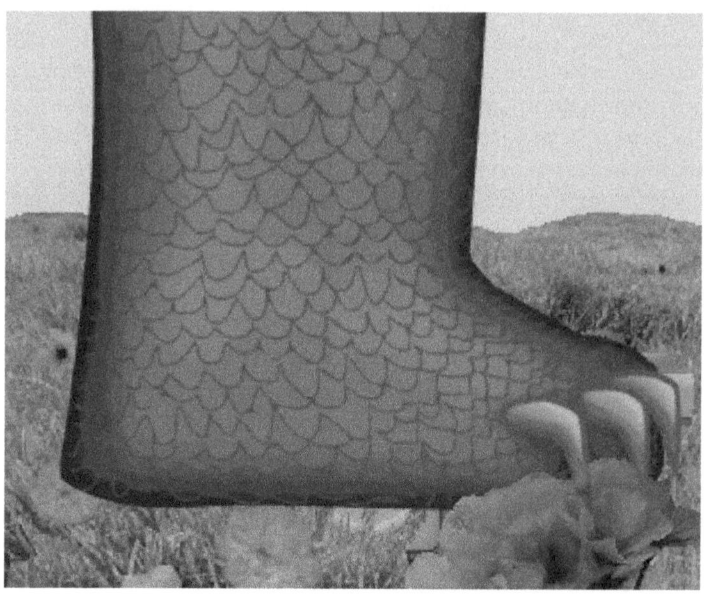

Figure 5.8 Technologies extinct image from EFF's Endangered Gizmos Campaign. Copyright 2005, Electronic Frontier Foundation. Used with permission. Source: www.eff.org/endangered.

promotes the advancement of knowledge and future cultural production by making works available to be built upon. Like their counterparts espousing the property stewardship narrative, they assert that the basis for this argument can be found in a "foundational principle" of copyright law. The foundational principle described by supporters of the commons is again traced back to the Intellectual Property Clause of the Constitution, "to promote the progress of science and useful arts, by securing for a limited time to authors and inventors the exclusive right to their respective writings and discoveries." The cultural conservancy narrative emphasizes that the primary, constitutional purpose of copyright law—to promote progress—is best supported by digital distribution technologies that facilitate the distribution of and access to intellectual and creative resources necessary to spur future creation. P2P United, an advocacy organization that represents a group of peer-to-peer technology industry companies and proponents including BearShare, Blubster, Grokster, eDonkey, and Morpheus, make this claim directly. Citing their objective as "Fighting for the Future of Peer-to-Peer Technology," one goal stated in their mission statement is to encourage the "widest possible use of P2P technology 'to promote the Progress of Science and useful Arts' consistent with the Constitution and the laws of the nation" ("Our Mission"). StreamCast Networks' Vice President and General Counsel Matthew Neco also supports this argument, asserting,

> [W]e are in times of change, but the change that will come from P2P is good, because in this case the advancement of arts and sciences for the benefit of the citizens of this great Country is then best served. And that is, after all, the reason copyright exists at all. ("Press Information")

The commons created through digital networks, these technology advocates argue, rests on the foundation of copyright law as described in the U.S. Constitution. This foundational principle is different from the foundational principle established in the property stewardship narrative, which asserts that copyright law's ultimate aim is to provide economic incentive to authors. In this way, the two narratives assert a restoration of an original "steady state" in copyright law, but the steady state in the cultural conservancy model focuses on limitations on copyright protections, while the property stewardship model emphasizes extensions to copyright laws.

Relying on language of "foundational principles" and connecting the value of digital technologies to the values of a democratic nation is a key rhetorical strategy in the cultural conservancy narrative. The references to democracy attempt to elevate the stakes above the defense of using peer-to-peer file-sharing services to download music and movies; now the networks are protecting the citizens of a country against corporate greed that threatens democratic freedoms. When StreamCast Networks distributed court documents pertaining to the *MGM Studios v. Grokster* case to the public using its Morpheus software, executive director Adam Eisgrau made this statement:

> America wants and needs to digitize our democracy just as we needed and wanted to take it to the air when broadcasting was a glimmer in an inventor's eye . . . . The fate of unfettered access to information and the freedom to invent better ways of helping the public receive and share it, both vital pillars of our democratic society, are the real issues before the Court. ("StreamCast Harnesses Power of Peer-to-peer Networks")

Comparing the freedom to build digital technologies to freedom of the press and identifying such freedoms as "vital pillars of our democratic society" suggests that the digital copyright debate is about more than technology development—it is about the foundational principles of democratic participation on which our country was established. Public Knowledge, another public interest group "dedicated to fortifying and defending a vibrant information commons," argues that civic discourse, free speech, and artistic, scientific, and technological development are all threatened by current trends in copyright law ("Why These Issues Matter"). In their mission statement, the organization asserts that its goal is "to promote the core conviction that some fundamental democratic principles and cultural values—openness, access, and the capacity to create and compete—must be given new embodiment in the digital age" ("Mission Statement"). In making this statement, the organization suggests a corollary relationship between digital copyright law and the freedoms we take for granted as citizens of a democratic nation.

This notion of "freedom" is a central tenet of the cultural conservancy narrative in the copyright debate. Many supporters of technology development draw parallels between the goals of a commons and those of a democracy: a community-governing system that does not limit freedom of expression nor access to information. Siva Vaidhyanathan makes this connection between the commons and democracy in his second book, *The Anarchist in the Library*:

> Both democracy and creative culture work best when raw materials are cheap and easy and easily distributed. Any cultural development that has made a difference . . . is really about communities sharing, moving ideas between and among people, revising, playing with theme and variation, and ultimately forming a consensus about what is good and what should stay around. (188–9)

Vaidhyanathan asserts that in debates about copyright and digital technology we should focus on the larger questions: "[s]houldn't our priorities be diversity and easy access to culture and information?" and "[s]houldn't we strive for lower levels of regulation of culture and information?" (189). Such goals of an intellectual commons, as opposed to intellectual property as private property, support what is seen by proponents of the cultural conservancy narrative as the larger democratic ideals in our culture, such as free speech, freedom of expression, diversity in political discourse, access to information, and the freedom to innovate.

This connection between fundamental democratic rights and what is at stake in this digital copyright debate is one made in a similar fashion by the entertainment industry. Entertainment industry representatives argue that digital technology development presents a threat larger than destruction of the established economic market for cultural goods; it also threatens to break down the democratic right to private property. For the technology companies and copyright activists, increased regulation of digital networks threatens core democratic freedoms of diversity in political discourse and access to information. In the 2005 Supreme Court brief filed by Grokster and StreamCast in *MGM Studios v. Grokster*, the defendants again make this connection between democracy and an information commons when describing their peer-to-peer file-sharing technologies in these terms: in a section titled "Benefits of Peer-to-Peer File Sharing," a legal brief from Grokster and StreamCast argues that communal management of peer-to-peer networks, rather than outside, centralized regulation, offers the utilitarian benefits of lower distribution costs and tremendous storage and bandwidth capacity, as well as "enhanc[ing] political freedom in those places where suppression of particular material might be attempted" (Grokster and StreamCast Br. 8). In addition to providing economic benefits, digital networks have value in their facilitation of the democratic freedom to access information where "suppression" might otherwise occur.

An amicus brief supporting the respondents in *Grokster*, filed by Public Knowledge in collaboration with the Consumer Federation of America, Consumers Union, and Free Press, asserts that the case "raises profound questions about how far our society should go in projecting state-conferred and constitutionally limited private monopolies into public forums where citizens rely on information and communications technology to enable expressive freedom" (Consumer Federation of America, Consumers Union, Free Press, and Public Knowledge Amicus Br. 3). The brief identifies peer-to-peer technologies as nothing less than "technologies of freedom," arguing that while content owners can challenge the legality of particular uses, the technologies themselves hold great potential as mechanisms for free speech and unfettered access to information. Such democratic freedoms, according to the technology companies and their advocates, are the underlying, proposed values of a commons enabled by digital technology. The commons relies on the notion that the more we make available intellectual resources for others to build upon, the more innovation will take place. The concept gives attention to the public interest as the privileged goal, rather than the pursuit of self-interest that is articulated in the property stewardship narrative. As such, a commons would mitigate the privatization of intellectual and creative goods and make copyrighted works available as resources that can be freely accessed and used by others. In this way, digital technology development is presented in the cultural conservancy narrative as heroic, saving endangered intellectual and creative resources from extinction by providing the access necessary for the creation of new works.

The technology companies and their supporters highlight the potential of digital technologies as "technologies of freedom," as enabling forces for creative activity and increased access to information. The notion of the commons and the strategy of linking it rhetorically to the environmental movement and the democratic values of freedom of expression and public access to information have the potential to make convincing arguments in the digital copyright debate. The metaphor of the commons allows participants in the debate to shift the focus of discussion from market value and private property to a conceptual framework in which a broader spectrum of social and democratic values has standing. And if rhetoric has the power to shape new meanings, then the articulation of the cultural conservancy narrative used in this debate has the potential to shape new cultural understandings of copyright and its relationship to technology.

In the public discourse of the digital copyright debate, however, it seems that the discourse of the commons has failed to establish a coherent message that sufficiently argues against the heightened rhetoric of theft and morality from the entertainment industries. One reason for this failure may be that the cultural conservancy narrative appears only at dispersed points in varied forms in the discourse of the debate, oscillating between analogies to an environmental movement ("endangered gizmos"), political freedoms (providing access "where suppression of particular material might be attempted"), and even feminist ethics ("sharing" and "responsibility"). Foucault views revolution as arising from "mobile and transitory points" or a "swarm of points of resistance," noting that "it is doubtless the strategic codification of these points of resistance that makes a revolution possible" (*History of Sexuality* 96). In the cultural conservancy narrative, it is perhaps the case that its instantiations simply have not yet been "codified," have not been repeated widely and reached large enough audiences.

Further, the competing discourse of property rights does not make sharing an easy concept to promote. The entertainment industry has criminalized file sharers through the rhetoric of theft and piracy, and employed scare tactics to remind users that their online activities are not anonymous and that they can be punished for downloading and uploading content. In many ways, the message they send is "don't share" as much as it is "don't steal." Unlike the dynamic ecological system of the commons, digital networks have been characterized as static storehouses of entertainment products, individualistically driven by users who rely on anonymity and obscurity in order to download the packaged and highly commercialized content that belongs to others. The concept of sharing doesn't communicate well enough the distinctions between the ideas of facilitating the consumption of entertainment products and of contributing to an information commons. This language of sharing makes it difficult for the cultural conservancy narrative to gain strength within our firmly capitalist, consumer-driven society.

And, finally, the principles espoused in the cultural conservancy narrative in the digital copyright debate fail to map closely to actual usage of many forms of digital networks, such as peer-to-peer file sharing. Critics assert that technology companies are hiding behind a smoke-and-mirrors effect, behind high-minded principles with the intent only to seek individual gain. The notion of the commons appears as justification for reproducing others' works without the responsibility for increased contributions, unlimited access without communal management, anonymity without a sense of responsibility, and individual gain without interdependence. The values of freedom, equality, and cooperation seem to have been used to support the right to freely download recorded movies and music. Jana Sawicki reminds those who study discourse that in order for resistant discourses to gain legitimacy, "practices of freedom" must be in place that represent new cultural norms and behaviors (qtd. in Lay, *The Rhetoric of Midwifery* 74). For these reasons, it appears that the discourse of the commons has not proven persuasive because it lacks coherence and potency in the current cultural climate, failing to make a clear distinction between a free pass to consume entertainment products and the freedom to access, build on, and contribute to an information commons.

In the property stewardship narrative of the digital copyright debate, the foundational principle of authors' proprietary rights has historically shaped the legal debate: the discussion has relied on boundaries drawn between private and public property, which can be geographically and physically separated, mapped, and divided. In response to such discourse, the cultural conservancy narrative has been introduced to describe another steady state of copyright management, relying on creative processes rather than products, decentralized control rather than property stewardship, and communal responsibility rather than individualized ownership. In this chapter, I have considered one rhetorical framework for rethinking intellectual property. Such a new model might be facilitated by what law scholar James Boyle refers to as an "invention" of the commons ("Second Enclosure Movement"), in this case a conceptual shift from thinking about intellectual property as owned land to intellectual property as common, and presently endangered, resources. The notion of a commons places value in the social life of intellectual property, rather than its economic worth. In fact, it questions the very primacy of the role of content owners and the foundational principle of authorial property. Instead, it positions digital technology as the hero of the copyright story, asserting its facilitation of important freedoms—to access information, to participate in shared governance, to speak, to create.

It is important to remember, however, that digital networks alone do not inherently constitute a commons. As I discuss further in the following chapter, peer-to-peer networks constitute a commons only when adopted as such through social norms and practices. Peer-to-peer file-sharing networks are often used in ways that run counter to the ethos of the commons, as a free pass to consume copyrighted works without the responsibility of contributing content. While the narrative of cultural conservancy may identify them as "technologies of freedom," when applied to some peer-to-peer file-sharing networks, this may be a misnomer. Participants adopting the cultural conservancy narrative would do well to look back to earlier articulations of the discourse of the commons, like that which appears on the Creative Commons Web site, and apply them to emphasize the need for an entirely new model of copyright that responds and adapts to actual productive activities as facilitated by a range of digital technologies. In this high profile and hotly contested debate, such discourse will need to be self-reflective, thoughtful, based on a clearly articulated value in distribution and community. It will need to clearly identify what may be lost by the commodification of information goods and the assertion that economic value is the only value of creative and intellectual works. This discourse needs to make a clear distinction between the right to reproduce recorded music and movies on peer-to-peer networks and the right to access information, introduce innovative technologies, and build on existing intellectual and creative works. A new discourse is needed that better explains the danger of recent legal trends—not their threat to a free pass to infringe copyright but their potential threat to our freedoms to participate in intellectual and creative activities.

6 "The Tension Between Two Values" Technology vs. Intellectual Property in *MGM Studios v. Grokster*

MGM Studios v. Grokster (2005), the most recent copyright case to reach the U.S. Supreme Court, was brought in 2001 by 28 of the largest entertainment companies against the makers of Grokster and StreamCast software products for their development of peer-to-peer file-sharing technologies. The case raises the issue of whether a distributor of a technology that may be used for copyright infringement should be held liable for contributing to the unlawful activities of its end users. Peer-to-peer file-sharing challenges the notion of copyrighted works as discrete, commodified goods, and has the potential for the cultural commons envisioned by copyright activists. Peer-to-peer networks allow users to bypass an intermediary, centralizing content controller and exchange content directly with other users in a client-client fashion. They operate on individual computers that connect directly with others' individual computers, meaning that peer-to-peer networks cannot operate without this type of peer-to-peer interaction. Further, peer-to-peer networks grow larger and stronger, not weaker, through the increased activity of users. These characteristics—distributed architecture, decentralized control, and facilitation of sharing—challenge a print- and analog-based model of copyright law. In this way, the balance formulated by copyright law between authors' rights and users' rights is thrown off kilter: the very structure of the balance no longer works the way it did in a pre-digital culture. While print- and analog-based intellectual and creative works required a content owner's stewardship (and, subsequently, incentives for entertainment and publishing industry involvement), on peer-to-peer networks these products can be reproduced and circulate in the public sphere without this stewardship. In *MGM Studios v. Grokster*, the Supreme Court responded to the introduction of such structures by ruling in favor of the content industries by assigning potential liability to Grokster and StreamCast Networks for the infringing uses of their networks. This ruling set a precedent for the relationship between technology innovation and copyright law in a digital age.

In this chapter, I examine the rhetorical frameworks outlined in the previous two chapters in the context of a specific case study, within the discourse operating in a single copyright court case. More specifically, I examine how the language from trained experts in copyright law defines the relationship between copyright and digital technology. To do so, I examine several of the key legal documents in the Supreme Court case, including

- The two opening briefs filed by the petitioners, including one from the Motion Picture Studio and Recording Companies and one from the Songwriters and Music Publishers;
- A brief filed by the respondents, Grokster and StreamCast Networks;
- The reply briefs filed by the Motion Picture Studio and Recording Companies and the Songwriters and Music Publishers;
- The judicial opinion, written by Justice Souter, joined by Justices Thomas and Scalia;
- A concurring opinion from Justice Ginsburg, joined by Justices Rehnquist and Kennedy; and
- A second concurring opinion from Justice Breyer, joined by Justices Stevens and O'Connor.

The perspective I assume in this chapter is not one of a law scholar analyzing the successes or failures of particular legal arguments in the case. Rather, I look at legal discourse from a rhetorical perspective, with an understanding that the language used in this case both shapes and is shaped by social and cultural understandings of the relationship between copyright law and digital technology (see Chapter 2 for more in-depth discussion of the role of rhetoric in the study of digital copyright law).

The language used in the *Grokster* case exemplifies the ways in which the U.S. legal system is currently working to redefine the relationship between copyright and digital technology. For instance, while "progress in the arts and sciences" is identified by the competing parties as a common goal, there is no inherently "right" or "natural" progression in creativity and innovation to be identified in the case; rather, the final ruling is based on constructed categories that distinguish particular types of innovation as welcome and others as unwanted or even destructive to the public good. And while the litigants and justices refer to an "appropriate balance" between competing interests, no particular model of copyright protection exists as the correct balance beyond that which the court defines. The rhetorical activities inherent in legal processes, what Stanley Fish refers to as law's "creative rhetoricity" ("The Law Wishes to Have a Formal Existence"), constitute a fair or just balance when a particular account or version of the story becomes the accepted reality of the situation in a final ruling.

Justice Souter, who wrote the judicial opinion for *MGM Studios v. Grokster*, asserts that "the tension between [] two values is the subject of this case" (11). He identifies the two values as 1) the value in the creation of intellectual property, made possible by the enforcement of copyright protection, and 2) the value in innovative communication technology development, enabled by limiting the incidence of liability for copyright infringement. The goal of the ruling, then, becomes one of "balance," or finding a fair state of copyright law that protects the interests of two types of innovation: artistic and intellectual creation and technology development. The ruling in the case must define a state of balance within this tension by asserting an "appropriate" level of regulation of cultural production. My analysis reveals that the case is a site of negotiation of the role of technology in cultural production, mediating between the notion of private reward for individual contributions based on a print-based model of production and the concept of new modes of creativity enabled by digital technology. As we will see, the rhetorical frameworks used in the legal arguments that seek to resolve this tension result in a transformed steady state of copyright law that requires the regulation of digital technologies through a new "inducement rule."

CASE BACKGROUND OF *MGM STUDIOS V. GROKSTER*

The legal history of *MGM Studios v. Grokster* can be traced back to 1999, when Shawn Fanning developed a technology called Napster, which was the first file-sharing application to gain wide popularity among Internet users for trading music files across the network. Not long after Napster was shut down as a result of the ruling in *A&M Records v. Napster*, a second generation of peer-to-peer file-sharing technologies emerged to take Napster's place. What separated this second generation of file-swapping services from Napster was a technological tweak that had major legal implications.

Napster allowed users to browse each other's computers and share copyrighted songs with one another, but it routed all of those transactions through its own centralized servers, maintaining an ability to monitor users and a level of control over how people used its network. That control was Napster's downfall. The judge ruled that since Napster had the ability to prevent copyright infringement, it had a responsibility to do so. The developers of the new services learned from Napster's mistake. Their software abandoned centralized servers, allowing users to connect directly with each other. In October 2001, the major music and movie companies sued developers of two of these new peer-to-peer file-sharing applications, Grokster and StreamCast Networks, for contributing to the theft of millions of copyrighted music and movie files. In 2004, the Ninth Circuit Court of Appeals upheld a lower court ruling that file-sharing software could be used for legitimate purposes, and as such was protected under the 1984 *Sony-Betamax* ruling (*Sony v. Universal Studios*). The Supreme Court agreed to hear the case in December of 2004, and on June 27, 2005, the Court reached the decision that the developers of peer-to-peer file-sharing technologies can be held liable for inducing the infringing activities of their users. This ruling was, in effect, in favor of the content industries, and soon motivated

Grokster to shut down their peer-to-peer file-sharing services. While the decision in *Grokster* was technically unanimous, the justices' perspectives on the issue were more diverse than the 9–0 vote would suggest. The justices split themselves equally in number across a majority opinion and two concurring opinions, each signed by three justices.

The home page displayed on the Grokster Web site shortly following the ruling presents the misleading message that the Court concluded that all use of peer-to-peer technologies is unlawful. The threatening language supporting this perception warns users

> The United States Supreme Court unanimously confirmed that using this service to trade copyrighted material is illegal. Copying copyrighted motion picture and music files using unauthorized peer-to-peer services is illegal and is prosecuted by copyright owners.
>
> Your IP address has been logged. Don't think you can't get caught. You are not anonymous. (Grokster home page)

Those users of peer-to-peer file-sharing services that are more technologically savvy may not be scared off by this message. They know that individual users cannot easily be traced by Internet protocol (IP) addresses assigned to their computers. IP addresses are usually assigned to an Internet service provider, a university, or a company, and they don't typically lead to a single computer, but rather only to a network of computers that share the address. However, for the general population, the message presented on the Grokster Web site is a grave warning about how using the service is "illegal" and can be "prosecuted" under the law. At the bottom of the screen are links to Web sites from content industry organizations, the RIAA and the MPAA, that present anti-piracy materials.

While the Supreme Court ruling does not explicitly rule that peer-to-peer networks, in general, are unlawful, this is the message now being communicated by the entertainment industry. At first glance, it appears that the legal discourse in this case relies heavily on the property stewardship model espoused publicly by the content industries. The ruling suggests that the Court does not treat the principle of the commons as a legitimate model for cultural production and instead supports a property ownership model. A closer look at the documents of the case, however, reveals the ways in which the legal narrative is not so one-sided. Within the briefs and arguments of the case, both the rhetoric of property stewardship as well as the rhetoric of cultural conservancy are present in the construction of a legal narrative of how copyright should operate in the digital age. Further, because the legal narrative is a formal, institutionalized version of the story, it carries different properties than that of the public narratives described in the previous two chapters. The legal narrative does more than to assume a steady state of copyright law based on intellectual property as owned property or as shared resources; it works to prescribe a new steady state. The legal narrative in *Grokster* functions uniquely to present a legitimate, authorized solution, or "coda," to the narrative of the copyright conflict presented by the introduction of peer-to-peer file-sharing networks. And, in *MGM Studios v. Grokster*, this conclusion is "transformative" rather than one based on "restoration" to a previously established steady state.

In order to justify a transformed state of copyright regulation, the rhetoric of the *MGM Studios v. Grokster* case demonstrates that cultural production in a digital age is different and, as such, requires new copyright law. In the pages that follow, I will show how, first, the legal discourse in the case establishes the ways in which digital cultural production is different by making clear distinction between welcome (analog and print) and unwelcome (digital) forms of innovation, and second, how it proves that, in order to continue to support cultural production, digital technology requires new liability standards. By showing how digital technology creates new conflicts within the activities of cultural production, the legal discourse operating in *MGM Studios v. Grokster* introduces a new, transformed state in which copyright law must be extended in order to protect intellectual property.

DEFINING "PROGRESS IN THE ARTS AND SCIENCES"

I'll begin my analysis of the "creative rhetoricity" in *MGM Studios v. Grokster* by looking at a commonality in the legal discourse among the contesting parties: the asserted goal of supporting the future creativity and continued innovation facilitated by copyright law. This goal is an undisputed point in the *Grokster* case; both the content owners and the technology companies agree that the purpose of copyright law is to stimulate creativity and innovation. The arguments from each party regarding this common goal of "advancement in the arts and sciences" sound surprisingly similar: the petitioners argue that "copyright's 'ultimate aim' is to provide an 'incentive to stimulate artistic creativity for the general public good,' " and "the Copyright Act must be construed in light of this basic purpose" (Motion Picture Studio and Recording Company Br. 31-2, citing *Sony*). And respondents emphasize the importance of the law in protecting "risk taking that produces innovation" and "safeguard[ing] the incentive to innovate" (Grokster and StreamCast Br. 24, citing *Verizon Communications v. Law Offices of Curtis V. Trinko*). Both assert that the ultimate goal of intellectual property law is to provide incentive for progress in the form of future creativity and innovation. But you'll notice that the type of creative activity that is valued is different for each. While the petitioners value "artistic creativity," which in the context of *Grokster* refers to the creation of works of music and film, the respondents value "technological advances," in this case the development of peer-to-peer networks. Both rely on discourse of "advancement" and "continuing innovation," and argue that the "foundational principles" of intellectual property law support future creation.

This discourse of "advancement," "progress," and "innovation" supports the notion that creative and intellectual contributions lead naturally to a more highly advanced, and better, society. Jean-François Lyotard describes this concept of "progress" as holding broader social or cultural meaning, as a "principle of a general progress in humanity." He writes, "this idea of a possible, probable, or necessary progress is rooted in the belief that developments made in the arts, technology, knowledge, and freedoms would benefit humanity as a whole" (77). The idea of progress is what Lyotard refers to as a "metanarrative," which he identifies as "hav[ing] the goal of legitimating social and political institutions and practices, laws, ethics, ways of thinking. Unlike myths, metanarratives look for legitimacy, not in an original founding act, but in a future to be accomplished, that is, in an Idea to be realized" (18). In other words, metanarratives tell the story of a future, improved social reality, with the hope of it becoming realized through institutional practices and perceptions. The metanarrative of social progress is based on the concept of a continual, linear, and evolutionary process through which individuals and societies become better. If the production of art, science, and technology improves society, in the metanarrative of progress operating in the legal discourse of this case, then it is the responsibility of copyright law to ensure the continuation of that production.

The legal discourse from both parties alike demonstrates a strong interest in such social progress, which takes priority over privatized reward. Equating progress in the arts and sciences with a superior state of society, the content owners and technology companies both emphasize the benefit of creativity and innovation (either artistic or technological) to the larger public good. While the legal briefs acknowledge that creators need incentives for their contributions, they emphasize the societal benefit of those creations, rather than individualized reward. The Motion Picture Studio and Recording Company brief asserts that a ruling in favor of the content industries "is both manifestly just and central to copyright law's goal of 'stimulat[ing] artistic creativity for the public good'" (Motion Picture Studio and Recording Company Br. 22, quoting *Sony*). The writers of the Songwriter and Music Publishers' brief agree, stating that if the respondents were "permitted to continue to erode this [economic] incentive, the losers will be not just the songwriters and music publishers, but the public at large" (Songwriter and Music Publisher Br. 21). The petitioners believe that a ruling in favor of Grokster and StreamCast would "threaten[] the artistic innovation that is central to our economic and cultural vitality" (Motion Picture Studio and Recording Company Reply Br. 11–2), and the respondents believe that ruling against Grokster and StreamCast would "threaten innovation" (14), and "cause real social harm" (Grokster and StreamCast Br. 8). Both the content owners and the technology companies in their legal briefs emphasize the significance of copyright law to social progress, and the benefits to society that arise out of innovation rather than benefits to the individual for private property ownership.

THE ROLE OF TECHNOLOGY IN SOCIAL PROGRESS

While both petitioners and respondents assert a value in continued innovation and progress in the arts and sciences, what is identified as the type of innovation that is most valued differs. Grokster and StreamCast, in an effort to show that peer-to-peer file-sharing software development should be protected for its contribution to social progress, position technology as valuable to creative processes in that it facilitates the exchange of intellectual property and participation in a community of like-minded researchers, readers, listeners, viewers and future creators. They assert that it aids all users and potential creators equally, as "[t]he software is wholly neutral" (Grokster and StreamCast Br. 2) as to the type of intellectual property exchanged on the networks, whether it be research data, public domain materials, or copyrighted music and movies. Further, respondents argue that peer-to-peer file sharing does not limit the future creation of works, as the content-owner community asserts, but rather aids in the formation of a creative community whose members share values and goals:

> The terms "network" and "service" in the context of this case . . . can easily conjure a misleading picture. As to "network": respondents do not own or control a "network" in the familiar sense. . . . [I]t is more of a self-forming community of common language speakers within hearing distance than a "network" in the familiar lay sense. (Grokster and StreamCast Br. 3–4)

The technology companies present an image that sounds similar to the cultural conservancy narrative espoused by copyright activists in public discourse: peer-to-peer networks form an innocuous, even healthy, mutually beneficial environment in which community members can gather and freely exchange materials. This environment for cultural production might even be described as "fertile," conducive to the creation of new works. Grokster and StreamCast invoke an environmental reference much like that found in the cultural conservancy narrative to show how peer-to-peer networks benefit the public by reducing "inefficiency" and "wasteful redundancy" that occurs in the storage of materials on central servers (Grokster and StreamCast Br. 7). On peer-to-peer networks, no resources are wasted; all are shared and recycled and reused, without using up unnecessary storage space and bandwidth. The technology companies attempt to show how technology contributes to social progress in that it facilitates natural, "self-forming communities of common language speakers" that contribute to the sustenance of a healthy, fertile environment of creative activity.

The content owner petitioners, however, break down the concepts of a healthy environment and productive community on digital networks by repeatedly positioning technology development as destructive to society, doing great harm to the possibility of advancement in the arts and sciences. A key rhetorical strategy used to break down the idea of a cultural conservancy facilitated by digital technologies is the reference to the development and use of digital networks as an illness or disease. The petitioners characterize sharing on peer-to-peer file-sharing technology as contamination that will threaten the livelihood of future creativity and social progress in general. Comparing peer-to-peer file sharing to a disease, petitioners claim that networks are "breeding grounds" for unlawful activity (Motion Picture Studio and Recording Company Br. 3) and are particularly harmful because of their "viral distribution" (Motion Picture Studio and Recording Company Br. 12). They see activity on peer-to-peer networks as dirty, unhealthy, even dangerous: use of peer-to-peer networks is "epidemic" (Motion Picture Studio and Recording Company Br. 12) and "parasitic" (Songwriter and Music Publisher Br. 11). Technology developers are "feeding at the trough of Internet piracy" (Songwriter and Music Publisher Br. 9). Along the same lines, petitioners also argue that legal backing of such networks is a form of "immunity." While the term "immunity" can refer to freedom or exemption from normal operation of the law, it can also refer to protection against a disease, in this case immunity for an agent responsible for the destruction of social progress. The content owners see a ruling in favor of peer-to-peer developers as endangering the vitality of advancement in the arts and sciences.

By presenting the development and use of digital technology as a disease and harmful to the public good, the petitioners position technological innovation as fundamentally opposed to intellectual and creative innovation. They argue against the development of peer-to-peer file-sharing software, which has objectionable "technological merit" (Motion Picture Studio and Recording Company Br. 42), and assert that it "fosters innovation of a most unwelcome kind" (49). This key rhetorical strategy, distinguishing between natural, healthy types of innovation and unnatural, destructive types, establishes the development of digital technology as hindering social progress and working against an environment in which the conditions of copyright law support advancement and evolution in cultural production and, ultimately, social progress.

This comparison between peer-to-peer file sharing and disease works directly against the notion of a commons circulating in public discourse in the digital copyright debate. While the metaphor of the commons relies on images of a healthy environment of cultural production in which technology species or intellectual property resources flourish and grow, the content industries present a view of technology as dangerous, potentially destroying any healthy environment conducive to rich creative activity. While the healthy environment presented by Grokster and StreamCast is alluring, the threat of disease and destruction is perhaps more powerful. The content owner petitioners assert that the natural, healthy state of cultural production is not a commons, but rather is characterized by a highly regulated model of exchange and distribution that maintains exclusivity of intellectual and creative works through control of technology development. They show technology development as destructive to an established healthy state that is based primarily on print and analog production and assert that a property ownership model can work to regulate the spread of disease (i.e., the spread of individual copies on peer-to-peer networks) by maintaining a level of healthy production (by ensuring exclusivity in works and economic reward for creators). To follow this metaphor further, we might conclude that if saving the environment for cultural production is the goal, regulating digital networks may be the necessary pesticide or vaccine for mitigating risk to the public. While the solution may pose its own risks and have some potentially dangerous effects, it may be necessary to prevent the unwanted onset of a larger problem.

DIGITAL IS DIFFERENT: APPLYING THE *SONY-BETAMAX* RULE TO *GROKSTER*

While each party attempts to define a natural, healthy state of cultural production in the *Grokster* case, the legal narrative of the ruling must show coherence with previous case law regarding copyright liability to justify its conclusion. In legal discourse, one method for establishing the legitimacy of a particular argument is by proving adherence to and consistency with prior legal decisions. This doctrine of case precedent, or *stare decisis*, requires that courts rely on the reasoning of past cases to support current legal decisions. As defined in *Black's Law Dictionary*, *stare decisis* means "[t]o abide by, or adhere to, decided cases." Each case that a court decides must be consistent with all previously established decisions of that court and all higher courts. The concept of *stare decisis* creates unity between current and previous cases and generates a sense of adherence to legal history that legitimizes new rulings. The arguments in the briefs and the decision in *Grokster* rely primarily on the invocation of one prior case that addressed the regulation of technology development, *Sony v. Universal Studios* (1984), or what is more commonly known as the *Sony-Betamax* case[12]. This Supreme Court case is central to the decision in *MGM Studios v. Grokster*, as it is the only recent copyright case that has laid out guidelines for secondary liability for copyright infringement, as described in its "substantial non-infringing use" doctrine. Despite the varying positions taken in the parties' arguments regarding the interpretation of the standard set in *Sony*, each uses the technique of *stare decisis* to show that the position argued for is consistent with that which was decided in previous case law. In terms of the narrative function of legal rulings, *stare decisis* works to rhetorically construct the legal system as a closed, static set of rules, a system relying on fact-finding and subsequent decision making to maintain its integrity over time. By situating the present decision in the case precedent of the *Sony* case, the ruling in *Grokster* appears to result from a stable system of copyright law that offers a just and appropriate balance of authors' and users' rights across history.

Legal narratives, more broadly, seek to create "a legitimate, canonical state of things that has been complicated by some human action in some particular context or setting" (Amsterdam and Bruner 141). The conclusion of a legal narrative must either restore a time-honored state of things or offer a transformed state that supports legal order within a complicated new context. While referencing the precedent of the *Sony-Betamax* case creates coherence with legal history, another key rhetorical strategy in the legal narrative of the *Grokster* case is that of creating a distinction between the new context of peer-to-peer file sharing and previous contexts for copyright decisions. By creating a clear distinction between analog and digital contexts for cultural production, the narrative supports new extensions of copyright law necessary to maintain legal order. A transformed state of copyright law, which requires the regulation of technology, becomes necessary to restore justice and conclude the story.

A primary method used in the judicial opinion for determining liability for Grokster and StreamCast is a close look at the case precedent of the "*Sony-Betamax* rule" adopted from *Sony v. Universal Studios*. The *Sony-Betamax* rule states that a designer, developer, or manufacturer of a technology (in this case, the VCR) is not liable for the infringing uses of the technology as long as the technology is "capable of substantial noninfringing uses." The rule was established to ensure that users' potential misuses of technologies to infringe copyright would not endanger the creation and release of new products and services to the marketplace. It enables a balancing of the interests of artistic innovation and technological innovation, allowing the creation of technologies such as photocopiers, the iPod, CD writers, and Internet routers, without fear of lawsuits. The *Sony* rule is often interpreted as strongly technology protecting. It makes it difficult for courts to find liability for dual-use technologies, or technologies that can be used for both infringing and noninfringing uses. The *Sony* rule prevents technology innovation from having to adjust to varied and regulatory legal restrictions and favors accommodations for technology developments that aid the creation and distribution of intellectual property. In this way, *Sony* protects technology developers from overly regulatory copyright laws and, as such, is often cited in legal arguments to support the notion of technology as a positive force in cultural production.

The litigants in *Grokster*, then, were faced with the task of establishing consistency with case history by showing that the ruling in this case meets the "capability" standard introduced in the *Sony* decision. The technology companies argued that *Sony* does not hold a developer or distributor of a new technology liable, even if there is "constructive" knowledge of infringing use, as long as the technology is "capable of significant noninfringing uses." They note that "[t]his software here meets that standard" (Grokster and StreamCast Br. 1). Their interpretation of the standard set in the case rejects the requirement of a "predominance test," applied by the content owners, for which a certain majority of noninfringing uses must be established. While the technology companies do not support a quantitative measurement for the *Sony* test, they note that even according to the petitioners' quantitative measurement, Grokster and StreamCast would meet the test. They compare the 10% of noninfringing uses identified by the petitioners to the acceptable "less than 9%" identified in *Sony* (Grokster and StreamCast Br. 20). Further, regarding the design change as a new *Sony* standard that petitioners propose, the respondents argue that such a standard "would impermissibly extend vicarious liability beyond the principal-agent context without congressional authorization . . . and would threaten innovation by subjecting product design to expensive and indeterminate judicial second-guessing, contrary to *Sony*" (Grokster and StreamCast Br. 14). Grokster and StreamCast Networks do not feel that changing technology design, even if it is possible, should be a requirement of *Sony*. In this way, *Sony* appears to support new technology developments and, one might argue, the resulting emergence of new modes of cultural production.

Despite this strong basis in case precedent that supports technology development, the ruling in *Grokster* supports regulating technology as a means for sustaining a property-based model of cultural production. While the legal decision has to prove adherence to and consistency with the prior *Sony-Betamax* decision, it is important to note that legal history as created through case precedent is a rhetorical construct that establishes similarities or differences between the facts of a case or the context presented and previous facts and contexts. In *The Archaeology of Knowledge*, Foucault identifies the theoretical problems posed by the use of such concepts of order and unity in the construction of a coherent history and, in examining the discursive practices of medicine and political economy, concludes that the connections that make up such continuities are, in fact, illusory. With this in mind, while the legal history of copyright appears as a unified, linear story of statutes and prior cases that lead to self-evident conclusions in the contemporary digital copyright debate, any history told includes gaps, substitutions, transformations, and discontinuities. Therefore, while precedent appears to favor Grokster and StreamCast in this case, rhetorically constructed discontinuities between previous case law and the current *Grokster* situation become the basis for departing from the "capability" standard set in *Sony*.

The ruling in *Grokster*, while favoring the regulation of technology, necessarily shows consistency with the standard formed in *Sony*. The ruling asserts that *Sony* "struck an appropriate balance" (23–24) and that this balance remains workable for *MGM Studios v. Grokster*. However, the ruling also asserts an important discontinuity or gap between the two cases, noting in particular the unique characteristics of peer-to-peer file-sharing networks that require *new* standards for liability in this case rather than relying solely on the *Sony* rule. In this way, the *Grokster* decision remains consistent with case precedent, yet shows that the facts of the *Grokster* case are different and, as such, warrant different standards. The primary difference identified between the two cases is a distinction between analog- or print-based creativity and digital creativity. The *Grokster* ruling makes this distinction first by identifying these unique characteristics of peer-to-peer file sharing "as never before" appearing:

> [D]igital distribution of copyrighted material threatens copyright holders as never before, because every copy is identical to the original, copying is easy, and many people (especially the young) use file-sharing software to download copyrighted works. (11)

Further, the Court recognizes that "when a widely shared service or product is used to commit infringement, it may be impossible to enforce rights in the protected work against all direct infringers" (12). Therefore, we might infer that it is the digital nature of the innovation, which makes it a "widely shared service or product," that led the Court to conclude that "the only practical alternative [is] to go against the distributor of the copying device" (12). Within this vastly different digital context, a restoration of copyright law is not possible. It is only through a transformation of the terms of liability that justice can be served.

One reason that digital is positioned as different than its analog counterpart is the scale of copying and distribution. Peer-to-peer technology differs from any former analog technology, such as the VCR, in that it enables simultaneous copying in large numbers. The ruling by the Court in the opening paragraphs states that the *Grokster* case presents unlawful activity on a grand level: "there is evidence of infringement on a gigantic scale" (4) and the "probable scope of copyright infringement is staggering" (5). The petitioners make this point in their briefs by arguing that "[a] copyrighted motion picture or sound recording in digital form—unlike prior media such as videotapes—can be copied and disseminated, swiftly and without denigration, an infinite number of times" (Motion Picture Studio and Recording Company Br. 12). They even go so far as to say, "[b]ecause so many people have joined Grokster and StreamCast, virtually all popular sound recordings and motion pictures are available for free on the services" (Motion Picture Studio and Recording Company Br. 4). While this statement is obviously not true—all sound recordings and motion pictures are not available on the networks—petitioners persuasively show that the scale on which the distribution and downloading takes place is massive. This is very different from the previous cases in which copies were imperfect and individual, without opportunities for wide distribution.

The content owners also argue that this case differs from *Sony* because Grokster and StreamCast did not demonstrate that the "principal or primary" use of their technology is noninfringing, as *Sony* did. They argue that Grokster and StreamCast services "lack 'commercially significant noninfringing uses'" (Motion Picture Studio and Recording Company Br. 18). For them, evidence for meeting the *Sony* rule is a quantitative measurement, and showing "significance" means showing a "principal" or "primary" use, presumably based on a majority of lawful uses over unlawful uses. The petitioners state,

> *Sony-Betamax* variously stated the quantum of noninfringing use required to make out the staple article of commerce defense. . . . But the Court declined to "give precise content to the question of how much use is commercially significant." (Motion Picture Studio and Recording Company Br. 30)

This notion of "primary" or "principal" use is established through numbers of commercial significance. The petitioners do not believe that "speculative or anecdotal evidence" regarding noninfringing uses is enough and compare it to their own supplied evidence, "expert analysis, based on a statistical sample, demonstrating that 90% of the files being traded on the respondents' services are known or very likely infringing" (Motion Picture Studio and Recording Company Br. 37). In order to establish the regulation of peer-to-peer networks as lawful, the petitioners demonstrated that "the facts" of the *Grokster* case show extenuating circumstances that warrant restrictions that weren't necessary in *Sony*. By emphasizing these aspects of the digital networks—scale of infringement and the failure to meet the principal use standard—petitioners point out that Grokster and StreamCast are the "polar opposite" of *Sony-Betamax* (Songwriter and Music Publisher Br. 23) and, as such, the *Grokster* case requires a ruling different from that in *Sony*.

Petitioners propose yet another unmet standard for meeting the *Sony* test: changing the design of the software by implementing any available means for preventing infringement. They assert that while it was not possible for Sony to design the VCR to prevent unlawful copyright while maintaining its lawful function of "time-shifting," Grokster and StreamCast have this capability. They write, "[t]he calculus is different here. Because Grokster and StreamCast have at their disposal ready methods for policing and limiting infringement, liability must be imposed to require them . . . to adopt those methods without interfering with the purported legitimate use of their services for sharing non-protected files" (Songwriter and Music Publisher Br. 17). They argue that Grokster and StreamCast, because they chose not to employ such protection measures, "intentionally exploit copyright infringement" (10). The petitioners cite "undisputed evidence" that shows that Grokster and StreamCast have knowledge of the infringement occurring on their services, and that they advertised their services to infringers, thus actively "encouraging and assisting" their users' infringement.

Because of these key differences between the Grokster and StreamCast technology and prior analog and print technologies, petitioners argue that Grokster and StreamCast are not shielded under the *Sony-Betamax* rule. It is the digital nature of the innovation, the development of a technology with capabilities available only in digital form such as mass distribution and the ability to control end users' activities, that content owners highlight as the reason that Grokster and StreamCast Networks do not meet the standards defined in the *Sony* case. And because this narrative of legal history shows how the current context is different—how digital is different—it requires a new, transformed state of copyright law in order to restore justice in its conclusion.

INTRODUCING THE "INDUCEMENT RULE"

Although the final ruling was unanimous, there was much contention in the decision regarding which interpretation of *Sony* is correct: the "capability" standard adopted by the technology companies or the standards referenced by the content owners. This contention led to a decision with two concurring decisions, each signed by three justices. Justice Ginsburg, in the first concurrence, argues that "[t]his case differs markedly from *Sony*" because it is based on insufficient evidence of noninfringing uses. If Grokster is "overwhelmingly used to infringe" and "this infringement was the overwhelming source of revenue from the products," then *Sony* provides no defense, according to Ginsburg's concurrence. Ginsburg argues for more convincing evidence of substantial noninfringing uses of the technology, denigrating the respondents' evidence as a "motley collection of declarations" (Ginsburg concurrence 6) and their arguments as based on "mostly anecdotal evidence, sometimes obtained second-hand" (5). She concludes that these details are not sufficient to meet the *Sony* standard when compared to the more reliable survey data supplied, "in the face of evidence, proffered by MGM, of overwhelming use of Grokster's and StreamCast's software for infringement" (Ginsburg concurrence 5–6). Rejecting a reading of *Sony* based on a standard of "capability," she instead argues for a standard that requires majority or substantiality of noninfringing uses.

In contrast, in a second concurrence Justice Breyer argues that "a strong demonstrated need for modifying *Sony* (as he views is attempted in Ginsburg's concurrence) has not yet been shown" (Breyer concurrence 18). He views a quantitative measurement for the *Sony* rule as a departure from case precedent and argues it may have a limiting effect on the creation, development, and marketing new technologies. Breyer argues that "the nature of . . . lawfully swapped files is such that it is reasonable to infer quantities of current lawful use roughly approximate to those at issue in *Sony*" (Breyer concurrence 5). Breyer, therefore, argues that 10% of noninfringing uses satisfies the *Sony* test, asserting "in quantitative terms these uses account for only a small percentage of the total number of uses of Grokster's product. But the same was true in *Sony*, which characterized the relatively limited authorized market as 'substantial'" (Breyer concurrence 6). He concludes that "*Sony*'s rule is clear," a standard based on "capability" of noninfringing uses. He does not see a reason for a departure from that standard, as the petitioners do, and notes he has "found nothing in the briefs or record that shows that *Sony* has failed to achieve the innovation-protecting objective" (Breyer concurrence 11). In this way, Breyer supports the "capability" standard, which he asserts is "strongly technology protecting" and "forward looking" (10).

Surprisingly, in the judicial opinion, Justice Souter chooses to sidestep the *Sony* issue altogether. He argues that there is no need to "rewrite" the *Sony* rule in *Grokster.* He rejects the parties' assertions of what he perceives to be new standards for the *Sony* rule, stating only that

> we do not visit *Sony* further, as MGM requests, to add a more quantified description of the point of balance between protection and commerce when liability rests solely on distribution with knowledge that unlawful use will occur. It is enough to note that the Ninth Circuit's judgment rested on an erroneous understanding of *Sony* and to leave further consideration of the *Sony* rule for a day when that may be required. (17)

In this way, Souter leaves the *Sony* rule open to interpretation, and does not attempt to clarify or modify the terms of the asserted "balance." Instead, in the *MGM Studios v. Grokster* ruling he introduces an entirely new standard for liability, the "inducement rule." The inducement rule is based on the fact that "MGM's evidence in this case most obviously addresses a different basis of liability for distributing a product open to alternative uses" (24). The Court identified the basis for the inducement rule in "purposeful, culpable expression and conduct" (19), or the intent to design a product to infringe. In the case against Grokster and StreamCast Networks the Supreme Court decision introduces a new rule for regulating technology development: technologists are liable when they intentionally "induce" that infringement, even if their products are capable of both legal and illegal uses. The Court found that even though the peer-to-peer software in question was, like the VCR, capable of noninfringing uses (such as sharing research information, public domain material, educational materials, secure licensed files, and more), peer-to-peer distributors could still be liable under a new "inducement" rule. This is the first time this inducement rule has been imported into copyright law (though it has roots in intellectual property law, namely in patent law).

The Court defines the rule of inducement:

> [O]ne who distributes a device with the object of promoting its use to infringe copyright, as shown by clear expression or other affirmative steps taken to foster infringement, is liable for the resulting acts of infringement by third parties. . . . The inducement rule . . . premises liability on purposeful, culpable expression and conduct. (19)

What amounts to "clear expression"? What kind of evidence suggests "purposeful, culpable expression and conduct"? The Court found that three features in the *Grokster* case were "particularly notable" in showing an "unmistakable" unlawful objective (21). First, company e-mails, advertisements, and other details showed that Grokster and StreamCast conceived and marketed themselves as "the next Napster" in an effort to supply services to former Napster users. Among this evidence was the fact that "Grokster's name is apparently derived from Napster." Second, the companies did not attempt to develop mechanisms that would limit infringing uses of their software. Third, the companies' business models relied on infringement because their advertising-based revenue increased as more infringing material became available (21–23).

Abiding by the principle of *stare decisis*, the Court clearly states that it does not intend to revisit the existing copyright liability doctrines from *Sony* in this case. The opinion in *Grokster*, then, does not offer a new reading of the technology-protecting *Sony* to apply to digital technology. Instead, the legal narrative creates a clear distinction between analog and digital cultural production and introduces a transformed state of copyright in its conclusion. This new, transformed state applies copyright law to regulate technology to fit a print- and analog-based model of cultural production through the introduction of a new rule. As an entirely new rule of liability, the inducement rule introduces a new level of restriction from the previous case law. In the past, other technologies like the VCR have been accepted as lawful technologies, despite their potential threats to established business models for cultural production. It is not until this most recent case addressing the unique characteristics of digital networks that the law has ventured to introduce new standards for regulating technology at the design and development stage.

By introducing new standards for advertising and technology development, technology companies will deal with a new level of uncertainty about what they can and cannot do in the development process. Such uncertainly may lead to the development only of technologies that work to support the current print- and analog-based model of copyright that relies on exclusive, self-contained products of intellectual and creative activity, or simply to fewer technological developments. As a result, there may be an absence of technologies that enable more community-based creative processes. If the legal narrative of digital copyright in *Grokster* seeks to differentiate between analog and digital creativity, and ultimately asserts a value in analog creativity over digital creativity, the ruling may have the effect of taming technology, and, in turn, taming cultural production. If we posit digital creativity as disease-ridden and requiring new modes of regulation, to quote Lawrence Lessig, are we "spraying DDT to kill a gnat?" ("Who Owns Culture?").

CREATIVITY VS. TECHNOLOGICAL INNOVATION IN *MGM STUDIOS V. GROKSTER*

In *MGM Studios v. Grokster*, the Supreme Court's final say is a unanimous decision that "one who distributes a device with the object of promoting its use to infringe copyright . . . is liable for the resulting acts of infringement by third parties using the device" (2). The judicial opinion for the case asserts that it intends to address a tension between the "competing values" of cultural production and technological innovation. The legal narrative attempts to resolve this conflict by proposing an "appropriate balance" in copyright law between competing interests. The justices and litigants, as well as advocates and consumers, have touted the term "balance" to refer to an ideal state of copyright law that acknowledges the need to provide incentives to authors while limiting their protections so that others have the freedom to develop new works. In the Supreme Court opinion in *Grokster*, the justices define an "appropriate balance" between technology innovation and artistic creativity as one necessitating new standards of liability to regulate the unique, and undesirable, capabilities of digital technologies.

Because of the Court's reluctance to revisit the *Sony* decision, the *Grokster* ruling does not break from or correct existing case law, namely the "capable of substantial noninfringing use" standard. While the majority of the justices (including two concurrences signed by three justices each) would have either expanded or contracted the *Sony-Betamax* doctrine, the Court as a whole asserts that it does not wish to reexamine the *Sony* precedent in the decision. The Court does not attempt to make a more quantifiable *Sony* rule, nor to fully embrace the "mere capability" standard. Instead, the legal narrative resolves the conflict by establishing a new category for liability, in which issues like how the product was marketed and how the technology was designed will be decisive on copyright infringement claims. In the legal discourse of *MGM Studios v. Grokster*, the Court shows a reluctance to reexamine case precedent in response to new models for cultural production in a digital age. Rather, what is determined to support progress in the arts and sciences is an amendment to copyright law to regulate technology development to fit the economic models existing for print and analog creativity. Such regulation requires a transformed state of copyright law that extends the terms of liability to technology developers themselves. The differentiation between digital and analog models of cultural production works to show how the new context for creative and intellectual activity requires a new, transformed state of copyright law.

The judicial opinion in the *Grokster* case examines the conflict between technology development and cultural production in a digital age. From the petitioners, we see the positioning of technology as an agent of intellectual and creative growth. Faith in technology as an inherently progressive force, leading to advancement in the arts and sciences, is based on a powerful metanarrative of social progress. On the other hand, the respondents present technology as a destructive force. As with the introduction of many new technologies, peer-to-peer file sharing has evoked a flurry of fears about its pandemic potential for spreading "disease" and "viruses" that will kill cultural production. The inducement rule presented in the ruling, in effect, regulates technology development to mitigate fears of these social ills and legal disorder. By introducing a new inducement rule, the legal narrative in *Grokster* concludes by transforming copyright law to create order within new and unfamiliar digital contexts. This conclusion also works to define creative activity on the Internet as business transactions between corporate authors and consumer citizens, reinforcing the protections given to an intellectual-property-as-exclusive-property model. The legal narrative in the *Grokster* ruling, rather than concluding with a return to a restored state of cultural production, tips toward an even more propertized cultural landscape by presenting a transformation of copyright law to regulate digital technology at the development stage.

7 Copyright on Campus
Shaping Digital Citizens through Anti-Piracy Messages

Using peer-to-peer file-sharing networks is not unique to college campuses. But recent studies assert, and at times overstate, the pervasiveness of unauthorized file sharing among university students. One study, presented in a 2004 report from the Pew Internet & American Life Project, indicates that 56% of full-time students download files and 35% share files on peer-to-peer networks, and 80% report that they do not care if the files are copyrighted (Madden and Lenhart 4–7). RIAA president Cary Sherman claims that college students not only download often, but that they do so more than the general population: "[a]ll the research we've seen indicates college kids as the most prolific illegal downloaders" (Cohn). To support this statement, he refers to the results of a survey conducted by Student Monitor from spring of 2006 that found that more than half of college students engaged in unauthorized downloading, and to research from the NPD market research firm that indicates that college students accounted for more than 1.3 billion illegal music downloads in 2006 ("RIAA Welcomes Bipartisan Push"). In 2005, the MPAA released the results of its own study presenting research on file sharing in terms of monetary losses: 44% of the motion picture industry's losses could be attributed to downloading by college students, they claimed. This figure turned out to be an overstatement, however, and in 2007 the MPAA revealed that there had been an error in the research process and the number was actually 15% (Green). While it is clear that college and university students do engage in downloading music and movie files on university networks, the existing research is inconclusive: there is no consistent evidence that students are *more* likely to engage in illegal file sharing than the general population.

Nevertheless, the music and motion picture industries have pursued legal action against higher education students specifically with great determination. While it may be that the content industries began the battle on college campuses with the intention of curbing file sharing among the most active participants on the networks, where they believed they were losing the most money, a more likely rationale for increasing efforts to discourage file sharing on college campuses is the fact that college students are easy targets. The content industries are not likely seeking large monetary compensation from lawsuits against students (college students usually have very little in their bank accounts). Instead, the entertainment industry may seek to influence what they perceive as a morally moldable population, to change the perception among young people that peer-to-peer file sharing is acceptable behavior. In what they often refer to as "educational materials" distributed to campuses, representatives of the entertainment industry and their supporters often assert a moral or ethical goal: to instill in students a particular code of ethics regarding peer-to-peer file sharing and, more generally, regarding the use of the Internet. In doing so, the anti-piracy messages targeting college campuses prescribe binary roles for students in their digital copyright narratives, on the one hand, as amoral or unethical criminals, making them villainous characters, or, on the other, as responsible consumers who pay for all content on digital networks.

The battle over peer-to-peer file sharing on college campuses has heated up since 2002, which marks the formation of the Joint Committee of the Higher Education and Entertainment Communities. The committee—whose members include, but are not limited to, Cary Sherman (president, RIAA), Dan Glickman (president and CEO, MPAA), Brit Kirwan (chancellor, University System of Maryland), and Graham Spanier (president, Penn State)—was created to "address matters of mutual concern, including the use of university networks for copyright infringement and the problem of unauthorized file sharing on university and college campuses" (Joint Committee). In the years since, the group has supported the entertainment industries' efforts to quell unauthorized peer-to-peer file sharing on college campuses. As a starting point, in 2004 the committee issued a report that offered the results of a "very informal survey" conducted by the RIAA of 55 doctoral institutions to assess what universities were already doing to educate students about the consequences of unauthorized downloading. They found,

> Over 80% of the institutions had online-accessible statements on P2P file sharing, with slightly more than a half of these statements addressing file sharing in some detail in the context of the institution's stance on P2P. However, less than 20% of detailed online institutional statements on P2P were incorporated into an institutional computer use or copyright policy. ("University Policies and Practices Addressing Improper Peer-to-Peer File Sharing" 2)

The committee concluded, "[t]hese data do suggest that institutions are beginning to address the issue of P2P file sharing with statements concerning file sharing likely to evolve into formal institutional policy positions" (2). And, in fact, many colleges and universities are—more than commercial Internet service providers—educating network users about the legal risks associated with illegal file sharing, creating policies that prohibit unauthorized file sharing, and punishing students who engage in it. However, despite the fact that the Joint Committee of the Higher Education and

Entertainment Communities recognizes that university officials have begun to respond to student file sharing on university networks, content industry representatives have recently pursued increasingly aggressive tactics against this particular population of file sharers.

RIAA lawsuits against individual file sharers among the general population began in 2003. The purported goal of these lawsuits, and particularly ones geared toward adolescents, teenagers, and college-aged file sharers, was "education." Cary Sherman, president of the RIAA, said of the lawsuit approach, "[e]nforcement is a tough-love form of education" (Knopper). While the initial rounds of lawsuits were not targeted specifically at university students, the RIAA soon began laying plans for extending their pursuit to college campuses. In 2005, Graham Spanier, president of Penn State, and Cary Sherman, president of the RIAA, coauthored an article that appeared in the *Chronicle of Higher Education* in which they presented a united front against what they described as an ethical struggle facing morally underdeveloped young college students. The article, titled "Thou Shalt Not Pirate Thy Neighbor's Songs," offered suggestions for university administrators to curb unauthorized file sharing on university networks, such as educating students of their "moral and legal responsibilities," employing "effective remedies against violators," and implementing anti-piracy software. The article, written in the wake of the *MGM Studios v. Grokster* decision, called the case a "wake-up call" and argued for increased awareness of file sharing on campuses, particularly for those campuses "that have yet to engage the issue" (Spanier and Sherman B24).

This article, representing a top university figure and the powerful RIAA, set the tone for the battle waged in higher education since. The authors note the stakes of ignoring the file sharing issue on campuses: rampant file sharing endangers academic learning by using significant bandwidth intended for academic purposes and introducing ominous-sounding "malicious viruses, worms, and Trojan horses." Further, the title of the article introduces an analogy between unauthorized file sharing and violation of the Bible's Ten Commandments, presumably a mix between "thou shalt not steal" and "thou shalt not covet thy neighbor." And the article concludes by suggesting that university administrators have a duty to take a more active approach to curbing file sharing on campus due to their obligation to lesson students on the immorality of theft:

> [T]o allow students to leave college believing that piracy is acceptable or even the norm fails a generation in more ways than one. . . . The promotion of theft, even in the digital age, should not be tolerated. A new generation of young adults looks to all of us for guidance. It is of service to no one to turn and look the other way. (B24)

If students are ethically naïve, "arriv[ing] on their campuses eager to use their institutions' high-speed connections to pirate songs, movies, games, and other creative content," then it is up to universities to provide the guidance needed to lead them toward more appropriate behavior.

The editorial was met with mixed reactions from the academic community, but the content industries were not deterred. In February of 2007, the conflict intensified when the RIAA sent "pre-litigation letters" to 400 students at 13 universities across the country. They also sent letters to university presidents to announce the new approach, calling it "a last resort." In the letters to presidents, Cary Sherman described "a reasonable role that campus administrators can play," including forwarding the pre-lawsuit letters to their students and directing them to two new RIAA-created resources. The first was a Web site for collecting "pre-litigation settlement" payments from illegal downloaders, allowing self-identified users to settle with the RIAA before a lawsuit was filed (http://www.p2plawsuits.com). The second was a free online "educational" video and brochure package created by the RIAA, titled *Campus Downloading*, that described the dangers of unauthorized file sharing for college students (http://www.campusdownloading.psu.edu).

Along with the letters to college campuses, the P2P lawsuits Web site, and the *Campus Downloading* materials, the RIAA launched an advertising campaign incorporating concepts developed by college marketing students enrolled in RIAA-EdVenture Partners classes. One advertisement, a "for sale" listing that looks similar to a classified listing or a Craigslist posting, describes "one slightly used identity" for sale by "Stew Pidd," warning of the security threat posed by sharing files on digital networks. The other includes an eye exam chart where in place of the letters the chart reads, "[i]f you can't see that illegal downloading is stealing then keep reading," with an anti-piracy message following ("What the Artists and Songwriters Have to Say"). The two advertisements, developed by university students themselves, appeared in campus newspapers across the country.

In May of 2007, Congress, namely the U.S. House Judiciary Committee's Subcommittee on Courts, the Internet, and Intellectual Property and the House Committee on Education and Labor, provided backing for efforts targeting higher education by sending letters to officials at 20 universities, and including a survey requesting detailed information about each university's anti-piracy efforts (MCloskey). The letter warned, "[i]f we do not receive acceptable answers [about what the universities are doing to curb unauthorized file sharing], Congress will be forced to Act" (Triplett).

And in October of 2007, the MPAA sent their own letter to the presidents of 25 colleges, asking them to adopt the anti-piracy software it developed called University Toolkit. The letter stated that the software "produce[s] a report that is strictly internal and therefore confidential to illustrate the level of file sharing" on campus networks (McLaurin). The MPAA offered the software for free, though their offer was rescinded just two months later when the software was found, ironically, to violate copyright laws. Along with the letter, university contacts received a copy of the MPAA's *Briefing Book on Campus Digital Piracy*.

The materials circulated by the RIAA, the MPAA, and Congress did not provide details on what the legal consequences for piracy are, although the punishment for violators ranges from five years of jail time to fines upwards of $150,000, or an average of $3,000 to $5,000 in a settlement. A new bill from Congress made the stakes even higher for college administrators: in addition to helping develop individual students' moral compasses and protecting their criminal records and personal bank accounts, administrators were also faced with struggling to secure federal funding for education at their institutions. The anti-piracy campaigns came to campuses as Congress was considering a higher education funding bill that would place new anti-piracy obligations on universities that participate in federal financial aid programs. The anti-piracy efforts coincided with the reauthorization of the Higher Education Act in the form of the 2008 Higher Education Opportunity Act (HEOA), which stipulates that universities develop plans to "effectively combat" the unauthorized distribution of copyrighted material and suggests that institutions use technology-based deterrents to monitor bandwidth users' activities and offer "alternatives" to illegal file sharing. The HEOA was signed by President George W. Bush on August 14, 2008, to reauthorize the HEA, which had not been reauthorized since 1998. The HEOA governs federal student aid, grants to institutions of higher education, and other programs.

The Act contains two provisions that address peer-to-peer file sharing: Section 488 and Section 493. In these sections, the HEOA requires that higher education institutions make annual disclosures informing their students that the unauthorized distribution of copyrighted materials may subject them to criminal and civil penalties. These disclosures must also describe the steps that the institutions will take to detect and punish illegal distribution of copyrighted materials by their students. In addition, institutions are required to certify to the Secretary of Education that they have developed plans to "effectively combat" the unauthorized distribution of copyrighted material. Although universities are not explicitly required to do so by the law, the Act suggests that institutions satisfy this requirement through the use of technology-based deterrents such as "bandwidth shaping" and "traffic monitoring to identify the largest bandwidth users." Finally, "to the extent practicable," institutions are required to offer alternatives to illegal file sharing, although the specific alternatives to be offered are not specified in the law.

The two major issues that have been raised by members of the higher education community about the HEOA are 1) the exorbitant cost of compliance—some estimates are as high as $500,000 per institution per year (Guess)—and 2) the potential violations of students' privacy. Regarding the former, critics note that the cost of compliance would likely be passed on to the students by way of tuition and fees, which, of course, contradicts the purpose of the Act, to make college more affordable. The latter issue regarding students' privacy is also troubling. One example of a technology-based deterrent is "traffic monitoring to identify the largest bandwidth users." This deterrent identifies individuals as probable violators of the law based solely on the amount of bandwidth they are using, regardless of the actual reasons for that use. Compliance with the vague federal requirement to deploy unproven technologies with considerable new costs has been understandably high among university administrators' concerns.

In addition to the efforts organized by the RIAA, the MPAA, university officials from top academic institutions, and Congress, other activist organizations have also sought to present anti-piracy messages that would appeal to the college student demographics. In the past several years these organizations have launched public Web sites and brochures of their own to deliver messages that speak directly to file sharers, with the intention of persuading them to stop unauthorized downloading and uploading. Whereas many of the anti-piracy materials presented publicly are aimed at a younger generation of file sharers or at a more general population, a few appear to speak directly to college-aged file sharers, including

- The 2003 Pro-Music Web site (http://www.pro-music.org), launched by an international coalition of music organizations that includes the IFPI, the Motion Picture Association European Office, and the International Video Federation. The Web site also presents a brochure, the *2007 Copyright and Security Guide for Schools and Universities*.
- The 2004 What's the Download Web site (http://www.whatsthedownload.com) and the What's the Download blog (http://www.whatsthedownloadblog.typepad.com). These materials are presented by the Recording Academy, with the help of an advisory board, comprised of 12 young music fans (aged 19 to 25) from across the country, and honorary board members, including Kelly Clarkson and Kanye West. The materials were announced at the 46th annual Grammy Awards and included a public service announcement, titled "Club," that aired on television.
- The 2005 MusicUnited Web site (http://www.musicunited.org) from the Music United for Strong Internet Copyright (M.U.S.I.C.) Coalition. The M.U.S.I.C. Coalition is comprised of 21 music organizations including the RIAA. The release of the Web site was accompanied by a poster campaign in 11 U.S. cities, urging the purchasing of music in lieu of unauthorized peer-to-peer file sharing, with the tagline of "Feed a Musician, Download Legally."

Together, these efforts from the content industry representatives, university officials from top academic institutions, Congress, and coalitions of entertainment industry supporters present campuses nationwide with a persuasive appeal for more proactive approaches to addressing the issue of unauthorized downloading among college students. The mandates for universities from Congress look surprisingly similar to the requests from the entertainment industry, which include directives asking higher education administrators to take a four-step approach:

- To inform campus communities on the unethical and illegal nature and consequences of unauthorized downloading through educational materials and policies.
- To discipline students and staff who violate policies.
- To employ technology deterrents to file sharing on university networks.
- To offer legal alternatives to unauthorized file sharing to network users.

It is the first point that is of most interest to the discussion of the rhetoric of the digital copyright debate. The call for increased education efforts provides the impetus for the distribution of the anti-piracy messages presented by various commercial and political groups to college students. And in the materials presented in the past several years by the RIAA, MPAA, and other entertainment industry supporters to higher education institutions, we can see a casting of college students in prescribed roles that are far from unbiased. These rhetorically constructed roles do more than inform students of the consequences of illegal file sharing; they also work to shape students' perceptions of "digital citizens," redefining their relationship to technology and to cultural production on the Internet. By creating narratives of the digital copyright "problem" that cast students as criminals at worst and consumers at best, these stories reaffirm traditional hierarchies of cultural production and support the binary positioning of producer and consumer of copyrighted works. As my analysis will show, such rhetorical work fails to recognize the complex roles of technology users as producers of content as well as consumers and, as such, offers obstacles to new models for cultural production online. Together, the anti-piracy narratives shape students' perceptions of their roles within digital culture, as they become political actors and digital citizens in their own right.

ANALYSIS OF ANTI-PIRACY NARRATIVES TARGETING UNIVERSITY COMMUNITIES

As shown in the preceding short history, college campuses have become the latest battleground in the digital copyright debate. In the carefully constructed narrations of the digital copyright problem and its solution, university students are strategically cast as villains, in the form of either naïve perpetrators or unrelenting criminals. In order to seek reform, students must move from this deviant role of thief to the role of the responsible consumer who "respects" intellectual property in the digital marketplace. Students become part of the problem in the digital copyright narratives told on campuses, and a transformation is needed—from criminal to consumer—to reach a restored steady state of cultural production. In addition to criminalizing a large population of our nation's young adults, the narratives introduced in anti-piracy campaigns targeting college students also serve as an instantiation of the property stewardship narrative and, as such, reinforce a particular model of cultural production as a linear process that necessitates the involvement and mediation of the music and movie industries.

Copyright and College Students' "Personal Value Systems"

In order to secure assistance from university officials in anti-piracy efforts, the entertainment industry representatives and supporters make several different appeals in their letters, videos, brochures, booklets, and public Web site content. These appeals attempt to explain the stakes of failing to address the piracy issue on campus, a necessary rhetorical move as the entertainment industries are asking universities to monitor students' Internet activity and to help to punish file sharers on an unprecedented level. First, the letters and materials seek support from university officials through a practical appeal, explaining how piracy endangers and wastes essential academic resources, namely in the form of security breaches on digital networks and excessive use of bandwidth. The anti-piracy messages point to the dangers of files carrying viruses or spyware, the fact that peer-to-peer file sharing takes up bandwidth intended for academic activity, and the network susceptibility to hacking that can come from sharing files. Pro-Music, for example, states that peer-to-peer networks are "notorious sources" of viruses, spyware, firewall compromises, resource drains, and hacking (*2007 Copyright and Security Guide* 3). The MPAA argues that reducing peer-to-peer file sharing would benefit the university community both in terms of protecting resources from security breaches as well as saving money, as it "eases computer demands & saves taxpayers money" (*Briefing Book* 9). The RIAA also points to monetary losses for universities by noting that illegal downloading "can be costly to the university administration in terms of resources such as excessive use of bandwidth and time spent on responding to infringement notices" (*Campus Downloading: Protect Yourself. Do It Legally.* 2). These practical concerns, of course, speak to key issues facing university officials, including the integrity of university resources and budgets. However, they may not provide compelling enough reason to monitor student activity and put forth an agenda from commercial entities like the RIAA or MPAA.

Another appeal the entertainment industry representatives and their supporters make is establishing common values with universities. Many of the anti-piracy materials posit that unauthorized downloading leads to a lack of "respect" for intellectual work. The entertainment industry representatives and supporters note university communities' interests in producing, and thus presumably protecting, intellectual property. As generators of intellectual and creative works, both the university and the entertainment communities presumably have a vested interest in ensuring that the rights associated with intellectual property are protected. The RIAA's *Campus Downloading* booklet asserts this common goal, stating, "[a]s with the entertainment communities, institutions of higher education place great value on works and expect others similarly to respect their efforts" (*Campus Downloading: Protect Yourself. Do It Legally.* 5). And the MPAA's *Briefing Book* echoes this sentiment by pointing out, "[c]olleges and universities comprise a large portion of the creators and developers of intellectual property and have a stake in the enforcement of copyright laws" (*Briefing Book* 9). Pro-Music frames the issue as one that is central to the university mission: "[p]erhaps most importantly, respect of intellectual property is essential to the academic mission; if it is not adequately protected, your own works are devalued, as well as works that you use and teach" ("Advice for Schools and Universities"). The language of "respecting" copyright laws is used widely when describing the conflict at the heart of the digital copyright debate in the anti-piracy narratives on college campuses.

Respecting intellectual property, on one level, means following the rules of legal authority by abiding by copyright laws. But respect also means recognizing the value of intellectual property. As Tarleton Gillespie points out about the use of the term in anti-piracy materials designed for K–12 classrooms, "while sometimes 'respect' refers simply to obeying a rule, as in to *respect the speed limit*, it can also mean to hold in high regard, to appreciate something for its inherent value, as in the command to *respect your elders*" ("Characterizing Copyright" 20). Just as the term is used frequently in anti-piracy materials for younger children, it is also used in messages aimed at college students. Respect refers to honoring protections offered to content owners by copyright law, and it also refers to valuing intellectual property in a particular way. Recognizing the value of intellectual property, as defined by content industry representatives, means honoring an economic value in copyrighted works as consumable goods. By abiding by the rules for commercial distribution and consumption of works, students should understand their role as consumers of intellectual and creative works produced by others, and should seek permission for each use or pay fees for each copy. While the anti-piracy messages acknowledge that members of the academic community produce work in addition to consuming it, they do not present students as producers when narrating the peer-to-peer file-sharing problem. Instead, in the anti-piracy narratives on college campuses, students remain firmly situated in the position of the consumer who values the goods produced by others.

The concept of teaching respect for intellectual property rights that is commonly cited as an underlying goal in educating students about the consequences of unauthorized file sharing transforms anti-piracy messages into efforts to shape future moral digital citizens. The language of respect and consequences for wayward actions reframes the copyright debate as a moral issue, and positions paying for content as a moral obligation. The issue of copyright on digital networks appears to have a clear-cut right and wrong, rather than involving the complex, circumstantial legal bargaining inherent in copyright law. In the anti-piracy narratives, college-aged file sharers appear as ethically unformed Internet users in need of moral guidance, thus, as part of the problem to be solved. Promoting respect for copyright has the underlying goal of molding college students into model digital citizens that respect the authority of the law and the marketable value of intellectual property rights.

Teaching ethical behavior through anti-piracy materials in the classroom is not limited to college-aged students. Many anti-piracy campaigns target much younger children in the K–12 schools. Professionally prepared educational materials are offered to schools nationwide, and individual teachers can incorporate them into regular classroom activities. As Gillespie notes in his study of anti-piracy campaigns available for K–12 classrooms, one reason for introducing the anti-piracy messages at a young age is that the audience is morally impressionable: "[m]ost of the campaign producers I spoke to also felt that young users, still forming their ethical precepts and moral reasoning, may be more open to pleas about the morality of these activities" ("Characterizing Copyright" 6). At the university level, it becomes a matter of forming responsible future citizens at the brink of their transition into independence and adulthood.

As the anti-piracy narratives demonstrate, responsible digital citizens exhibit respect for copyright by being loyal consumers of intellectual property, by engaging the digital marketplace. Penn State president Graham Spanier offers, "we have some level of responsibility for the well being of millions of young men and women who, while in the transition from adolescence to adulthood, are massive consumers of entertainment products at the same time they are developing personal value systems" (*Briefing Book* ii). Spanier presents a close relationship between two roles that he assigns to college students, as young adults forming "personal value systems" and as "massive consumers." While Spanier suggests that these two roles be addressed simultaneously, he does not make note of alternative roles; many students who are active Internet users are also *producers* of creative and intellectual works and active *participants* in digital culture. Spanier suggests that the natural role for students is that of passive consumers and, therefore, that their value systems necessarily consist of respecting consumable goods produced by others. With this statement, he attempts to equate responsible citizens with loyal consumers in the digital world.

While materials geared toward younger children may present prescribed forms of moral behavior, the educational materials aimed at college students attempt to skirt around didacticism by taking the stance that college students should ultimately make their own decisions regarding peer-to-peer file sharing. The implication is that if students understood more fully the ramifications of unauthorized downloading, they would choose not to do it. The Recording Academy's Web site, titled What's the Download, gains credibility among college-aged file sharers by noting its contributors: an advisory board made up of "12 young music fans (aged 19–25)" and "honorary board members" including pop music artists Kelly Clarkson and Kanye West. In one section, the Web site addresses college-aged audiences by offering "[s]tuff to think about before you click the 'Download Now' button or copy your friend's CD." The page addresses, and rebukes, the various reasons file shares may choose to download music, including "everybody's doing it" and "I think the laws about downloading and copyright are dumb." The page directs students to view the issue as a question of ethics: "[m]ost people would agree that we all have a little voice inside our head that tells us whether something we're doing is right or wrong. Brainiacs call this a 'code of ethics,' and every person's code is unique" ("What's the Controversy: Thinking Twice"). Playing on issues of identity and individuality that appeal to most young adults, identifying a code of ethics as "unique" positions the issue of digital copyright as one that affects each individual differently, based on his or her personal set of morals. Based on this unique code of ethics, the Web site suggests, the reader can use the information presented to make his or her own decision regarding personal beliefs about file sharing. Ultimately, the What's the Download Web site leaves it open to the student's sound judgment; it is the individual's decision whether or not to continue to download music. Prefacing its anti-piracy message, it reads, "[t]ake a look, and see if you—and your personal code of ethics—agree or disagree with these issues. Thinking about them will help us come to a decision about the part each of us wants to play in the downloading controversy" ("What's the Controversy: Thinking Twice"). The Web site appears to give the college-aged viewer individual agency, the ability to choose where he or she stands on the issue of downloading music from peer-to-peer networks. This iteration of the anti-piracy narrative places college students in the role of naïve Internet user uninformed about the consequences of unauthorized downloading. The goal becomes educating them on the issues and then leaving them to make better choices. A quotation from Spanier in the concluding seconds of the RIAA's *Campus Downloading* video likewise acknowledges students' right to make up their own minds on the issue; however, he ultimately presents one choice as "right": "whatever your choices are for music, make the right one. It's your life."

It is likely that college students, who engage regularly in practices of critical reading in their academic activities, will easily recognize the bias in these messages. They will likely see the anti-piracy messages for what they are: arguments about why peer-to-peer file sharing is wrong. In order to show that peer-to-peer file sharing is the wrong choice, the familiar, central metaphor between file sharing and theft is used in the anti-piracy messages. One of the more obvious comparisons appears on the Web site MusicUnited.org, presented by an alliance of 21 music industry organizations advocating against file sharing. The Web site gives reasons "why you shouldn't steal music" ("Why You Shouldn't Do It"). The language of "file sharing" isn't introduced on the page at all, and instead the Web site refers to the activity of downloading music on peer-to-peer networks only as "stealing." The What's the Download Web site presents a similar message: "downloading and swapping music illegally is just like stealing a CD from a store" ("What's the Controversy: The Lowdown"). The content on these sites and others compare file sharing to stealing, showing it to be a legal and moral offense. Further, in response to the question "[h]ow do I know if I am downloading music legally?", the FAQ page of the What's the Download Web site presents the broad claim, "[a]s a general rule of thumb: if you are using a P2P network, then you are likely downloading illegally" ("What's the Controversy: Just the FAQs"). This message, as it relies on the rhetorical hedge "generally," remains technically true to copyright law. However, such broad statements about the illegality of peer-to-peer networks simplify a rather complex message about copyright into a clear-cut matter of legal right and wrong.

Other examples equating peer-to-peer file sharing with stealing emphasize not breaking the law but rather the immoral nature of theft. A message that appears on one page of the MusicUnited Web site notes the social stigma attached to stealing: "[m]ost of us would never even consider stealing something—say, a picture or a piece of clothing—from a friend's house. Our sense of right and wrong keeps most of us from doing something so selfish and antisocial" ("Who Really Cares?")[13]. In this comparison, the theft referred to is not that which takes place in a store setting but rather theft from a friend, an even more egregious act. The act becomes a crime not only in the legal sense but an act of betrayal by breaking the trust of a friend. This act could subject the perpetrator to legal consequences as well as to harsh judgment from others for the deviant behavior for being "selfish and antisocial."

Given the message that file sharing is stealing and that stealing is both a legal and ethical offense, the only "right" decision for college students to make is against file sharing on peer-to-peer networks. Anti-piracy messages solicit college administrators' assistance in educating students about copyright and enforcing consequences, but also in instilling a strong sense of file sharing as unethical. The MPAA materials argue that "[c]onsistent enforcement of the campus policy reaffirms that stealing is fundamentally wrong" (*Briefing Book* 11). Insofar as universities support the ethical development of students at a time when they are forming their "personal value systems," university administrators have an obligation to steer them in the right direction in the digital copyright debate. The message is not one that stops at warning of the legal consequences of file sharing but also extends to a moral and ethical lesson: "[i]llegal downloading and distribution of movies, music, and software is stealing, and thus universities have an ethical as well as legal responsibility to address such activity" (*Briefing Book* 6). Beyond a legal obligation, it becomes the "responsibility" of universities to guide the development of future ethical citizens in digital culture.

Students as Criminals

In the previous examples, college-aged file sharers are presented as future digital citizens whose moral and ethical value systems are in formation. This role positions students as innocent in their role as file sharers, with the assumption that once they acquire more knowledge about copyright and file sharing, they will be able to make more ethical decisions about their use of peer-to-peer networks. This role as naïve computer user is one that students inhabit frequently in the anti-piracy narratives repeated on college campuses; however, students are at the same time often cast in a more devious role, as villainous characters in the form of copyright "criminals." Lawrence Lessig bemoans the "copyright wars" in which "apparently the 'terrorists' are our kids." In an article appearing in *U.S. News* titled "Prosecuting Online File Sharing Turns a Generation Criminal," Lessig argues,

> We call our kids crooks; after a while, they believe it. And like black marketeers in Soviet Russia, they live life getting comfortable with the idea that what seems "obvious" and "reasonable" to them is a crime. They get used to being criminal. . . . This fact is deeply corrosive. As with Prohibition, it is profoundly corrupting. And over time, it will only weaken our kids' respect for the law.

Whereas the intent of this chapter isn't to explore the psychological effects of labeling a generation of children and young adults as "criminals," it is fruitful for this discussion to explore the rhetorical effect of such use of language on how we, as a culture, understand copyright and cultural production in a digital age. By criminalizing college-aged students, the label works discursively to redefine what the Internet should be: a digital marketplace, a commercial space in which students are consumers and "others" are the producers.

By relying on stiff legal language and threats of legal consequences, the anti-piracy messages use scare tactics to strong-arm students into compliance. By equating file sharing with theft using casual, familiar language in a statement like "downloading music is like stealing a CD from a store," the activity has already been identified as immoral. In many of the anti-piracy messages this language is coupled with more formal legalese, such as the following message from Pro-Music's *2007 Copyright and Security Guide for Schools and Universities*, to state explicitly that such activity is criminal: "the laws of virtually every country make it both a civil and a criminal offence to make illicit copies, distribute, and/or make available a third party's materials on the internet without their permission" (3). Without giving specifics, these materials broadcast to student file sharers that their actions are punishable, either within the university setting or through the legal system. Different from the naïve perpetrator described previously, the infringer in this narrative is a knowing criminal; the student who understands that file sharing is "wrong" but continues to engage in it does so with disregard for the authority of the law. Casting students as unrelenting criminals positions them as juvenile delinquents with no respect for copyright law or for the value of intellectual property. Playing on the larger narrative of young people as rebellious, these campaigns present file sharing as a deviant counteractivity, not only unfair to artists and copyright owners but destructive to the social fabric of digital culture.

Examples of students as criminals are many, but perhaps the most notable are the characters presented in the *Campus Downloading* video produced by the RIAA and viewed by university students during their orientation to campuses nationwide. The eight-minute video begins by featuring several college-aged students on a university campus reflecting on why they continue to download music on peer-to-peer networks when they know their actions are unlawful. One female student looks particularly obstinate when she proclaims, "I know people say it's bad and everything, but, I mean, they're not gonna kick me out of school for it." Another female student offers the typical "it won't happen to me" justification: "I don't really think anything can happen to me. I guess a lawsuit, maybe, but I don't really foresee that happening." And a male student shrugs and reports that he'll continue to do it until he gets caught: "[y]eah, when you download from the Internet, it's like you're anonymous. Who's gonna know?" These students, presumably actors rather than real-life students speaking from their own experiences, appear fearless in the face of what are harsh consequences for illegal and immoral activity. Their faces represent juvenile delinquents with no remorse for a crime. In response to their apathy on the issue, the slightly older male narrator of the video, in an ominous tone, says, "[o]h yeah? So you think it can't happen to you. You need to meet Derek."

These students' immature obstinacy is contrasted with reflections from real-life UNC-Charlotte student Derek "Mickey" Borchardt. Derek recalls the day when a campus police officer came to get him from his morning Spanish class to take him to his room, where there was an FBI agent waiting for him. He was being charged with copyright infringement based on his peer-to-peer file-sharing activity on the university network. Derek reports that he has difficulty "knowing for the rest of my life, I'm gonna hafta explain, forever, why I'm a felon. That's never gonna go away." This scene sounds more like one from a movie, with an FBI agent rushing in to capture a hardened criminal, and not like the life of a middle-class college student in North Carolina. In a later interview in which he reflects on the experience, Derek describes his "shame" at getting caught and of "knowing I'd stolen the property of others like me who are passionate about the art of music." He also describes his "fear for the future [he'd] recklessly damaged" (Borchardt). Derek shows remorse for his actions, and his story stands as a warning to those students who believe they are exempt from punishment. The two roles being portrayed here are, on the one hand, the obstinate teen with no respect for the law and, on the other, the criminal who has been punished severely for a crime. The intended message of the clip is for the viewer to understand that such rebellious and deviant behavior exhibited by the first group of students can lead to them down a path of the life of a criminal, as exemplified by Derek.

On the Campus Downloading Web site, on a page devoted to "Information for Parents of College Students," the RIAA describes file sharing as a crime and students as criminals: "[i]t's against the law and offenders can be prosecuted in criminal court and sued for damages in civil court." The students here are referred to as "offenders" who can be "prosecuted." And in describing the Internet, the page offers a continuum of roles for Internet users, from "seemingly innocent teens to the hardest of hardened criminals":

> The Internet is a tremendous learning tool that represents a great technological advance for society. But caution should be exercised—everyone, from the most seemingly innocent teens to the hardest of hardened criminals, is out there surfing cyberspace with very few rules (and even less enforcement) to maintain order.

In this excerpt, students are only "seemingly innocent," perhaps understanding file sharing to be illegal or unethical but continuing to engage in it. It is also possible that students as file sharers could be the "hardened criminals" who fail to acknowledge any "rules" in cyberspace. These rules, presumably referring to copyright law, "maintain order" in the virtual environment, and without their enforcement, the Internet becomes dangerous territory, corrupting the youth of today.

The notion of file sharing as a dangerous issue facing teenagers and young adults finds parallels with a mixture of messages circulating in the media associated with societal ills. At various times, the anti-piracy messages show likenesses to anti-drug messages and national security threats. First, what the late Jack Valenti has called the entertainment industry's own "terrorist war" (Lessig, "Prosecuting Online") sounds reminiscent of both the "war on drugs" waged by students, parents, and school officials in the late 1990s and the more recent "war on terror" declared by the Bush administration. An example that shows likenesses between piracy, drug trafficking, and national security threats and anti-piracy messages targeting college students is the image titled "The Pyramid of Internet Piracy" included in the *Briefing Book* distributed to campuses by the MPAA. In the image we see a sinister positioning of file-sharing students as contributors to the epidemic of "Internet Piracy." The red-and-black color scheme and pyramid style are similar to the familiar images circulating in mainstream media describing national security threat "levels" from the U.S. Department of Homeland Security. In addition, the typeface is reminiscent of the "green screen" of first-generation personal computers, and though probably intended to offer a visual representation of security threats immanent in high-tech society, invokes an ironic futuristic look.

The pyramid itself narrates the way in which Internet piracy creates a social problem by presenting levels of danger in acts of pirating movies, organized according to the source of the activity ("suppliers," "release groups/top sites," "facilitators," and "file sharers/downloaders") and levels of threat based on number of copies produced (from <100 to 10,000,000s). The notion of "suppliers" certainly parallels the language of anti-drug messages, and the description of this group includes a reference to deviants in the form of "thieves who camcord films in theaters." The file sharers appear at the bottom of the pyramid, not as the source of the problem but as important contributors who make it widespread. The image, with rows and rows of red-and-white anonymous figures, positions students as the unthinking army, a terrifying group forging ahead to do dangerous work. The diagram integrates images of war, national security threats, and drug trafficking all in one small space in its representation of the dangers of

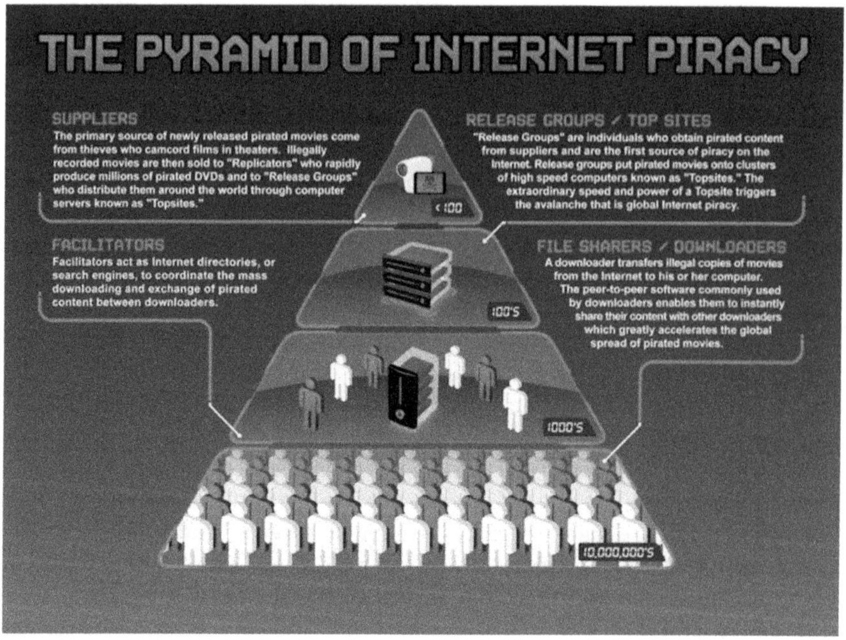

Figure 7.1 "The Pyramid of Internet Piracy" from MPAA's *Briefing Book on Campus Digital Piracy*. Copyright 2007, Motion Picture Association of America. Used with permission. Source: www.mpaa.org/BestPracticesBriefingBook.pdf.

file sharing on a global level. In this narrative of destruction, students are dangerous allies to the enemy.

In another representation in the *2007 Copyright and Security Guide for Schools and Universities*, college administrators suspecting their campus populations to be sharing files on peer-to-peer networks are given a list of "[w]hat to look out for," which includes warning signs of illegal activity. The list includes signals such as "staff and students show little awareness for regulations," "systems administrators see evidence of large amounts of files being traded on their networks," and "there are regular problems with computer viruses" (4). These warning signs invoke the messages parents have received regarding the signs of drug abuse, such as disrespect for family or school rules, and evidence such as rolling papers and plastic baggies or a sudden drop in grades. The warning signs, presented as a checklist, give readers the sense that file sharing behavior is illicit, something to be "caught" and punished. These anti-piracy messages position students, at various times, as petty thieves, terrorists, drug dealers, or personal drug users. Each of these roles, of course, is hyperbolic, but the rhetorical effect is the same—young file sharers are threats to society and should be punished accordingly.

Students as Consumers: Entering the Digital Marketplace

As described in Chapter 2, narratives contain a conflict, but they also contain a resolution, a return to a steady state of affairs. As such, they operate rhetorically by defining deviance as the cause of conflict, and normalcy as the resolved state at the point of conclusion. In the anti-piracy narratives circulating on college campuses, college students are cast in roles of villains, disruptive to the steady state or normalcy in Internet activity. In casting students as naïve and ethically unformed or as criminals, the anti-piracy messages must also present an alternative; the stories cannot end by criminalizing the nation's youth, future digital citizens with political agency, with no hope of redemption. In the anti-piracy narratives, the alternative, transformed role for students becomes that of the responsible digital consumer. The narrator in the *Campus Downloading* video warns, "if you're downloading and sharing music with your friends and not paying anything for it, you'd better think twice. You're probably breaking the law" and even goes so far as to say, "if it's free, it's not legal." The focus of these statements is on the lack of payment and the cost ("free") of the transaction, positioning the egregious act as the file sharer's failure to engage in a commercial transaction. The return to a normative role requires appropriate behavior from college-aged music and movie fans, which consists of paying for digital content. The goal of the anti-piracy messages becomes one of shaping students into digital consumers.

The suggested alternative to the role of criminal for the college student file sharer is the loyal consumer/music fan who pays for Internet content. The anti-piracy materials present positive images of students inhabiting this

Figure 7.2 Images from Campus Downloading Web site. Copyright 2007, Recording Industry Association of America. Source: campusdownloading.psu.edu.

role in photographs of college-aged individuals consuming digital content. Figures 7.2, 7.3, and 7.4 show a sampling of such images, taken from two different sources, in which images of students as consumers are presented. In the images, students are engaging in common activities of the music and movie fan/consumer, including listening to their music on an mp3 player or on a laptop, or purchasing a CD in the store. The images, and many others like them in anti-piracy materials, display students passively consuming

Figure 7.3 Headphones image from MusicUnited Web site. Copyright 2009, Music United Coalition. Source: http://www.musicunited.org/11_pressroom.html.

Figure 7.4 Music store image from MusicUnited Web site. Copyright 2009, Music United Coalition. Source: www.musicunited.org/11_pressroom.html.

digital content, participating in the digital marketplace, or shopping in a place of business. The positive nature of these images—bright colors, healthy and happy college-aged individuals enjoying the works they are consuming—stands in stark contrast to the vision of the unethical copyright criminal and, as such, suggests that this role is the right or appropriate one for students to inhabit.

According to the anti-piracy narratives circulating on college campuses, as consumers/fans, students have an important role to play in the digital copyright conflict: to do no less than save music and movies from extinction. The villains in the copyright story told on college campuses are file-sharing students themselves, who either unwittingly commit an unethical act or knowingly steal intellectual property. The danger presented by their actions is the demise of cultural production. In order to save the future of music and movies, they must move from this deviant position to that of the digital consumer. As the What's the Download Web site points out, consumers can protect "the future of music" by compensating the "music makers":

> Imagine a world where new music wasn't produced. Where great artists were discouraged from creating new songs. Where musicians stopped

> writing new beats because they knew it would be impossible to make a living. Whatever we each may think about music companies and the profits they make on music, the fact is that making records is expensive. It also costs money to discover, develop, and promote new talent. To keep relevant and new music alive, we need to support the music makers, doing everything from going to concerts to legally purchasing music. ("What's the Controversy: Who Pays?")

Students can save the future of cultural production, then, by becoming consumers who purchase music from those who produce digital content. Likewise, in the *Campus Downloading* video, the narrator asks college students to consider "[l]ife without music. College without music. Can you imagine?" The implied message is that if students fail to assume their role as consumers, music will go away.

*****

The conclusion of the stories about peer-to-peer file sharing as captured in the anti-piracy materials targeting college campuses describes the legal, moral, and socially appropriate role for students to assume. In doing so, the narratives also present a larger argument about the role of the Internet in cultural production and what digital culture should look like. By casting file-sharing students as criminals turned reformed digital consumers, the stories define the Internet as what the RIAA refers to as a "digital marketplace" (*Campus Downloading: Protect Yourself. Do It Legally.* 4), as a means for mass distribution of content. This narratives, which prescribe a role for digital networks as a means for distribution—to help Internet users buy, consume, and enjoy creative and intellectual work that is produced by others—reify a particular model of cultural production that relies on a clear distinction between consumer and producer. In this version of the story, Internet users cannot be both consumers *and* producers in cultural production and the Internet cannot be a site for creative and intellectual activity. An alternative role for Internet users, of course, does exist. The "digital author" has been widely touted, within the field of composition and rhetoric and beyond, and college classrooms are often venues for teaching about the production of online content and participation in digital culture. However, according to the anti-piracy materials presented on college campuses, in order to preserve the very future cultural production, students must assume the role of loyal consumers who respect copyright law and the value of digital content as consumable goods.

8 Toward a New Rhetoric of Copyright

Defining the Future of Cultural Production

At the outset of my research on the digital copyright debate, I was optimistic about the possibility of finding a new rhetoric of copyright that was mobilizing the debate in the ways that Andrea Lunsford and Susan West envisioned over a decade ago, toward a reconceptualization of authorship based "not in ownership but in owning up to our situatedness within a network of others who shape our language and our notions of how we may be—and whose value, like our own, depends on our very connectedness. (403)" I was hopeful about what I perceived as actions and discourses of resistance to the recent history of copyright law among participants in the debate. The widespread use of digital technology in the activities of cultural production made "the commons" seem to be a realistic alternative to the property ownership model of copyrighted goods. In addition, I noted the powerful language of sharing and community that emerged from copyright activists and technology supporters, sounding similar to the network envisioned by Lunsford and West. It seemed to me that the information commons, finding support in digital communication technology development, user activities, and public discourse, could surface as a feedstock for economic innovation and as a catalyst for creative activity on the Internet. Unfortunately, the commons as a unified new model of cultural production has failed to gain strength in the debate to date, and the notion of a cultural conservancy on digital networks has yet to come into fruition. However, despite the recent legal trajectory toward more strict copyright protections and the powerful discourse of property ownership that characterizes the contemporary debate, I remain hopeful about the potential for change in the digital copyright landscape.

In the past decade, Internet users have made visible the fact that the current legal structure for regulating intellectual property does not work well in practice, and other models that are not supposed to work are in fact facilitating creative and intellectual activity. Digital networks complicate the notion of copyrighted works as discrete packages of consumable goods and make certain types of nontraditional collaboration, including forms of copying, common practice. The balance maintained by copyright law over the years between technology development and creativity online now seems off kilter. The very structure of copyright law no longer works the way it did in a print-based culture. Whereas print- and analog-based intellectual and creative works required a publisher's or content owner's stewardship, in a digital age these works are produced and can reach the public without requiring mediation. And we have already witnessed the effects of attempting to retrofit the law within a culture of digital production. New rules attempting to maintain this print- and analog-based model of intellectual property such as digital rights management and the inducement rule seem extreme in their attempts to tightly control technological innovation to fit copyright law.

So, why does the print- and analog-based model of ownership persist in copyright law? From an intellectual standpoint, if there is nothing to anchor intellectual property rights where they are except utilitarianism (the idea that a property-based model of intellectual property produces more good than any other possible structure), it would no longer be so. As James Porter and Danielle DeVoss point out, this utilitarian justification for contemporary copyright law has recently come under considerable scrutiny (3–4). They cite James Boyle, who notes the fallacy in the assertion from the "copyright maximalists" that "the more intellectual property rights we create, the more innovation" ("Deconstructing Stupidity"). Boyle uses Europe's Database Directive as an example, showing how its model of providing strong copyright protection over databases has not helped Europe compete with the U.S. information industry. Although strong copyright protections can lead to short-term benefits for established industries, such protectionism does not demonstrate a strong correlation with increased development and creativity over time. In fact, there is evidence that alternative models of copyright may, in fact, heighten both cultural production and economic development. Lessig notes the example of the free software movement in Brazil, which has helped to increase its wealth and develop the potential of its technology industry (Koman). Because the current model of copyright cannot be justified based on a purely utilitarian or economic argument, we might look to other explanations for its persistence in the legal system.

Generally speaking, the property stewardship model of copyright likely retains its privileged position because of a more deeply embedded set of cultural values in private property and economic reward for individual labor. A system of authorial property recognizes authorship as individual and proprietary, and authored works as discrete and privately owned. While these values are neither necessarily nor inevitable, new values in cultural production introduced by users of digital technologies face an overwhelming challenge when seeking widespread adoption and validation through the law. Internet users, technology developers, and copyright activists must do more than demonstrate that their activities are economically advantageous; they must also establish a fundamental shift in cultural values, from a value in consumerism to a value in sharing and participation in digital culture.

While digital networks have the potential to facilitate more creative activity through the protection of an intellectual and creative commons, they can do so only with a shift in cultural values. Faith in technology as an inherently progressive force, leading to social and cultural advancement, is based on the powerful metanarrative of progress that is interwoven into the ethos of U.S. culture. However, such an optimistic view of technology as inherently progressive is, of course, an illusion. Whenever a new technology arrives, it typically also evokes widespread fear about what social ills it may lead to, and how it may be a threat to culture, morality, and society. Such fears, in turn, often play out in the form of limitations on the revolutionary nature of technology, either through social norms or through institutional control. In an analysis of the rhetoric of the digital copyright debate, we see clearly fears of peer-to-peer file-sharing technology and what it may mean for the social, economic, and moral fabric of our culture. In arguing for the regulation of peer-to-peer networks through copyright law, for instance, the content industries and their supporters at various times liken file sharing to theft, terrorism, drug abuse, and epidemic disease, and attribute to it the breakdown of the moral and democratic values of our society. The content owners would have us believe that creative and intellectual activity is best encouraged by limiting distribution and maintaining exclusivity in intellectual works as property, which requires the regulation of digital technologies. They fear digital technology not only because the advancement of technology changes the marketplace (after all, they too have benefited from advancement in digital technology, as evidenced in the market for VCR and DVD rentals) but because of the conceptual, long-term shift in cultural production that the technology represents. Alternative models for creative and intellectual activity have the potential to threaten their very existence.

It is largely through rhetoric that these fears become widespread. Through narrations of the digital copyright conflict, participants in the debate define the copyright problem as one of saving cultural production from extinction. If actions aren't taken to restore a normative state of cultural production, participants argue, then intellectual and creative activity will cease altogether. Different groups of participants in the debate have differing views on what a steady state of cultural production looks like and what redress or restorative actions should be taken to resolve the current conflict. Each presents their version of the story as the objective retelling of the facts of the debate. Rhetorical analysis of the public and legal narratives of the digital copyright debate reveals which assumptions about copyright law are legitimized in contemporary discourse sometimes at the expense of others. These assumptions have important implications for the future of the online debate surrounding copyright law and, more generally, for the future of cultural production in a digital age.

THE RHETORICAL WORK OF NARRATIVES IN THE DIGITAL COPYRIGHT DEBATE

A primary rhetorical structure used to present arguments in the digital copyright debate is that of the narrative, and different narratives from various participant groups offer competing versions of the digital copyright saga. Storytelling serves to argue for particular structures of intellectual property regulation outside of the didactic, combative, and formal rhetoric of the legal system. The narratives in the digital copyright debate take the form of multimedia presentations, "statements of the case" in legal briefs, and dramatic characterizations of file-sharing "pirates" and copyright "dinosaurs" in comic strips, brochures, and on Web sites. Each story is structured around a steady state, or proper balance in copyright law, a threat or conflict that disrupts the steady state, and a resolution. These narratives conclude by showing how a particular legal action rights an important injustice against a creator, copyright owner, or property steward, with the ultimate, shared goal of a healthy state of cultural production. Inherent in these narratives are "morals of the story" that lesson Internet users on their roles as ethical digital citizens.

The competing narratives from the technology companies, content industries, justices, and litigants contain some common features. One important commonality is the reliance on the "foundational principles of copyright law" and the principle of "legal history" to support the proposed resolution to conflict. The use of this feature by the entertainment industries gains authority by suggesting coherence with what is perceived as the natural evolution or trajectory of copyright law. Their story assumes that technological regulation is a necessary means to ensure proper management of the private property of intellectual works, a management system that has worked throughout the history of copyright in the U.S. It presents the role of the content industries as a necessary mediator in the production of intellectual works, protecting incentives necessary for maximizing creativity in a time when emerging technology threatens continued development. The technology supporters and copyright activists likewise cite the foundational principles of copyright law as justification for their model of the commons, although these principles are different from the exclusivity valued by the proponents of the property stewardship model. Rather than assuming that exclusive ownership of private property must be maintained for cultural production to flourish in a digital age, the cultural conservancy narrative seeks support in the notion of progress through shared access to intellectual and creative resources. Supporters of an information commons emphasize that the primary purpose of copyright law is to promote progress and that this principle is best supported by allowing digital technologies to facilitate widespread sharing and open access.

Another powerful thread that runs through most, if not all, of the narrative structures in the debate is the rhetoric of technological determinism. Participants in the debate often assume the inevitability of the role of technology in society as either progressive or destructive. In turn, these assumptions function to establish the relationship between technology and copyright law as either mutually beneficial or adversarial, respectively. On the one hand, the unpredictability of digital technology is perceived as a threat to the stable system of copyright law, which relies on legal code created for an analog world. New technologies that do not fit within the existing system of cultural production challenge the very stability of the law. This line of reasoning assumes that technology development will inevitably lead to lawlessness on digital networks and other social ills, and asserts that regulating technology development and use is necessary to maintain the law's authority. In this way, the rhetoric of technological determinism works to support legal developments, such as the *Grokster* ruling, that seek to control technology development. At the same time, other participants in the digital copyright debate who support less restrictive copyright protections also rely on this rhetoric of technological determinism. They argue for the inevitability of technology to lead to a digital commons and seek to establish it as vital to democratic freedoms of speech, access to information, and citizen participation.

This framework of technological determinism is detrimental to the goals of copyright revisionists, however, because it fails to highlight the role of *users* as participants and political actors in the shape of digital culture. Talking about technology in this way—as a determining agent—reveals an overly simplistic view of the role of technology in our society. Martin Heidegger, in *The Question Concerning Technology,* addresses the problems caused by technological determinism, more specifically, the tendency to understand the world as a series of problems that are either caused by technology or amenable to technological fixes. This is what he calls a "technological understanding" of the world. He writes,

> The essence of technology is by no means anything technological. Thus we shall never experience our relationship to the essence of technology so long as we merely conceive and push forward the technological, put up with it, or evade it. Everywhere, we remain unfree and chained to technology whether we passionately affirm or deny it. But we are delivered over to it in the worst possible way when we regard it as something neutral. (4)

A more appropriate approach, and one that breaks free from the rhetoric of technological determinism that characterizes the current digital copyright debate, is to reconceptualize the problem in terms of users of technology. If we agree that a new rhetoric is needed to better describe new modes of cultural expression in a digital age, we need to recognize that this framework should not position technologies as neutral; rather, technologies have implications as they are employed by users within a social context. Digital technologies are not inherently good or bad, but are used within certain social, institutional, and legal constraints towards certain ends. Narratives that present technology as either the problem or the solution in the digital copyright narrative, without situating that technology in the context of user behaviors and emerging practices for creative and intellectual activity, fail to directly address the role of users in redefining cultural production in a digital age.

PRIVILEGING PROPERTY STEWARDSHIP

It is within the specialized legal rhetoric of recent court cases and legislation that narratives negotiate status as the correct story of copyright. Institutionalized support for regulating technology through copyright law legitimizes the property stewardship narrative, in which creative works retain exclusivity, ownership is individualized, and access is granted only by buying discrete, commodified packages of copyrighted goods. For instance, *MGM Studios v. Grokster* establishes a clear distinction between welcome (analog- and print-based) and unwelcome (digital) forms of creativity by introducing the notion of peer-to-peer file sharing as a "disease" or a "virus," and subsequently argues that, in order to continue to support analog- and print-based creativity, new liability standards are required for technology developers. And the anti-piracy campaigns on college campuses that are used by universities to meet requirements of the Higher Education Opportunity Act (HEOA), which stipulates that universities advise students on the legal consequences of file sharing, prescribe single-faceted roles for students as consumers in a digital marketplace. Initially cast as naïve or amoral Internet users, students must grow and transform into responsible digital consumers who pay for Internet content. These examples demonstrate how the narrative of property ownership emerges as a privileged story of copyright in its deployment through the institutionalized systems of the law, Congress, and the university.

A question posed at the beginning of this book is "how is it that in the digital copyright debate one particular narrative appears rather than another?" That is, how is it that one story becomes the true or accepted story in the digital copyright conflict? While my methodology does not allow for conclusive evidence of cause and effect, rhetorical analysis of the debate illuminates possible reasons for the strength of the property ownership narrative and the failures of narratives of resistance. Situating my analysis within theoretical frameworks regarding the role of rhetoric in resistance sheds some light on the current status of competing narratives in the digital copyright debate.

Foucault's theory of resistance to power structures, and in particular the role of discourse in contributing to change, helps to explain why the property stewardship narrative persists as the privileged story of copyright. To begin, when considering issues of power as they relate to the outcome of the conflict, one might assert that it was the property stewards—the entertainment industries—who have the most political power and, thus, the most influence in the debate. As Jessica Litman notes, who has a seat at the bargaining table will affect the trajectory of the digital copyright conflict. In the *Grokster* case, for example, not only did the entertainment industries have more established and more highly successful business models, but they also had a long history of copyright negotiation, much more than the new and inexperienced technology companies and user advocates. And in the case of copyright messages targeting college campuses, the HEOA stipulations about "educating" campus communities about copyright forced university officials, who vulnerably seek government funding in a time of economic uncertainty, to deliver anti-piracy messages. From a Foucauldian perspective, however, the operation of power in the digital copyright debate extends farther than the notion of a dominant group holding sovereignty over subjected groups. Rather, power operates at multiple points of everyday life not only in the legal and governmental realms but also through the discourses that occur at localized sites to define what is and is not acceptable in the use of digital technologies for intellectual and creative activity. Discourse in these public and social realms defines social values, which are then, in turn, deployed through institutionalized systems. From this perspective, we can begin to see the importance of discourse in the trajectory of the digital copyright debate.

As I noted in Chapter 2, for Foucault power operates through discourse, where certain narratives emerge as truthful or legitimate. Further, Foucault asserts that shifts in established power structures rely on the "deployment of discourse" at "mobile and transitory points of resistance" (*History of Sexuality* 96). In order to gain strength, this deployment must come together to form a "dense web that passes through apparatuses and institutions, without being exactly located in them" (96). The property-based discourse of the digital copyright debate exhibits this strong, impenetrable web, repeated by many participants representing different perspectives—the content industry representatives, university presidents, college students, moviemakers, and pop musicians, to name a few. Because it is widespread and consistent, operating at "multiple and transitory points," it is more likely to find a voice in the formal institutions of the law, the government, and the university.

On the other hand, the deployment of the discourse of the commons remains weak, lacking such "density" and power in the context of ongoing debate. While the discourse of the commons has gained strength among legal scholars and through grassroots efforts like Creative Commons, in the current digital copyright debate it appears only at dispersed and fragmented points that are not yet coherent and cohesive enough to mobilize groups or individuals in a way that leads to change. As such, the narrative of cultural conservancy fails to present itself as a compelling story about how intellectual property should be regulated in a digital age. Instead, it appears diluted and ill defined, which leaves it open to accusations from the content industry of "smoke and mirrors." As a case in point, petitioners in *MGM Studios v. Grokster* assert that the principles of communal responsibility and sharing in the peer-to-peer file-sharing debate fail to map closely to actual usage of their networks. They argue that the technology companies are "hiding behind such high-minded principles when they are running businesses designed to profit from copyright infringement" (Songwriter and Music Publisher Reply Br. 1–2). The language of sharing, democratic freedoms, and an interest in the public good that comes from access to information appears as insincere justification for the reproduction of entertainment goods for personal consumption without compensating creators.

And in fact, the content owners are correct in pointing out that the widespread use of peer-to-peer networks does lack the characteristics of a true commons; users download works without contributing new ones, enjoy unlimited access without communal management, hide behind anonymity without a sense of responsibility, and reap the benefits of individual gain without a larger public good. The values of freedom, equality, and cooperation inherent in the discourse of the technology companies and copyright activists get lost amidst what appears to be a defense of the right to freely download recorded movies and music. In order for the discourse of the commons to elicit change in the digital copyright debate, it would need to increase its density among groups and individuals in a definitive way, coming from even more dispersed sites rather than existing only within fairly specialized discourses of copyright activists and scholars. In addition, it would need to be heard from Internet users themselves who are also producers of content, who move beyond the role of passive consumers

An interesting occurrence in the debate is that participation from actual creators, artists, and technology users is rather rare or, when present, weak. Weighing-in by artists or creators in support of technology developers in the digital copyright debate is limited, and doesn't extend far into public forums. The content industry, on the other hand, receives backing from artists and others who participate in a particular type of music- and moviemaking dependent on property stewards: recall the RIAA's MusicUnited Web site on which successful artists offer their arguments against file sharing, or consider the 11-minute documentary presented on the MPAA's RespectCopyrights Web site that shows various individuals involved in the Hollywood movie production process, from mail room to set design to director. These same kinds of testimonials from technology developers, users of digital networks, or creators who rely on digital technology for alternative modes of composing do not appear as frequently in public realms. Perhaps the voices of those engaged in the production of intellectual works who may personally suffer the consequences of overreaching copyright laws are not heard clearly. Stories not only from creators of traditional forms of media and content, but also from musicians who rely on remixing existing sound clips, independent moviemakers, and even amateur artists, authors, and creators who access, reuse, and repurpose digital materials may be able to offer a more complete picture of what is at stake in the debate. These testimonials could show that the digital copyright debate affects more than the music downloader who is trying to get something for free. They would demonstrate that the intellectual and creative activities on the Internet are hindered by overly protective copyright law. The power of the discourse of property in the digital copyright debate, then, may reside in the fact that it is a clearly articulated and consistent narrative that appears from various groups at various sites over a large network of relations.

In addition, there is a stark difference between the discourse of property rights based on dark, threatening images of theft, crime, and disease and the discourse of the commons based on sunny pastures and images of a healthy environment. The content owners equate file sharers with carjackers, a computer mouse with a weapon, downloading with shoplifting, and file sharing with the spread of disease or even terrorism. These destructive images no doubt serve as strong counterarguments to any positive images presented by technology developers and their supporters. The message communicated is that digital technology is destructive to cultural production and the very democratic ideals of our nation. As we have seen in the discourse of theft that is used to justify regulating technology, such scare tactics have a great impact on both the public perception and political action. It is much more difficult to establish something as safe or moral when it has already been posited as dangerous or unethical. In the discourse of the digital copyright debate, the extremist rhetoric of the content owners may require more direct counterattacks from their opposition. Establishing how regulating technology and restricting access to information is itself destructive to intellectual and creative production—a common value among participants in the debate—may help to counteract the vicious attacks from the property stewardship narrative on the destructive role of digital technology in cultural production. And this discourse may need to do more than create an anonymous villain who endangers technology "species," and instead identify who or what is responsible for a truncated future for cultural production on the Internet.

Finally, we should not forget that technology developers and copyright activists face the very serious challenge of having not only to present a compelling argument regarding the utility of digital technology for cultural production, but they also have to define and defend a cultural shift in values in cultural production. A particular articulation of a new discourse (like "the commons" in the digital copyright debate) is not alone liberating, but rather it is only through the cultural adoption of a new viewpoint of the "right" or "correct" form of copyright and cultural production that legal change can happen. The shift from a model based on natural rights of authors and property ownership to one based on community and sharing has proven difficult, particularly in the context of a debate involving high-profit business and large media companies.

Mike Markel notes the slowness of copyright law in adapting to new digital technologies. Citing Anne Wells Branscomb, he describes her use of the metaphor of copyright law as dinosaur, a common metaphor used in discourse about copyright and one that was alluded to in the EFF's Endangered Gizmos campaign. Branscomb writes,

> The law will lumber along like an unwieldy dinosaur wending its way to extinction if it cannot keep up with the pace of change in this new

> interactive, information-intense environment. But the law is by nature conservative, attempting to bring order only as fast as consensus can be reached among social groups willing to conform to norms they believe are fair and workable. (qtd. in Markel 198)

As Branscomb points out, new legal forms of copyright require the forward-looking adoption of new values in cultural production, which is difficult within the context of the conservative and slow-moving institution of the law. It is only when social groups have come to consensus about the role of digital technology in the future of cultural production that copyright law might respond with a new trajectory.

The ongoing balancing of power between copyright law and social perceptions and behaviors demonstrates the ways in which dominant and resistant power structures inform and influence one another in the digital copyright debate. While courts make laws, those laws carry meaning only so far as the public understands and obeys them. Copyright law may seem to denote clear distinctions between lawful and unlawful uses, but it is more often the case that the specific terms of copyright develop out of practice. As L. Ray Patterson and Stanley W. Lindberg note in their landmark text *The Nature of Copyright*,

> Most Americans think of law as consisting of written rules in the form of legislative statutes or court decisions. But law also grows out of what people actually do, that is, out of custom. Even the most comprehensive legal statute is skeletal in content, while court decisions tend to be fact-intensive (resolving disputes between litigants over specific, concrete issues). Between these two poles, therefore, there is an enormous amount of room for private action, and consistent private action can essentially "make" law by reshaping existing customs (or even creating new ones) that may subsequently be honored by the courts. (*Nature of Copyright* 9–10)

If Patterson and Lindberg are correct, then the ways in which the public perceives and acts on copyright law can largely determine what the law means. As we have seen through reports from Pew Internet & American Life Project, BigChampagne, and other empirical researchers of peer-to-peer usage, citizens continue to share files despite recent court rulings and lawsuits that posit such files sharing as unlawful. The RIAA wins settlements, but these legal actions do not seem to have a direct effect on actual usage patterns. And since the 2005 *Grokster* ruling, we have witnessed continued developments in new technologies that allow users to "work around" the law and find means for continuing to share files. As stated in an April 2006 *CNET News* report, for instance, college students are now employing programs such as Direct Connect (DC++), MyTunes, and OurTunes to share files on universities' local area networks (LANs) in an effort to avoid sending and receiving files on the public Internet (Terdiman). And since 2005, the Web site YouTube has gained popularity as a public space where users can upload, view, and share video files. Such social activities are evidence that while the law may attempt to restrict social behavior, individuals can use technology to find ways to work around even legal barriers. As Patterson and Lindberg suggest, laws alone won't change behavior on a large scale, nor will they stop the development of digital technology. Instead, it appears that change in the legal climate for cultural production may follow only from widespread adoption of a new set of cultural practices, beliefs, and discourses.

RHETORIC AND PRAXIS IN THE DIGITAL COPYRIGHT DEBATE

The day after of the Supreme Court decision in *MGM Studio v. Grokster* was announced, James Porter and Martine Rife published a paper on the implications of the case, in which they describe what they perceive as the direct impact of the ruling on the work of educators and writing teachers. Of import for writing instructors and researchers, they assert, is the concept of "intention" that gains strength in the case. They show concern for the responsibility placed on university instructors and administrators for closely monitoring their digital writing and teaching spaces. They write that the case sends the message that writing instructors can no longer "'turn a blind eye' to copyright infringement, even by others, if it is occurring in/across/through an electronic space that you are responsible for—that is, where you have set up an electronic 'intermediary space' (e.g., your class web site, your blog)." In addition, they note the emphasis on a "good faith" standard in copyright decision making: "you are not responsible for infringements by others if you are acting in good faith to promote respect for copyright and if the intermediary service or server you are sponsoring clearly is intended for 'substantial noninfringing purposes.'" While *MGM Studios v. Grokster* addresses a context that seems far removed from the academic world (one of Hollywood movies and popular music, entertainment industries and technology companies), the practical impact of the case on writing teachers and researchers should not be overlooked.

I am less concerned about direct impact of the *Grokster* case, however, than I am about the role of the ruling as one instance in a larger trend toward increasing regulation of digital technology through copyright law. This trend is moving toward increasingly restrictive copyright laws that control technology in an effort to "save" cultural production. Despite a history of balance between technology innovation and copyright protections, the law now regulates digital technologies that appear to threaten established business models and markets for copyrighted works as consumable goods. The indirect implication of the recent history of copyright law is the reification of a pre-digital mode of cultural production that is based on a binary relationship between producer and consumer of content. This trajectory is of great concern to rhetoric and writing scholars who recognize that cultural production—including writing—in the digital age often arises out of activities that run counter to this model of production, like transformative reuse and remixing of existing materials and user participation in the development of content online.

An underlying assumption in this book is that researchers studying rhetorical practices in online debates surrounding legal issues can help shape public debate and, ultimately, future legal decisions. This is perhaps a controversial point, that rhetoric researchers can influence public policy and law. As research in rhetoric and writing studies takes a more critical turn—seeking to critique in addition to describe rhetorical activities—the question of what we might *do* in light of critical perspectives on issues arises. If we identify particular practices, ideologies, and/or situations as problematic or destructive to something we value, how do we facilitate change? As our research reveals problematic practices and situations, we have a responsibility to explore how our research might contribute toward some sort of positive action.

Scholars studying the public and legal discourse of the digital copyright debate might challenge inherent cultural biases through critical rhetorical praxis. Praxis, or putting ideas into practice, occurs when individuals are able to reflect upon and exert agency within a particular context by bringing together theoretical insight and practical action. Patricia Sullivan and James Porter define the term: "[p]raxis, then, is a 'practical rhetoric,' focused on local writing activities (practice), informed by general principles (theory), and calling upon prudential reasoning" (*Opening Spaces* 26). Studies of the rhetoric of the digital copyright debate provide theoretical insight into deliberations about copyright law, but it is my hope that they will also facilitate action based on social actors' reflections on these insights. Viewing critically the discourse operating in the digital copyright debate can help participants to see how particular rhetorical frameworks have the potential to distort important issues and/or contribute to undesirable outcomes. It follows that the critics of the debate—legal experts, copyright activists, technologists, creators, and general Internet users—will likely desire a more compelling, responsible, and persuasive rhetoric of copyright to counteract both the damaging property talk and the failures of the cultural conservancy narrative.

Research in rhetoric reveals that the law is a site of institutionalized rhetorical processes. Analysis of the rhetoric of the digital copyright debate makes visible the discursive structures operating in the legal arena of copyright law and identifies spaces where change might be possible. Following I share a framework for change for rhetoricians and compositionists who seek copyright reform that, if adopted at multiple, localized points, could influence the ongoing debate about cultural production and have the potential to positively shape digital culture at large. This change is not change in the sense of a large-scale revolution of copyright law itself. Rather, this change happens in the form of mobilizing sites of resistance in the digital copyright debate.

So, what might praxis in the digital copyright debate look like within our discipline? I should state explicitly that I do not condone downloading copyrighted music files from peer-to-peer file-sharing networks as a substitute for purchasing licensed copies. In fact, such behaviors actually work against emerging new models for copyright in that file sharers remain in the role of consumers of content without becoming producers or participants in digital culture. Following are more practical, but more importantly reflective, recommendations for what we can do—what we should do—as rhetoric and writing scholars and teachers in light of the insights learned from analysis of the digital copyright debate.

Teaching Digital Creativity

In our teaching practices, writing instructors need to more openly acknowledge the range of "allowable" copying, reuse, and remixing of copyright works that is inherent in much digital composing. We can begin by looking to recent studies of composition processes to paint a more complete picture of composing activities in the digital age. As Porter and DeVoss argue, "remixing is key to digital writing." As many documents are digital creations that appropriate other digital works—photos, graphics, layouts, templates, coding, audio and video files, etc.—the ability to compose documents with multiple media, to publish this writing quickly, to distribute it to mass audiences, and to allow audiences to interact and become co-composers of new texts challenges many traditional notions and practices of the composition classroom. However, as plenary speaker at the 2004 Conference on College Composition and Communication, Lessig argues that our students are part of a "remix culture," that is, characterized by "creativity mixing with other creativity." Lessig asks the question "[w]ill writing be allowed?" and points to the many writing activities that many students encounter—which include remixing texts to express ideas—that are illegal without permission. As instructors, we can encourage this type of reuse and remixing through classroom assignments and discussions that allow students to maximize the potential for using new media for creative development (for more on Lessig and "remix culture," see "Who Owns Culture?").

One major obstacle to teaching digital creativity in the composition classroom is the notion of plagiarism adopted on most college campuses. Even if we ask students to engage in composing practices that require collaboration, interactions, and remixing, we need to remember that these practices may break the rules that students have learned about textual ownership, authorship, and plagiarism. As John Logie argues in "Cut and Paste:

Remixing Composition Pedagogy for Online Workspaces," "the policies addressing the use and circulation of texts by students will serve to intimidate and, ultimately, stifle" those practices that rely on reuse and remix (303). Plagiarism policies on many campuses serve to identify copying and remixing as a violation of academic code. Students (and instructors) may find it difficult to distinguish between allowable copying versus piracy and plagiarism, which they know to be disallowed. Logie cites Rebecca Moore Howard, who argues,

> The plagiarist is the thief who is not original, but derivative; who works not in solitude, but in the company of others' texts; and who pirates from these texts and represents the piracy as his or her own. For the representation of plagiarism, the most important property of authorship is that of morality. The property of morality is itself dependent on the belief that originality, proprietorship, and autonomy are "natural truths" about "real" authorship rather than cultural arbitraries. (qtd. in Logie 304–05)

Her characterization sounds similar to what I have described of the property ownership rhetoric in the public digital copyright debate. Assignments that challenge this rhetoric of theft can help students to distinguish between theft and remixing, recognizing the gray areas that exist between original composition, plagiarism, copying, and remixing.

In addition, to become responsible digital citizens, college students need to do more than to passively consume content online; they must also become active contributors to content. With the rise of social networks, digital production technologies, and widespread Internet usage in general, the production of online content has become decentralized and disintermediated. The lines between producer and consumer of content in digital spaces have blurred, and amateur creation and distribution are on the rise. Because the vast majority of our students are already participating online through blogs, discussion boards, Web sites and wikis, and social networking, we are presented with a unique opportunity to ask them to reflect on this shift from Internet *user,* or consumer of content, to Internet *participant*, inhabiting the dual role of consumer and contributor to content.

A New Rhetoric of Copyright

In addition to teaching digital production and participation in the writing classroom, it is important that we also ask our students and colleagues and other interested parties to understand the implications of the language of property and theft that pervades our cultural discourses on copyright. The entertainment industry has introduced the powerful and concise sound bite that copying a copyrighted work without permission from the copyright owner is equivalent to stealing another's property.

Based on this abstract moral principle—"do not steal"—the content companies have effectively obscured the many ways in which copying and reuse of materials is acceptable and desirable. Instead, they have created binaries, such as theft versus originality and free copying versus paying royalties, that neglect the range of activities that fall between these binaries, such as fair use. We can talk to students, faculty, and administrators on our campuses about how the law may not be so black and white, and challenge the assumption that royalties must be paid for any use of copyrighted material.

Further, if we want to overcome the discourse of theft and piracy, we need to find our own ways of talking and thinking about cultural production on the Internet. Conceiving of file sharing as theft and intellectual property as privately owned goods shapes more than our understanding of copyright law; it also shapes our understanding of what type of cultural production should be allowed. To begin, we might understand that many Internet users are also creative participants who inhabit the dual roles of consumer and producer of content online. We would do well to continue to conduct research that seeks to better demonstrate the range of activities based on copying, reusing, and repurposing digital content that are contributory and valuable within digital culture. We need to uncover through research that the rules for what can be copied, by whom, and with what attribution will vary depending on context and purpose. But it is only by approaching Internet users as creators, composers, authors, and, most importantly, active participants in a dynamic digital culture that we can better understand the need to move beyond considering seemingly universal rules of "do not copy" and "give credit" to a more complex understanding of the norms of cultural production in a digital age.

In addition, writing instructors and researchers should move to discuss issues not only in terms of the current rules for legal behaviors but also in terms of how rhetoric and discourse shape those rules. One way to enable this process is through the careful consideration of a new rhetoric of copyright for a digital age. As copyright law scholar Litman notes in her book *Digital Copyright*, "[i]f you're dissatisfied with the way the spoils are getting divided, one approach is to change the rhetoric" (79). As an example of the power of rhetoric in the copyright landscape, Litman, in a chapter called "Choosing Metaphors," illustrates how content industries have successfully repurposed language to significantly alter the intellectual property debate. She specifically maps the evolution of the word "piracy" as used by the content industry, showing its shift in meaning from an illegal profiteering activity based on counterfeit copying to, more broadly, any file-sharing activity regardless of legality. This rhetorical shift—toward one focused on accusing citizens of stealing, even plundering, private property—has effectively, and to our detriment, changed the way the public speaks about, and therefore perceives, the morality of file sharing.

Based on the analysis of existing rhetoric of the debate, I suggest a four-part framework for a new rhetoric of copyright that is democratic, user-based, action-oriented, and unified.

- *Democratic.* One successful rhetorical strategy of the digital copyright debate is identification of the democratic principles inherent in copyright law. Both the content owners and copyright activists agree that copyright law supports certain democratic values—such as advancement in the arts and sciences—but disagree on how best to achieve that goal. A new rhetoric of copyright would do well to root arguments in this common value, focusing on the productive processes online and the ways in which participation in creative activity has the potential to increase with the use of digital technologies. Rather than looking to copyright's recent history, participants in the debate might look farther back to the origins of copyright, which had the goal of encouraging socially beneficial, culturally significant intellectual and creative activity. This activity relies not on drawing boundaries between who is allowed to access works, who participates, and in what ways, but instead would allow users the freedom to innovatively shape digital culture from within.
- *User-based, not technology driven.* Much of the rhetoric of the digital copyright debate relies on technological determinism—the notion of technology as either inherently progressive or destructive. It is the users, however, that define how technology will be applied to conform to or resist certain models of cultural production. A new rhetoric of copyright could shift the focus from technologies as leading to progress or social ills. Rather, the heroes in a new rhetoric of digital copyright could be Internet users themselves, as participants in digital culture, as amateur creators, as contributors within a system of interactive and relational engagement that leads not only to economic rewards but to greater intellectual and creative insights.
- *Action-oriented.* In order for a new rhetoric to gain strength, it will need to be supported by ethical actions. Some commercial entities, such as Flickr and Facebook, have begun to recognize the economic value of free content and a participatory Internet and now harness Web 2.0 technologies to turn a profit (see Shuen's *Web 2.0: A Strategy Guide* for an in-depth discussion of how this business strategy works). Copyright activists must support their rhetoric with similar success stories, demonstrating how the debate is not about downloading information for free. Instead, a new rhetoric of copyright based on the notion of a participatory Internet must rely on visible sites of online participation, of individual users embracing their roles as contributors to digital culture and providing something of value to others.
- *Unified.* If change is only possible if enacted at "mobile and transitory points of resistance," a new rhetoric will need to come not only from

an exclusive group of trained legal experts and academics, but also through more public channels: in the classroom, at university forums, in online spaces. We need to form more unified arguments about what's at stake in the digital copyright debate, the very future of cultural production on the Internet. By making rhetorical appeals toward this common end, a new rhetoric of copyright might be able to show how expansions to copyright laws negatively affect different groups—teachers, researchers, archivists, technology developers, music fans, amateur moviemakers, composers of mash-ups, fan-fiction writers, and more. Much like James Boyle's suggestion of an "environmental movement" for intellectual property law, a new rhetoric of copyright needs to assert a common goal—saving digital culture—that will unite differentiated parties with seemingly competing interests.

LOOKING AHEAD: INTELLECTUAL PROPERTY STUDIES IN RHETORIC AND COMPOSITION

Interest in intellectual property issues among rhetoric and composition scholars now has an established history. One marker of continued interest is the ongoing success of the CCCC Intellectual Property Caucus, which has been convening since 1994. Scholarship in rhetoric and composition on intellectual property issues during the past 15 years or so has focused on several lines of inquiry, from examining the relationship between composing processes and the concept of authorship, to studying forms of digital authorship introduced with new technologies, to the more recent discussions about the implications of copyright law on teaching and writing practices. Looking forward, I argue that we might build on this existing research and offer a unique contribution to the study of intellectual property by shifting the focus of our research from the issue of distribution to that of participation online.

DeVoss and Porter, in an excellent article titled "Why Napster Matters to Writing: Filesharing as a New Ethic of Digital Delivery," make a convincing case for the relevance of the copyright debate to the study of writing and composition by asserting that the practice of file sharing pertains to the fundamental reasons for why people write and share their writing in the first place. They argue, "[f]rom a rhetorical perspective, Napster represents a crisis in *delivery*, the often-neglected rhetorical canon. Napster has fundamentally changed the national landscape regarding the digital distribution—and thus delivery—of documents" (179). Along the same lines, in his analysis of the peer-to-peer file-sharing debate in *Peers, Pirates, & Persuasion*, John Logie makes a similar claim. He says that

> Digital media offer opportunities to efficiently archive and access the bulk of artistic and intellectual work created since the dawn of

> humanity. *This is not an overstatement.* The potential intellectual and social utility of these now-hypothetical archives is staggering. Our challenge is to engage in a principled argument about how best to achieve this goal. (italics in original, 21)

Both of these works seek to establish what's at stake in the digital copyright debate. DeVoss and Porter and Logie make important contributions to intellectual property scholarship by showing how copyright laws may limit access to cultural works that are needed for scholarship, teaching, and writing. DeVoss and Porter note the importance of "delivery" for writers in a digital age, and Logie recognizes the value of "archiving" in cultural production. These discussions rightly point out that legal decisions that govern access to copyrighted material and the discourse of the digital copyright debate endanger the potential of the Internet to distribute content or deliver information.

While issues of delivery and distribution are of interest to writing scholars, the field is perhaps more closely connected with issues of production of content. As demonstrated in the preceding chapters, one consequence of the current rhetoric of the digital copyright debate is the reification of a binary between those who consume and those who produce content on the Internet. The arguments about distribution are important and have strong implications for what Internet users have access to online, but tend to cast Internet users as consumers of cultural goods. Given our field's focus on composing and production, rhetoric and composition scholars are uniquely situated to move the debate forward by more explicitly acknowledging the interrelated nature of consumption and production in a digital age.

Two persistent claims in the digital copyright debate currently provide the discursive foundation for public characterizations of cultural production. Both claims potentially obscure the debate, specifically in terms of what it means for how we produce and participate—or, how we write—within digital culture:

- *The Internet delivers content.* The rhetoric of the digital copyright debate, firmly rooted in the metaphor of property ownership, relies on the notion that the Internet is a storehouse or archive for access to copyrighted goods. This emphasis serves to reinforce a view of the Internet as a space for distribution of finished products. These characterizations sustain the notion that the Internet's most valuable use is to deliver content, and assert that the Internet may be lessened if artists and producers become too fearful or face too many obstacles to distributing their works online. By focusing on access to information by consumers, the digital copyright debate may not move beyond a reification of industry dynamics: a sharp divide remains between producer and consumer of content, as the Internet is positioned as a distribution technology that facilitates the exchange of producers' finished products.

- *Internet users are consumers of products.* This second claim that appears in the public discourse of the digital copyright debate supports the consumer-producer binary that is neither necessary nor inevitable online. If the Internet is to be used primarily as a distribution mechanism for cultural goods, then users become consumers of those goods. Lessig, in his new book, *Remix*, challenges this assumption by extolling the virtues of a "read-write" culture online, in which many users participate actively in contributing to its value, rather than a "read-only" culture, in which users act solely as consumers of content delivered by a few producers. While only occurring in limited spaces at present, this new mode of production positions Internet users as co-contributors in creating value. Within such models of community-based production, the value of the interaction is not so much the product itself but the mode of production: a participatory Internet in which more users move fluidly from the position of consumer to the position of contributor.

Rhetoric and composition scholars, experts in the activities of composing and producing texts, have much to offer in terms of problematizing these two claims. In addition to studying the digital copyright debate as a challenge to the future of the Internet as a site for distribution, we would also do well to reveal the implications of copyright law for the complete range of activities involved in cultural production: the social processes through which a culture circulates, consumes, *and* produces creative and intellectual works. Rhetoric and composition scholars, by uncovering the activities of participation online, can show how the digital copyright debate affects more than how copyright should regulate a marketplace for creative and intellectual goods. It also shapes the future of digital culture.

Appendix A

RESEARCHER AS ACTIVIST IN THE DIGITAL COPYRIGHT DEBATE

The goals for this book were twofold. First, I wanted to identify and characterize the current rhetoric operating in the high-profile digital copyright debate. But my purpose was not only descriptive. I also had as a goal the emancipation of the debate from the existing, limited rhetorical frameworks and, ultimately, challenging the cultural assumptions about how intellectual property should be regulated in a networked age. I attempt to achieve a balance between these two equally important roles, as researcher and as advocate in the copyright debate. This balance requires that, as a researcher, I situate the discussion in an ongoing conversation, employ systematic methods, and collect evidence on which to base claims and theoretical insight about the nature of the debate. It also requires that I offer recommendations based on key findings so that others might apply these theoretical insights to practice. I realized through my analysis that the rhetorical study of intellectual property cannot have one without the other: critical rhetorical praxis requires both theory and action, each being based on and influencing the other.

One difficulty in managing my two roles as researcher and advocate is the reputation that has developed around those engaged in copyright activism. Copyright activists are often called "copyfighters," attaining a status that is similar that which "hackers" suffered a decade ago. The term "copyfighter" is generally used to apply to those individuals who participate in efforts to influence reforms in intellectual property law. However, copyfighters are often also taken to be extremists, outlaws, perhaps doing good but through questionable means. A well-known blog called "Copyfight" defines the terminology, recognizing this tension: "[t]he copyfight is the battle to keep intellectual property tethered to its purpose, understanding that when intellectual property rights are pushed too far, they can end up doing exactly the opposite of what they're intended to do" ("What Does 'Copyfight' Mean?"). While I recognize the dangers of labeling copyright advocacy as a "fight" (it conjures up images of "war" that reinforce the inflated rhetoric of the entertainment industry), copyright scholars participate in an uphill battle when seeking policy change and legal reform. Though my stance may not be one of a "fighter," I would call scholars "participants" and "contributors" to ongoing contentious conversations with the end goal of renegotiation of the copyright bargain.

My own activities concerning copyright reform have included participation in the annual Intellectual Property Caucus at the Conference on College Composition and Communication, sharing my research at disciplinary and interdisciplinary conferences, working on a copyright information and education outreach program at a previous institution, and serving on an intellectual property committee at my current university. My role in these activities is to work to make the specialized, legal, and institutional discourse of copyright understandable, fair, and accessible to the community that relies on it. While there are various fronts on which these discussions can take place, in particular I participate as an expert in rhetoric and writing studies, with the hope of helping various participants in the debate better understand the implications of the language we use in the debate.

There has been, recently, a shift toward more action-oriented research, or at least research that explores rhetoric's role in civic engagement and public discourse. Researchers studying the rhetoric of intellectual property fall within this category of researchers who explore the role of rhetoric in a high-profile public and legal debate. However, our work may not seem directly action oriented. Our research will not likely result, in a direct way, in quick and responsive revisions to laws, nor will it enjoy such widespread exposure as other types of political discourse. The work of intellectual property researchers in rhetoric and writing studies, however, can effect change in more subtle ways through the process of revealing ideologies. Through analyses of discursive processes to reveal structures of power, knowledge, and control, this work can contribute to a heightened awareness that can lead slowly to shifts in thinking. An activist research stance in copyright scholarship requires adoption of new rhetoric and new understandings of how intellectual property should be regulated in a digital age.

Appendix B

COPYRIGHT LEGISLATION AND COURT CASES

This appendix contains information on selected copyright legislation and case law regulating the use and development of digital communication technologies current at the time of this writing. The following table includes the title of each act or case, the date on which it occurred, and the details relevant to this study. Note that the information presented is intended to show a progression of increasingly regulatory legal restrictions over intellectual property particular to the development of new technologies. It is not intended to be comprehensive.

Table B.1 Brief History of Legislation and Court Cases Affecting Digital Copyright

Legislative Action or Court Case	Date	Relevant Details
Sony Corp. of America v. Universal City Studios, Inc.	1984	• Also known as the "Sony-Betamax case." • Ruled that the making of individual copies of television programs for the purposes of "time-shifting" is a fair use. • Also ruled that the manufacturers of video-recording devices could not be held liable for contributing to users' infringing uses if the product is "capable of substantial non-infringing uses."
Digital Millennium Copyright Act (DMCA)	1998	• Prohibits acts of circumventing a technological protection measure used by content owners to prevent access to works (e.g., encrypting DVDs). • Prohibits the manufacture, sale, or distribution of tools and technologies that make circumvention possible. • Includes a number of exceptions, but these exceptions have been criticized for being too narrow or for limiting users' fair use rights.

(*Continued*)

Table B.1 Continued

Legislative Action or Court Case	Date	Relevant Details
Copyright Term Extension Act (CTEA)	1998	• Extended the duration of copyright protection 20 years, from life of the author + 50 years to life of the author + 70 years, or 95 years for corporate authorship.
A&M Records, Inc. v. Napster, Inc.	2001	• Ruled that Napster, the provider of peer-to-peer file- sharing software, could be held liable for contributory infringement and vicarious liability. • Argued that because Napster had the capability to monitor and control users' infringing behaviors, they had a responsibility to do so. • Made a distinction between "space-shifting" and the *Sony* standard of "time-shifting," arguing that the shift to digital format was not a personal use but a distribution of the file. • The original Napster service has been shut down, but has been relaunched in a new form, as a pay service.
Re: Aimster Copyright Litigation	2003	• Ruled that it was not enough for Aimster's file- sharing service be capable of noninfringing uses, but that it must be able to *demonstrate* substantial noninfringing uses. • Aimster's technology design prevented them from awareness of whether the uses of their services were infringing or noninfringing. The Court argued that such "willful blindness is knowledge" and ruled that Aimster committed contributory infringement.
Eldred v. Ashcroft	2003	• Challenged the Copyright Term Extension Act (CTEA). • Brought by Eric Eldred, a noncommercial Internet publisher of public domain texts that were retroactively assigned copyright protection by CTEA. • Lawrence Lessig, representing Eldred, argued that the CTEA was unconstitutional because it violated the "limited times" provision in the copyright clause. • Ruled that the CTEA did not violate the "limited times" clause because the extension was limited and not perpetual.

(*Continued*)

Table B.1 Continued

Legislative Action or Court Case	Date	Relevant Details
RIAA/MPAA lawsuits against individuals	2003-present	• Lawsuits against individual file sharers who download and distribute copyrighted materials. • Targets include college campuses.
Inducing Infringements of Copyrights Act (Induce Act)	2004	• Proposed in the U.S. Senate to amend the Copyright Act (Title 17, Chapter 5). • Would extend the definition of copyright infringement by introducing the concept of "intentional inducement." • "Intentional inducement" is defined as intentionally aiding, abetting, inducing, or procuring an infringement of copyright "by acts from which a reasonable person would find intent to induce infringement."
MGM Studios, Inc. v. Grokster, Ltd.	2005	• Ruled that Grokster and StreamCast Networks, file sharing companies, could be held liable for contributing to the infringing activities of their users. • Grokster and StreamCast were found to be inducing infringement based on their marketing strategies and the fact that they did not employ available technological means for monitoring and preventing infringing uses.
Higher Education Opportunity Act	2008	• Reauthorized the Higher Education Act for the first time since 1998. • Governs federal student aid, grants to institutions of higher education and other economic programs. • Stipulates that universities develop plans to "effectively combat" the unauthorized distribution of copyrighted material and suggests that institutions use technology-based deterrents to monitor bandwidth users' activities and offer "alternatives" to unauthorized file sharing.

Notes

1. While the decision in *Grokster* was technically unanimous, the justices' perspectives on the issue were more diverse than the 9–0 vote would suggest. The justices split themselves equally in number across a majority opinion and two concurring opinions, each signed by three justices. I discuss the justices' points of agreement and dissent in more detail in Chapter 6.
2. John Logie challenges this distinction between the classical author and the modern author through an analysis of the concept of authorship in the work of Quintilian ("I Have No Predecessor"). While Quintilian has traditionally been positioned as a "vehicle," as imitative of his predecessors, or as a compiler and synthesizer of works by others more than a contributor himself, Logie shows how Quintilian makes subtle authorial claims, such as asserting that he will tread on new ground and authorizing his own editions. Karen Burke LeFevre also asserts consistencies in conceptions of authorship in ancient and modern times. Arguing against this "great divide" in concepts of authorship, LeFevre's critique of understandings of invention shows the continuities between Plato's views and modern conceptions as, ultimately, solitary activities.
3. Further, both Lange and Litman argue it is the public domain that allows this concept to persist, as it works to establish the balance between protecting authors' rights and the public interest. Although I have not read more recent works by Lange, it is safe to say that Litman does not think the public domain has been able to successfully achieve this desired balance in light of more recent developments in digital copyright (for more recent discussion of the public domain by Litman, see *Digital Copyright*).
4. In 2001, the entertainment industry enjoyed initial success, winning its high-profile battle against the leading first-generation file-sharing system at the time in *A&M Records v. Napster*. In 2003, the Seventh Circuit confirmed a lower court ruling that helped shut down the Aimster peer-to-peer network in *Re Aimster Copyright Litigation*. When the Ninth Circuit ruled in favor of Grokster in *MGM Studios v. Grokster* in 2003, the circuits split in their treatment of file-sharing technology, and the issue became situated for Supreme Court review. For more information on the inconsistencies of these three important court opinions, see Fred von Lohmann's "IAAL: What Peer-to-Peer Developers Need to Know about Copyright Law."
5. Cognitive linguists William Labov and Joshua Waletsky, in their study of first-person oral narratives, also make this distinction, asserting that linguistic forms employed in narratives create a sense of separation between the initial scene or steady state and the subsequent conflict or troubling moment.
6. Examples of legal cases that address issues of copyright in online works based on the metaphor of physical property are many: in deciding whether

a company was entitled to adopt its competitor's registered trademark in a site's metatags, the court in *Brookfield v. West Coast* compared the metatag to a billboard that deceptively advertised the competitor's store as its own; in *Fonovisa, Inc. v. Cherry Auction*, the court considered infringing music files online as comparable to the exchange of infringing copies of records sold at swap meets; and in *A&M Records v. Napster*, in deciding the legality of Napster the court ruled that making copies of files and distributing them online was to be considered "space-shifting," a more serious offense than the "time-shifting" that occurred in the taping which occurred in the use of Betamax players in *Sony v. Universal Studios*.

7. Former MPAA President Jack Valenti's rhetoric is now infamous among those who follow copyright debates. Beginning with the perceived threat of an early technology, the VCR, to the movie industry, Valenti employed hyberbolic rhetoric to describe the threats posed by new technologies. In 1982, Valenti proclaimed that the VCR "is to the American film producer and the American public as the Boston Strangler is to the woman home alone" (Castonguay). More recently, in 2002, he declared war on peer-to-peer file-sharing technologies: "[w]e're fighting our own terrorist war," he reported to the *New York Times* (Harmon). For more on Jack Valenti's rhetoric in the peer-to-peer file-sharing debate, see John Logie's "A Copyright Cold War?" and Chapter 4 of Tarleton Gillespie's *Wired Shut*.
8. Having said that, it is not difficult to see that the efforts of the two consumer awareness Web sites cited in this chapter, MusicUnited.org and Respect-Copyrights.org, fail miserably on many counts at making connections with their target audience, presumably teenagers and young adults. For instance, the MusicUnited.org Web site uses outdated slang terms like "It's a Drag!" in a prominent location, showing that the contributors to the site are not connected with the language of their target audience. The error of using slang incorrectly is no doubt one of the quickest ways to appear "uncool" to young consumers.
9. This point is not new or particular to the digital age; it was made clear as early as 1813 in a passage from Thomas Jefferson's frequently cited letter written to Isaac McPherson:

   > If nature has made any one thing less susceptible than all others of exclusive property, it is the action of the thinking power called an idea, which an individual may exclusively possess as long as he keeps it to himself; but the moment it is divulged, it forces itself into the possession of everyone, and the receiver cannot dispossess himself of it.

   While Jefferson is talking here about patents, the sentiment can be applied readily to copyrightable works as well.
10. Models for managing productivity based on the commons are certainly not absent from our culture. David Bollier, cofounder of the organization Public Knowledge, asks us to consider the many working examples of the commons that operate successfully—including community gardens, blood donation, and software development (see *Silent Theft*).
11. The movies were selected, out of twelve submissions, as the winners of a contest held in fall 2003. A panel of independent judges chose winners based on three criteria: Communication of Creative Commons' Mission (40%), Creativity (30%), and Technical Merit (30%). Three winners were awarded a selection among technological tools such as a PowerMac G5 computer or an Apple iPod.
12. For a detailed breakdown of the different interpretations of the *Sony* rule in *MGM Studios v. Grokster*, see "The Grokster Scorecard" by Jonathan Band.

13. This same material appeared on the original version of the RIAA's Music United Web site, which was intended for a general population of peer-to-peer file sharers, in 2005. The Web site has since been updated and much of its content altered; however, the creators of the revised version of the site must have deemed this quote powerful enough to use it again for this more targeted audience of college students.

Bibliography

2007 Copyright and Security Guide for Schools and Universities. 2007. International Federation of the Phonographic Industry (IFPI). 13 July 2009. <http://www.pro-music.org/Content/GuidesAndResources/advice_for_universities.php>.

A&M Records, Inc. v. Napster. No. 00-16401 and 00-16403. 9th Cir. US Ct. of Appeals. 12 Feb. 2001.

"Advice for Schools and Universities." 2009. Pro-Music. 13 July 2009. <http://www.pro-music.org/Content/GuidesAndResources/advice_for_universities.php>.

"Agreement on Guidelines for Classroom Copying in Not-for-Profit Educational Institutions with Respect to Books and Periodicals." House Rep. 94-1476. 19 March 1976.

Amsterdam, Anthony G., and Jerome Bruner. *Minding the Law.* Cambridge: Harvard UP, 2000.

"Anti-piracy." 2005. Recording Industry Association of America. 7 Aug. 2005. <http://www.riaa.com/issues/piracy/default.asp>.

Architectural Works Protection Act. Pub. L. 101-650. 1 Dec. 1990.

Aughton, Simon."P2P Activity Doubles in Two Years." *PC Pro.* Oct. 2005. 9 Apr. 2006. <http://www.pcpro.co.uk/news/78525/p2p-activity-doubles-in-two-years.html>.

Baake, Ken. *Metaphor and Knowledge: The Challenges of Writing Science.* Albany: SUNY Press, 2003.

Band, Jonathan. "The *Grokster* Scorecard." 2005. Electronic Frontier Foundation. 9 Apr. 2006. <http://www.eff.org/IP/P2P/MGM_v_Grokster/summary.pdf>.

Barlow, John Perry. "The Economy of Ideas: A Framework for Rethinking Patents and Copyrights in the Digital Age." *Wired* 2.03 (1994). 9 Apr. 2006. <http://www.wired.com/wired/archive/2.03/economy.ideas.html>.

———. 2000. "The Next Economy of Ideas: Will Copyright Survive the Napster Bomb? Nope, but Creativity Will." *Wired* 8.10 (2000). 9 Apr. 2006. <http://www.wired.com/wired/archive/8.10/download_pr.html>.

Barthes, Roland. "The Death of the Author." *Image—Music—Text.* New York: Hill & Wang, 1977. 142–48.

Biesecker, Barbara. "Michel Foucault and the Question of Rhetoric." *Philosophy and Rhetoric* 25 (1992): 351–64.

Bizzell, Patricia, and Bruce Herzberg. *The Rhetorical Tradition: Readings from Classical Times to the Present.* New York: St. Martin's Press, 1990.

Bleistein v. Donaldson Lithographing Co. No. 117. Supreme Ct. of the US. 2 Feb. 1903.

Bollier, David. *Silent Theft: The Private Plunder of Our Common Wealth.* New York: Routledge, 2002.

Bolter, Jay David. *Writing Space: Computers, Hypertext, and the Remediation of Print*. 2nd ed. Mahwah, NJ: Lawrence Erlbaum, 2001.

Borchardt, Mickey. "Sinking a Music Pirate." *Los Angeles Times*, 3 Apr. 2006. 13 July 2009. <http://articles.latimes.com/2006/apr/03/opinion/oe-borchardt3>.

Boyle, James. "Deconstructing Stupidity." *Financial Times*, 21 Apr. 2005. 9 Apr. 2006. <http://news.ft.com/cms/s/39b697dc-b25e-11d9-bcc6-00000e2511c8.html>.

———. "Foucault in Cyberspace: Surveillance, Sovereignty, and Hard-Wired Censors." 23 Mar. 1998. Working paper. Social Science Research Network. 13 July 2009. <http://papers.ssrn.com/sol3/papers.cfm?abstract_id=11468>.

———. "The Second Enclosure Movement and the Construction of the Public Domain." *Law and Contemporary Problems* 66 (Winter/Spring 2003): 33–74. Apr. 2006. <http://www.law.duke.edu/journals/lcp/articles/lcp66dWinter-Spring2003p33.htm>.

———. *Shamans, Software, Spleens: Law and the Construction of the Information Society*. Cambridge: Harvard University Press, 1996.

Briefing Book on Campus Digital Piracy. 2007. Motion Picture Association of America. 13 July 2009. <http://www.mpaa.org/BestPracticesBriefingBook.pdf>.

Britt, Elizabeth C. *Conceiving Normalcy: Rhetoric, Law, and the Double Binds of Infertility*. Tuscaloosa: University of Alabama Press, 2001.

Brookfield v. West Coast. No. 98-56918. 9th Cir. US Ct. of Appeals. 10 Mar. 1999.

Buranen, Lise, and Alice M. Roy, Eds. *Perspectives on Plagiarism and Intellectual Property in a Postmodern World*. New York: SUNY Press, 1999.

Burke, Sean. *Authorship: From Plato to the Postmodern*. 1995. Edinburgh: Edinburgh University Press, 2000.

Campus Downloading. Recording Industry Association of America. 13 July 2009. <http://campusdownloading.psu.edu/>.

Campus Downloading DVD. Recording Industry Association of America. 20 Oct. 2009. <http://www.campusdownloading.com/dvd.htm>.

Campus Downloading: Protect Yourself. Do It Legally. Recording Industry Association of America. 20 Oct. 2009. <http://campusdownloading.com/pdf/campusdownloading_booklet.pdf>.

Castonguay, Sylvie. "50 Years of the Video Cassette Recorder." *WIPO Magazine* Nov. 2006. 13 July 2009. <http://www.wipo.int/wipo_magazine/en/2006/06/article_0003.html>.

Cohen, Julie E."Copyright, Commodification, and Culture: Locating the Public Domain." *The Future of the Public Domain*. Eds. L. Guibault and P. B. Hugenholtz. Kluher Law International, 2006. 121–66.

Cohen, Julie E., Lydia Pallas Loren, Ruth Gana Okediji, and Maureen A. O'Rourke. *Copyright in a Global Information Economy*. New York: Aspen Law & Business, 2002.

Cohn, Emily. "RIAA Targets College Students." *The Cornell Daily Sun* 28 Feb. 2008. 13 July 2009. <http://cornellsun.com/node/28168>.

Cone, Justin. *Building on the Past*. 2003. Creative Commons Moving Images Contest. 10 May 2006. <http://mirrors.creativecommons.org/movingimages/Building_on_the_Past.mpg>.

Consumer Federation of America, Consumers Union, Free Press, and Public Knowledge Amicus Br. *MGM Studios, Inc. v. Grokster, Ltd.*, 545 U.S., 125 S. Ct. 2764 (2005).

Copyright Act of 1976. Pub. L. 94-553. 19 Oct. 1976. 27 Oct. 1998.

Copyright, Plagiarism, and Intellectual Property. Spec. issue of *Kairos: A Journal for Teachers of Writing in Webbed Environments* 3.1 (1998).

Copyright Term Extension Act of 1998. Pub. L. 105-298.

DeVoss, Danielle, and James Porter. "Why Napster Matters to Writing: Filesharing as a New Ethic of Digital Delivery." *Computers and Composition* 23.2 (2006): 178–210.

Digital Millennium Copyright Act. Pub. L. No. 105-304. 28 Oct. 1998. 112 Stat. 2860.

Donaldson v. Becket. 98 Eng. Rep. 257. 1774.

"Donny the Downloader." 2009. The American Society of Composers, Authors and Publishers. 13 July 2009. <http://www.ascap.com/resource/dtd/>.

Eisenstein, Elizabeth L. *The Printing Press as an Agent of Change.* 2 vols. Cambridge: Cambridge University Press, 1979.

Eldred v. Ashcroft. No. 01-618. Supreme Ct. of the U.S. 15 January 2003.

"Endangered Gizmos." 2005. Electronic Frontier Foundation. 1 Mar. 2006. <http://www.eff.org/endangered/>.

Eubanks, Philip. *A War of Words in the Discourse of Trade: The Rhetorical Constitution of Metaphor.* Carbondale: Southern Illinois University Press, 2000.

Feist Publications v. Rural Telephone Service. No. 89-1909. Supreme Ct. of the US. 27 Mar. 1991.

Fish, Stanley. "The Law Wishes to Have a Formal Existence." *The Fate of Law.* Eds. Austin Sarat and Thomas R. Kearns. Ann Arbor: University of Michigan Press, 1991.

———. "Rhetoric." *Critical Terms for Literary Study.* Eds. Frank Lentricchia and Thomas McLaughlin. Chicago: University of Chicago Press, 1990.

Fonovisa, Inc. v. Cherry Auction. No. 94-15717. 9th Cir. U.S. Ct. of Appeals. 25 Jan. 1996.

Foucault, Michel. *The Archaeology of Knowledge.* New York: Barnes and Noble, 1972.

———. *The History of Sexuality: An Introduction. Vol. 1.* New York: Vintage, 1990. NY: Random House, 1978.

———. *The Order of Things: An Archaeology of the Human Sciences.* London: Tavistock, 1970.

———. "Two Lectures." *Power/Knowledge: Selected Interviews and Other Writings, 1972–1977.* Ed. Colin Gordon. Brighton, England: Harvester Press, 1980. 78–108.

———. "Space, Knowledge, Power." *The Foucault Reader.* Ed. Paul Rabinow. Pantheon, 1984. 239–56.

———. "What Is an Author?" *Textual Strategies: Perspectives in Post-Structuralist Criticism.* Ed. Josue V. Harari. Ithaca, NY: Cornell UP, 1979. 141–60.

Fraser, Nancy. *Unruly Practices: Power, Discourse, and Gender in Contemporary Social Theory.* Minneapolis: University of Minnesota Press, 1989.

Gillespie, Tarleton. "Characterizing Copyright in the Classroom: The Cultural Work of Anti-Piracy Campaigns." *Communication, Culture, & Critique* 2.3 (2009): pre-press ms.

———. *Wired Shut: Copyright and the Shape of Digital Culture.* Cambridge: MIT Press, 2007.

Gilligan, Carol. *In a Different Voice: Psychological Theory and Women's Development.* Cambridge: Harvard University Press, 1982.

Ginsburg, Jane C. "The Concept of Authorship in Comparative Copyright Law." 10 Jan. 2003. Columbia Law School Pub. Law Research Paper No. 03-51. 12 July 2009. <http://papers.ssrn.com/sol3/papers.cfm?abstract_id=368481>.

———. "A Tale of Two Copyrights: Literary Property in Revolutionary France and America." *Tulane Law Review* 64.5 (May 1990): 991–1031.

Goldstein, Paul. *Copyright's Highway: From Gutenberg to the Celestial Jukebox.* New York: Farrar, Straus, & Giroux, 1995.

Green, Kenneth C. "The Movie Industry's 200% Error." *Inside Higher Ed* 29. Jan. 2008. 13 July 2009. <http://www.insidehighered.com/views/2008/01/29/green>.

Grokster and StreamCast Br. MGM Studios, Inc. v. Grokster, Ltd., 545 U.S., 125 S. Ct. 2764 (2005).

Grokster homepage. 2005. 20 Mar. 2006. <http://grokster.com/>.

Guess, Andy. "The Costs of Policing Campus Networks." *Inside Higher Ed*. 20 Oct. 2008. 13 July 2009. <http://www.insidehighered.com/news/2008/10/20/p2p>.

Gurak, Laura J. *Persuasion and Privacy in Cyberspace: The Online Protests over Lotus Marketplace and the Clipper Chip*. New Haven, NJ: Yale University Press, 1997.

Gurak, Laura J., and Johndan, Johnson-Eilola, Eds. *Intellectual Property*. Spec. issue of *Computers and Composition* 15.2 (1998).

Halbert, Debora J. *Intellectual Property in the Information Age: The Politics of Expanding Ownership Rights*. Westport, CT: Quorum, 1999.

Hardin, Garrett. "The Tragedy of the Commons." *Science* 1968. 15 Aug. 2005. <http://www.sciencemag.org/cgi/content/full/162/3859/1243>.

Harmon, Amy. "Black Hawk Download: Pirated Videos Thrive Online." *New York Times*, 17 Jan. 2002. 10 June 2005. <http://www.nytimes.com/2002/01/17/technology/circuits/17VIDE.html>.

Hartsock, Nancy. "Foucault on Power: A Theory for Women?" *Feminism/Postmodernism*. Ed. Linda Nicholson. New York: Routledge, 1990.

Havelock, Eric A. *The Muse Learns to Write: Reflections on Orality and Literacy from Antiquity to the Present*. New Haven, CT: Yale University Press, 1986.

Heidegger, Martin. "The Question Concerning Technology."*The Question Concerning Technology, and Other Essays*. Trans. William Lovitt. Harper & Row, 1977. 3–35.

Heines, Marjorie, and Tricia Beckles. "Will Fair Use Survive? Free Expression in the Age of Copyright Control." Dec. 2005. Free Expression Policy Project. Brennan Center for Justice at NYU School of Law. 13 July 2009. <http://www.fepproject.org/policyreports/fairuseflyer.html>.

Hekman, Susan J., Ed. *Feminist Interpretations of Michel Foucault*. Penn State University Press, 1996.

Herrington, TyAnna. *Controlling Voices: Intellectual Property, Humanistic Studies, and the Internet*. Carbondale: Southern Illinois University Press, 2001.

Higher Education Opportunity Act. HEOA, Pub. L. 110–215. 2008.

Howard, Rebecca Moore. *Standing in the Shadow of Giants: Plagiarists, Authors, Collaborators*. Stamford, CT: Ablex, 1999.

Hunter, Dan. "Cyberspace as Place and the Tragedy of the Digital Anticommons." *California Law Review* 91 (2003): 439–520.

"Information for Parents of College Students." 2009. Campus Downloading. Recording Industry Association of America. 13 July 2009. <http://campusdownloading.psu.edu/info.htm>.

Jefferson, Thomas. *The Writings of Thomas Jefferson*. Eds. Andrew A. Lipscomb and Albert Ellery Bergh. 20 vols. Washington, DC: Thomas Jefferson Memorial Association, 1905.

Joint Committee of the Higher Education and Entertainment Communities Technology Task Force home page. Educause. 13 July 2009. <http://www.educause.edu/EDUCAUSE+Major+Initiatives/PeertoPeer/JointCommitteeoftheHigherEduca/1204>.

Kaufer, David S., and Kathleen Carley. "Some Concepts and Axioms About Communication: Proximate and at a Distance." *Written Communication* 11.1 (1994): 8–42.

Knopper, Steve. "RIAA Will Keep On Suing." *Rolling Stone*, 9 June 2005. 13 July 2009. <http://www.rollingstone.com/news/story/7380412/riaa_will_keep_on_suing>.

Koman, Richard. "Remixing Culture: An Interview with Lawrence Lessig." 24 Feb. 2005. O'Reilly Policy Development Center. 10 Apr. 2006. <http://www.oreillynet.com/pub/a/policy/2005/02/24/lessig.html>.

Krim, Jonathan. "File Sharing Firms Can Be Held Liable: Ruling Aids Entertainment Industry." *Washington Post*, 28 Jan. 2005: A1.

Labov, William, and Joshua Waletsky. "Narrative Analysis: Oral Versions of Personal Experience." *Essays on the Verbal and Visual Arts*. Ed. J. Helm. Seattle, WA: University of Washington Press, 1967. 12–44.

Lakoff, George, and Mark Johnson. *Metaphors We Live By*. 2nd ed. Chicago: University of Chicago Press, 2003.

Landow, George P. *Hypertext: The Convergence of Contemporary Critical Theory and Technology*. Baltimore: Johns Hopkins University Press, 1992.

Lange, David. "Recognizing the Public Domain." *Law and Contemporary Problems* 44.4 (1982): 147–78.

Lay, Mary M. "Midwifery on Trial: Balancing Privacy Rights and Health Concerns after 'Roe v. Wade.' " *Quarterly Journal of Speech* 89.1 (Feb. 2003): 60–77.

———. *The Rhetoric of Midwifery: Gender, Knowledge, and Power*. New Brunswick, NJ: Rutgers University Press, 2000.

LeFevre, Karen Burke. *Invention as a Social Act*. Carbondale: Southern Illinois University Press, 1987.

Lemley, Mark. "Place and Cyberspace." *California Law Review* 91 (2003): 521–43.

Lessig, Lawrence. "The Architecture of Innovation." *Duke Law Journal* 51 (2002): 1783–1802.

———. *Free Culture: How Big Media Uses Technology and the Law to Lock Down Culture and Control Creativity*. New York: Penguin, 2004.

———. *The Future of Ideas: The Fate of the Commons in a Connected World*. New York: Vintage, 2002.

———. "Prosecuting Online File Sharing Turns a Generation Criminal." *U.S. News & World Report*. 22 Dec. 2008. 13 July 2009. <http://www.usnews.com/articles/opinion/2008/12/22/prosecuting-online-file-sharing-turns-a-generation-criminal.html>.

———. *Remix: Making Art and Commerce Thrive in the Hybrid Economy*. New York: Penguin Press, 2008.

———. "Who Owns Culture?" 7 Apr. 2005. Introduction to lecture with Jeff Tweedy. New York University Library. 11 May 2006. <http://www.videobomb.com/posts/show/2121>.

Licklider, Joseph C., and Robert W. Taylor. "The Computer as a Communication Device." *Science and Technology* (Apr. 1968): 12–31.

Litman, Jessica. *Digital Copyright*. Amherst: Prometheus, 2001.

———. "The Public Domain." *Emory Law Journal* 39.4 (Fall 1990): 965–1023.

Locke, John. *Second Treatise of Government*.1690. 10 Apr. 2006. <http://www.constitution.org/jl/2ndtreat.htm>.

Logie, John. "A Copyright Cold War? The Polarized Rhetoric of the Peer-to-Peer Debates." *First Monday* 8.7 (2003). 9 Apr. 2006. <http://www.firstmonday.org/issues/issue8_7/logie/>.

———. "Cut and Paste: Remixing Composition Pedagogy for Online Workspaces." *Internet-Based Workplace Communications: Industry and Academic Applications*. Hershey, PA: Idea Group Inc., 2005. 299–316.

———. " 'I Have No Predecessor to Guide My Steps': Quintilian and the Roman Construction of Authorship." *Rhetoric Review* 22.4 (2003): 353–73.

———. *Peers, Pirates, & Persuasion: Rhetoric in the Peer-to-Peer Debates.* West Lafayette, IN: Parlor Press, 2006.
Lunsford, Andrea. "Rhetoric, Feminism, and the Politics of Textual Ownership." *College English* 61.5 (1999): 529–44.
Lunsford, Andrea A., and Lisa Ede. *Singular Texts/ Plural Authors: Perspectives on Collaborative Writing.* Carbondale: Southern Illinois University Press, 1990.
Lunsford, Andrea, and Susan West. "Intellectual Property and Composition Studies." *College Composition and Communication* 47.3 (1996): 383–411.
Lyotard, Jean-François. *The Postmodern Explained: Correspondence 1982–1985.* Trans. Don Barry, Bernadette Maher, Julian Pefanis, Virginia Spate, and Morgan Thomas. Eds. Julie Pefanis and Morgan Thomas. Minneapolis: University of Minnesota Press, 1992.
Madden, Mary, and Amanda Lenhart. "Music Downloading, File-sharing, and Copyright." July 2003. Pew Internet Project Data Memo. Pew Internet & American Life Project. 13 July 2009. <http://www.pewinternet.org/~/media/Files/Reports/2003/PIP_Copyright_Memo.pdf.pdf>.
Markel, Mike. *Ethics in Technical Communication: A Critique and Synthesis.* ATTW Contemporary Series in Technical Communication, Vol. 14. Westport, CT: Ablex, 2001.
McBride, Sarah, and Ethan Smith. "Music Industry to Abandon Mass Suits." *Wall Street Journal,* 19 Dec. 2008: B1.
McCloskey, Paul. "Congress Warns University Presidents on P2P File Sharing." *Campus Technology.* 15 May 2007. 13 July 2009. <http://campustechnology.com/articles/2007/05/congress-warns-university-presidents-on-p2p-file-sharing.aspx>.
McLaurin, Stewart. Letter to university president. 24 October 2007. 13 July 2009. <http://blog.washingtonpost.com/securityfix/MPAA%20Letter1.pdf>.
MGM Studios, Inc. v. Grokster, Ltd. No. 04-480. Supreme Ct. of the U.S. 27 June 2005.
MGM v. American Honda Motor Company. No. 94-8732. Central Dist. of California. 29 Mar. 1995.
Milar v. Taylor. 98 Eng. Rep. 201. 1769.
"Mission Statement." Public Knowledge. 10 Apr. 2006. <http://www.publicknowledge.org/about/what/mission>.
Motion Picture Studio and Recording Company Br. *MGM Studios, Inc. v. Grokster, Ltd.*, 545 U.S., 125 S. Ct. 2764 (2005).
Motion Picture Studio and Recording Company's Reply Br. *MGM Studios, Inc. v. Grokster, Ltd.*, 545 U.S., 125 S. Ct. 2764 (2005).
MusicUnited.org. 2009. Recording Industry Association of America. 7 Aug. 2005. <http://www.musicunited.org/>.
Netanel, Neil. "Copyright and a Democratic Civil Society." *Yale Law Journal* 106 (1996): 292–386.
No Electronic Theft Act. Pub. L. No. 105-147. 16 Dec. 1997.
No Electronic Theft (NET) Act (Introduced in House). 25 July 1997. H.R. Rep. 105-339, 105th Congress, 1st Sess. 13 July 2009. <http://thomas.loc.gov/cgi-bin/query/D?c105:1:./temp/~c1056vphqG::>.
Ong, Walter. *Orality and Literacy: The Technologizing of the Word.* 2nd ed. New York: Methuen, 1988.
"Our Mission." P2P United. 20 June 2005. <http://www.p2punited.org/mission.php>.
Patterson, L. Ray, and Stanley W. Lindberg. *Copyright in Historical Perspective.* Nashville, TN: Vanderbilt University Press, 1968.
———. *The Nature of Copyright: A Law of Users' Rights.* Athens, GA: University of Georgia Press, 1991.

Pew Internet & American Life Project. "Music Downloading, File Sharing, and Copyright: A Pew Internet Project Data Memo." 1 Jan. 2003. 10 Apr. 2006. <http://www.pewinternet.org/PPF/r/96/report_display.asp>.

Piracy—It's a Crime. Motion Picture Association of America. RespectCopyrights.org. 7 Aug. 2005. <http://www.respectcopyrights.org>.

"Piracy of Intellectual Property." Statement of Marybeth Peters. The Register of Copyrights before the Subcommittee on Intellectual Property, Committee on the Judiciary. 25 May 2005. U.S. Senate, 109th Congress, 1st Sess. 13 July 2009. <http://www.copyright.gov/docs/regstat052505.html>.

Porter, James E., and Danielle Nicole DeVoss. "Rethinking Plagiarism in the Digital Age: Remixing as a Means for Economic Development?" Paper presented at WIDE Research Center 2006 Conference. 24 Apr. 2006. <http://www.wide.msu.edu/conference/wdk_plagiarism_FINAL.doc>.

Porter, James E., and Martine Courant Rife. "*MGM v. Grokster*: Implications for Educators and Writing Teachers." 28 June 2005. Wide Research Center. Michigan State University. 10 Apr. 2006. <http://www.wide.msu.edu/widepapers/grokster/>.

"Press Information." Grokster. 10 June 2005. <http://www.grokster.com/press.html>.

Press Release. 29 June 2005. Motion Picture Association of America. 7 Aug. 2005. <www.mpaa.org/MPAAPress/2005/2005_03_29.doc>.

"Products." StreamCast Networks. 10 June 2005. <http://www.streamcastnetworks.com/FullProducts.html>.

"Quick Guide." Grokster.10 June 2005. <http://www.grokster.com/us/help/quick.html>.

Re: Aimster Copyright Litigation. No. 02-4125. 7th Cir. U.S. Ct. of Appeals. 30 June 2003.

RespectCopyrights.org. Motion Picture Association of America. 7 Aug. 2005. <http://respectcopyrights.org/content.html>.

Rheingold, Howard. *The Virtual Community: Homesteading on the Electronic Frontier*. Reading, MA: Addison-Wesley, 1993.

"RIAA Statement on *MGM v. Grokster* Supreme Court Ruling." 27 June 2005. Recording Industry of America. 7 Aug. 2005. <http://www.riaa.com/news/newsletter/062705.asp>.

"RIAA Welcomes Bipartisan Push for University Accountability on Campus Piracy." 2 May 2007. RIAA Newsroom. 13 July 2009. <http://www.riaa.com/newsitem.php?news_month_filter=5&news_year_filter=2007&resultpage=&id=83022480-6BBB-8334-F603-22A672A57C34>.

Rose, Carol. "The Several Futures of Property: Of Cyberspace and Folk Tales, Emission Trades and Ecosystems." *Minnesota Law Review* 83 (1998): 129–82.

Rose, Carol M. *Property and Persuasion: Essays on the History, Theory, and Rhetoric of Ownership*. Boulder, CO: Westview, 1994.

Rose, Mark. *Authors and Owners: The Invention of Copyright*. Cambridge: Harvard University Press, 1993.

Samuelson, Pamela. "The Copyright Grab." *Wired* 2.01 (Feb. 1996). 13 July 2009. <http://www.yoz.com/wired/2.01/features/copyright.html>.

Samuelson, Paul A. "The Pure Theory of Public Expenditure." *The Review of Economics and Statistics* 36.4 (Nov. 1954): 387–89.

San Martin, Melissa. "Copyright Law: The Relevance of Bad Faith to a Fair Use Analysis." *Journal of Technology Law & Policy* 9.2 (Dec. 2004). 13 July 2009. <http://grove.ufl.edu/~techlaw/vol9/issue2/martin.html>.

Sarat, Austin, and Thomas R. Kearns, Eds. *The Rhetoric of Law*. Ann Arbor: University of Michigan Press, 1996.

Sawicki, Jana. *Disciplining Foucault: Feminism, Power, and the Body*. New York: Routledge Press, 1991.

Seibert, Sheryl. *Mix Tape*. 2003. Creative Commons Moving Images Contest. 10 May 2006. <http://mirrors.creativecommons.org/movingimages/Mix_Tape.mov>.

Sherman, Cary. Letter to university presidents. 28 Feb. 2007. 13 July 2009. <http://www.acenet.edu/AM/Template.cfm?Section=CEOs&Template=/CM/ContentDisplay.cfm&ContentID=20643>.

Shuen, Amy. *Web 2.0: A Strategy Guide*. O'Reilly, 2008.

Songwriter and Music Publisher Br. *MGM Studios, Inc. v. Grokster, Ltd.*, 545 U.S. 125 S. Ct. 2764 (2005).

Songwriter and Music Publisher Reply Br. *MGM Studios, Inc. v. Grokster, Ltd.*, 545 U.S. 125 S. Ct. 2764 (2005).

Sony Corp.of America v. Universal City Studios, Inc. No. 81-1687. Supreme Ct. of the U.S. 17 Jan. 1984.

Spanier, Graham, and Cary Sherman. "Thou Shalt Not Pirate Thy Neighbor's Songs." *Chronicle of Higher Education* 52.15 (2 Dec. 2005). B24.

Spigelman, Candace. *Across Property Lines: Textual Ownership in Writing Groups*. Carbondale: Southern Illinois University Press, 2000.

"StreamCast Harnesses Power of Peer-to-Peer Software to Share Supreme Court Documents with Global Audience." StreamCast Networks. 10 June 2005. <http://www.streamcastnetworks.com/pdf/StreamCast%2003_01_05_supreme_court_documentss_on_p2p.pdf>.

"Studios File First Wave of Suits against Online Illegal File Traders." 16 Nov. 2004. Motion Picture Association of America. 7 Aug. 2005. <http://www.respectcopyrights.org/11-16-04_Lawsuit_Press_Release.pdf >.

Sullivan, Patricia, and James E. Porter. *Opening Spaces: Writing Technologies and Critical Research Practices*. New Directions in Computers and Composition Studies. Greenwich, CT: Ablex, 1997.

"Tales from the Public Domain: Bound by Law." Center for the Study of the Public Domain." Duke Law. 13 July 2009. <http://www.law.duke.edu/cspd/comics/>.

Terdiman, Daniel. "Studios, RIAA Target Student Piracy." *CNET News* 27 Apr. 2006. 10 May 2006. <http://news.com.com/2100-1025_3-6066118.html>.

Tonson v. Collins. London. 96 Engl. Rep. 169. 1761.

Triplett, William. "Congress Threatens Colleges." *Variety*, 2 May 2007. 13 July 2009. <http://www.variety.com/article/VR1117964133.html?categoryid=16&cs=1>.

UMG Recordings v. MP3.com. No. 00-472. Southern Dist. of New York. 4 May 2000.

"Unintended Consequences: Five Years Under the DMCA." Electronic Frontier Foundation. 7 Aug. 2005. <http://www.eff.org/IP/DMCA/?f=unintended_consequences.html>.

"University Policies and Practices Addressing Improper Peer-to-Peer File Sharing." Apr. 2004. Education Task Force, Joint Committee of the Higher Education and Entertainment Communities. 13 July 2009. <http://www.educause.edu/ir/library/pdf/CSD3092.pdf>.

Vaidhyanathan, Siva. *The Anarchist in the Library: How the Clash Between Freedom and Control Is Hacking the Real World and Crashing the System*. New York: Basic Books, 2004.

———. *Copyrights and Copywrongs: The Rise of Intellectual Property and How It Threatens Creativity*. 2nd ed. New York: New York University Press, 2001.

———. "The State of Copyright Activism." *First Monday* 9.4 (April 2004). 13 July 2009. <http://firstmonday.org/htbin/cgiwrap/bin/ojs/index.php/fm/article/view/1133/1053>.

van Houweling, Molly. "Cultivating Open Information Platforms: A Land Trust Model." *Journal of Telecommunications and High Technology Law* 1.1 (2002): 309–23.

Viacom International v. YouTube. Complaint filed withSouthern Dist. of New York. 13 March 2007.

von Lohmann, Fred. "IAAL: What Peer-to-Peer Developers Need to Know about Copyright Law." Jan. 2006. Electronic Frontier Foundation. 10 Apr. 2006. <http://www.eff.org/IP/P2P/p2p_copyright_wp.php>.

Warner Bros. v. RDR Books. No. 07-9667. Southern Dist. of New York. 14 Jan. 2008.

Wetlaufer, Gerald B. "Rhetoric and Its Denial in Legal Discourse." *Virginia Law Review* 76 (1990): 1545–97.

"What the Artists and Songwriters Have to Say." MusicUnited.org. 13 July 2009. <http://www.musicunited.org/3_artists.html>.

"What Does 'Copyfight' Mean?" 30 July 2005. *Copyfight* weblog. 12 Apr. 2006. <http://copyfight.corante.com/archives/2005/07/30/what_does_copyfight_mean.php>.

"What's the Controversy: Just the FAQs." What's the Download. The Recording Academy. 13 July 2009. <http://www.whatsthedownload.com/whats_the_controversy/faq/>.

"What's the Controversy: The Lowdown." What's the Download. The Recording Academy. 13 July 2009. <http://www.whatsthedownload.com/whats_the_controversy/the_low_down/>.

"What's the Controversy: Thinking Twice." What's the Download. The Recording Academy. 13 July 2009. <http://www.whatsthedownload.com/whats_the_controversy/thinking_twice/>.

"What's the Controversy: Who Pays?" What's the Download. The Recording Academy. 13 July 2009. <http://www.whatsthedownload.com/whats_the_controversy/who_pays/>.

White, James Boyd. *Heracles' Bow: Essays on the Rhetoric and Poetics of the Law*. Madison: University of Wisconsin Press, 1985.

"Who Really Cares?" MusicUnited.org. 13 July 2009. <http://www.musicunited.org/1_whocares.html>.

"Why These Issues Matter." Public Knowledge.10 Aug. 2005. <http://www.publicknowledge.org/issues/why>.

"Why You Shouldn't Do It." MusicUnited.org. 13 July 2009. <http://www.musicunited.org/4_shouldntdoit.html>.

Woodmansee, Martha. "The Genius and the Copyright: Economic and Legal Conditions of the Emergence of the 'Author.' " *Eighteenth-Century Studies* 17.4 (1984): 425–48.

Woodmansee, Martha, and Peter Jaszi. "Introduction." In *The Construction of Authorship: Textual Appropriation in Law and Literature*. Eds. Martha Woodmansee and Peter Jaszi. Durham, NC: Duke University Press, 1994. 1–14.

Yen, Alfred C. "Western Frontier or Feudal Society?: Metaphors and Perceptions of Cyberspace." *Berkeley Technology Law Journal* 17 (2002): 1207–61.

Index

For Product Safety Concerns and Information please contact our EU
representative GPSR@taylorandfrancis.com
Taylor & Francis Verlag GmbH, Kaufingerstraße 24, 80331 München, Germany

www.ingramcontent.com/pod-product-compliance
Ingram Content Group UK Ltd.
Pitfield, Milton Keynes, MK11 3LW, UK
UKHW021300190926
475701UK00009B/93

* 9 7 8 0 4 1 5 6 3 6 4 4 5 *